As Rare as Rain

AS
RARE
AS
RAIN

Federal Relief
in the Great Southern Drought
of 1930–31

NAN ELIZABETH WOODRUFF

UNIVERSITY OF ILLINOIS PRESS

Urbana and Chicago

Publication of this work was supported in part by
a grant from the Andrew W. Mellon Foundation.

Library of Congress Cataloging in Publication Data

Woodruff, Nan Elizabeth, 1949–
  As rare as rain.

  Bibliography: p.
  Includes index.
  1. Disaster relief—Southern States—History.
2. Droughts—Southern States—History.   3. Depressions—
1929–United States.   4. American National Red Cross—
History.   I. Title.
HV555.U62A139   1985   363.3′492   84-16143
ISBN 0-252-01161-9 (alk. paper)

For
Virginia Parks Woodruff
and
Wallace Green Woodruff

Contents

Preface

The summer and winter months of 1930–31 were trying times for rural southerners. Beginning in the spring of 1930 a severe drought gradually crept across twenty-three states, concentrating its greatest damage in the southern states of Arkansas, Kentucky, Louisiana, Mississippi, Tennessee, and West Virginia. The areas suffering most within these states were in the plantation counties in the Arkansas and Mississippi River Deltas and the Appalachian Mountain counties in Kentucky and West Virginia. Nature could not have found a more desperate region to inflict its vengeance upon, for during the two decades prior to 1930, sharecroppers, tenant farmers, and planters had suffered the ravages of the boll weevil and high wartime prices, followed by the collapse of the cotton market, indebtedness and foreclosures, the Mississippi River Flood of 1927, and the beginnings of the Great Depression in 1929.[1] The small farmers and coal miners of Kentucky and West Virginia had fared little better as they had seen their land gutted by timber and coal companies, suffered displacement from their land, and saw wages decrease.[2] The drought came as a final blow in a sequential chain of natural and economic misfortunes.

This is a study of the Great Southern Drought of 1930–31. It describes the responses of President Herbert Hoover, the American Red Cross, and the U.S. Congress to the tremendous human suffering created by the disaster. Since the drought occurred in the midst of a national depression, the issue of relief to the drought victims became intertwined with that of unemployment relief. Consequently, the drought introduced into Congress the debate over the role of the federal government in providing aid to the nation's needy. Fearing the emergence of a welfare state, Hoover argued for a relief program based on local voluntarism and self-help. According to this view, local communities would raise funds to help the needy in their communities. Hoover asked the Red Cross to administer the drought relief program because the agency had been chartered by Congress to provide relief to disaster victims and because its organizational structure reflected the ideology of local self-help. However, as the number of starving people increased during the winter of 1930–31, several congressmen insisted that the drought and depression called for bolder action. They questioned the adequacy of charitable relief and argued for a federal program that would provide aid for those suffering from both drought and unemployment. As congressional demands for greater federal involvement increased, Hoover pleaded unsuccessfully with the Red Cross to accept responsibility for all forms of relief. The debate over drought relief was a rehearsal for the controversies that would characterize the 1930s, for it centered on the question of responsibility for the welfare of the American people. Hoover succeeded in 1931 in preventing the passage of a massive relief measure, but his victory was short-lived. For the drought probably prepared at least rural southerners for the acceptance of the massive programs that would come with President Franklin D. Roosevelt's New Deal.

The drought also proved the fallacy of local voluntarism, for in the plantation counties the relief committees consisted of a planter, merchant, banker, and county judge. These men used Red Cross relief to retain control over their labor force and to insure that their workers picked cotton at a 50 percent wage reduction. In the coal-mining regions the local committees were comprised of men related to the coal mine owners who used relief to starve striking miners back to work. And in the Appalachian Mountain counties the local committees viewed the disaster as a providential act to rid the mountains of the "unfit." The rural South and Appalachia were poor laboratories to test the methods of local voluntarism.

As Rare as Rain provides a vivid picture of the misery and suffering that followed in the wake of the disaster, and it describes the ways in which sharecroppers, tenant farmers, planters, coal miners, company owners, and mountaineers responded to the calamity and the efforts to administer relief. For many southerners, the Red Cross program was their first experience with outside relief, and they greeted the prospects of a dole with mixed feelings. This book also presents a final glimpse of the plantation system of sharecropping and tenant farming and the class relationships defining that structure before the massive changes wrought by the New Deal and World War II. Thus, the drought not only played a significant role in American history, but it was also a crucial event in the last years of the plantation economy that had emerged from the ashes of the Civil War. There is here, too, a rare opportunity for viewing the different Souths—that of the sharecroppers and that of the coal miners and mountaineers.

A brief note on organization. The first six chapters focus largely on Arkansas, for the drought hit hardest there, and it struck only three years after the Mississippi flood of 1927. Thus Arkansans simply lacked the resources to care for their own, and the Red Cross administered the largest portion of its relief operation in that state. The last two chapters focus on the Appalachians. Although the Red Cross relief program was not as extensive there, it encountered problems that revealed both important similarities and variations from that of the Delta.

I have received the help of a number of people during the course of this study. Rudolf A. Clemen, Jr., and his staff at the American Red Cross National Headquarters in Washington, D.C., helped me locate most of the primary sources used in this study, and they offered me a wonderful place to work. The staffs of the Herbert Hoover Presidential Library, the National Archives, and the American Friends Service Committee Archives also aided me in finding relevant materials. The College of Charleston provided funding for the revisions and typing of the manuscript, and Dorothy Winchel and Susan Sweatt patiently typed several drafts.

A number of individuals took time from their own work to read and comment upon various drafts. I am especially indebted to Pete Daniel, who taught me southern history and who read so many versions of the drought, beginning with the dissertation, that he probably feels that he lived through the disaster. Louis Harlan and Harold Woodman not only read through the entire manuscript and offered suggestions, but they have also continued to offer their generous support of my work, and I thank them for it. Theodore Rosengarten also read the entire manuscript and offered helpful suggestions regarding organization. Patricia Cooper, Clarence Davis, George Heltai, Donald Ritchie, Julie Saville, Irene Silverblatt, and Raymond Smock read various chapters and provided not only their comments but also a great deal of moral support as well. I am grateful to them all. I also thank Richard Wentworth and Susan Patterson for their editorial advice. Of course I accept total responsibility for all errors that might appear in this book.

Finally I would like to express my appreciation to my family—to Angela, George, Sam, and Woody—for their constant support and interest. This book is dedicated to my parents, who taught me a great deal about southern history.

Notes

1. For a discussion of the southern economy during these years, see William J. Carson, "Banking in the South: Its Relation to Agricultural and Industrial Development," *Annals of the American Academy of Political and Social Science* 153 (1931), 210–23; Rupert Vance, *Human Factors in Cotton Culture* (Chapel Hill, 1929); and David L. Wickens, "Adjusting Southern Agriculture to Economic Changes," *Annals of the American Academy of Political and Social Science* 153 (1931), 193–201.

2. For a discussion of Appalachia and the coal and timber industries during these years, see David Corbin, *Life, Work, and Rebellion in the Coal Fields: The Southern West Virginia Miners, 1880–1922* (Urbana, 1981); Ronald D. Eller, *Miners, Millhands, and Mountaineers: Industrialization of the Appalachian South, 1880–1930* (Knoxville, 1982); John Gaveta, *Power and Powerlessness: Quiescence and Rebellion in an Appalachian Valley* (Urbana, 1980).

AS
RARE
AS
RAIN

1

Dog Days of Despair

Summers in the Arkansas and Mississippi Deltas are hot and humid. Green fields of rice and cotton, with intervening gardens of foodstuff, extend to the horizon over the flat alluvial plain laced with rivers and streams. An occasional brown cropper shack intrudes upon an otherwise idyllic scene, a reminder that the region is not the Arcadia it appears to be. One of the most fertile areas in America, it is also one of the poorest. When the drought crept across the Delta in the summer of 1930, the once emerald verdure of cotton burned to shriveled stalks.

The terrain, browned to parchments of baked earth, reflected the color of the sordid shacks that dotted its former verdant landscape. The scorched land and the dilapidated homes painted a picture that revealed more accurately the squalor of the country than a normal summer scene. As late July approached, thermometers reached record highs of over 100°. Streams dried up and water became a luxury, not just in the Delta, but in all the southern states affected by the drought. Tenant houses, seldom comfortable under better circumstances, became even less bearable in the intense heat.

In normal times the crops were planted by the end of July when credit was cut off at the commissary until picking season began in late September. For two months croppers fed their families by fishing and hunting, while revivals provided the major source of entertainment. Late summer was go-to-meetin' time as evangelists traveled through, breathing hell-fire and brimstone. Rural southerners cleansed their souls through singings, shoutings, and gyrations, capped off by a rededication to the Lord—an expiation providing not only escape from the boredom of farm life but also serving to vent frustrations emerging from a life of rugged survival and, more often than not, open exploitation.[1]

The drought interrupted this aged cycle. Having no crops to tend, croppers sat in their homes, which had often been located in the middle of cotton fields that lacked shade trees—without ice water, without a breeze—and gazed upon the charred stalks that they had planted up to their front porch steps. Without crops, the planter could not borrow money to furnish his workers with food and implements. Many croppers had planted gardens to supplement their diets, but vegetables had long since withered like the cotton. There would be no more fish to catch or game to hunt. Nor would there be crops to pay the rent. Without money they could not travel to look for other employment, and, even if they left, who would hire them? The timber had long since been cut, and the oil fields near Texarkana had been shut down by the Depression. So most families stayed in their cabins and endured the torrid summer. Parents wondered how they would feed their children in the cold winter months ahead, who would clothe them, where the fuel would come from to heat the cardboard-papered houses. Perhaps they hoped the Red Cross would feed them, as it had done in the Mississippi flood of 1927, but hope was as rare as rain in the summer of 1930. So they sat and waited. There was little else that they could do.

The drought of 1930 was one of the worst in American climatological history. In contrast to previous droughts, which had been intensive but short in duration, that of 1930 gradually grew worse and lasted for almost a year. From March to May only 57 percent of the normal percipitation fell in West Virginia, Kentucky, Indiana, Illinois, and Missouri, the least rainfall on record. By late July and August conditions worsened as Virginia, West Virginia, Kentucky, Arkansas, and Missouri averaged only 41 percent of their usual rainfall. (See Table 1.) By the first of September, the dry weather had persisted for nine months in the mid-Atlantic and for six months in the Ohio and Mississippi River valleys.[2] Instead of green fields ripe unto harvest, the earth turned brown beneath the cloudless copper skies.

July proved to be the hottest month. In St. Louis on July 11 temperatures reached 105°, and twenty people succumbed to the heat. Three days later the toll had climbed to 110. Torrid weather continued into late July, with record-breaking temperatures in several Arkansas and Kentucky cities and communities: Little Rock 104°; Conway 113°; Harrison 107°; Dardanelle 108°; and in Kentucky, Paducah and Bowling Green registered 108° and Louisville reached 104°[3]. Mid-July has always been the "dog day" weather in the South, but in 1930 it seemed the canicular days would last forever.

TABLE 1

Comparison of Actual Rainfall in Inches
during June, July, and August of 1930
with the Average Rainfall for
the Corresponding Period in Previous Years.

State	1930	Previous Years	Percentage of 1930 to Previous Years
Alabama	9.41	14.25	66
Arkansas	4.19	11.53	35
Georgia	11.46	15.34	75
Illinois	6.36	10.63	60
Indiana	6.45	10.54	61
Kansas	8.72	10.38	84
Kentucky	5.26	12.12	43
Louisiana	9.04	16.22	56
Maryland	5.83	12.49	47
Mississippi	6.33	13.54	47
Missouri	6.82	12.62	54
Montana	3.53	5.30	67
New Mexico	6.75	6.56	103
North Carolina	11.13	16.19	69
North Dakota	5.58	8.39	67
Ohio	6.22	11.16	56
Oklahoma	6.56	9.73	67
Pennsylvania	7.90	12.68	62
South Carolina	11.62	16.46	71
Tennessee	6.36	12.71	50
Texas	4.71	8.44	56
Virginia	6.83	13.26	51
West Virginia	6.97	13.11	53

SOURCE: *American National Red Cross Relief Work in the Drought of 1930–31*
(Washington, D.C., 1931), 97.

Scorching heat blistered the crops. Arkansas, one of the hardest hit states, lost from 30 to 50 percent of its crops, with cotton yielding only 48 percent of normal production. Soybeans and corn registered a complete loss. Kentucky, another severely affected state, yielded only 25 to 50 percent of its tobacco and corn, while oats and hay were a total loss.[4] The destruction of forage and grain led to the lowest feed storage in the area since 1901.[5] In Virginia a correspondent traveling through the Shenandoah Valley depicted the countryside as "overdone toast, drooping apple orchards and withered cornfields." The drought, he wrote, threatened to be the worst tragedy since the days of Sheridan's Raiders.[6] At the same time an observer noted that a crow would need to carry rations as it crossed the valley.

Five months with almost no rain brought disaster beyond crop failures. Fires destroyed thousands of acres in the Monongahela National Forest in West Virginia, and others swept across the Shenandoah Valley, Nantehala and Pisgah, North Carolina, and Natural Bridge, Virginia.[7] Little Rock experienced 293 fires in July.[8]

People in both urban and rural areas hauled water from long distances, as the drought diminished the South's usually abundant sources of water. For example, the Mississippi River, which flooded its banks three years before, reached, in late August, its lowest ebb since records had been kept. In Cairo, Illinois, the gauge registered 8.4 feet and only 4 feet in New Madrid, Missouri. Below Hickman, Kentucky, the river dropped so low that two submerged barges from the 1927 flood appeared and were dug out. Hickman had suffered greatly during the flood, and, as the climate reversed, it endured the drought. Dust clouds blew across the river into town, and barge loads were reduced 50 percent so they could be towed across the river.[9]

As the rivers and streams slowly evaporated, fish died by the thousands and polluted the surrounding vicinities. Nor was life necessarily better for the surviving creatures. Grown bull frogs hopped about but never learned to swim because of dried ponds.[10] Animals died from lack of forage and water. To defend against thirsty wildlife, some farmers padlocked their wells and guarded them with shotguns. Still others drove their cattle to the low-ebbed rivers.[11]

The immediate human reaction to the heat and dry weather resembled to some extent that of the wildlife. People searched for water—indeed, for any means to relieve the distress. In East Tennessee and Kentucky individuals filed trespassing suits against families who had forcibly used their wells. One woman, denied water from a neighbor's spring, retaliated by filling the well with kerosene, and in Memphis police blamed a series of robberies over a forty-eight-hour period on unemployment due to drought and the heat.[12]

Little Rock, Arkansas, became an oasis for those driven from the land. During the first two weeks of July a steady stream of applicants filed into the city's Social Welfare Bureau seeking aid, adding strain to a quickly diminishing budget. Jobless or not, all city dwellers withered in the heat. Air conditioners had yet to cool the humid South, and most

6

families lived in two rooms without any refrigeration. Lacking ice, they had no fresh milk or food.[13] But humans, like other natural victims, persevered as best they could.

By late July there was no indication that the drought would break and that rain would water the baked earth. Agencies traditionally involved in the rural South like the Agricultural Extension Service and the American Red Cross ordered surveys of the stricken counties. The reports described extensive destruction and misery.

A visit to the plantation counties in Arkansas convinced Red Cross representative Evadne Laptad that many sharecroppers would be destitute by winter. Diseases such as typhoid had rapidly increased, especially among black sharecroppers, though physicians were not reporting the cases. Pellagra was also on the rise due to lack of milk and vegetables, and in the southwestern counties infantile paralysis was spreading quickly. Laptad predicted the entire state would eventually need relief. She captured the tragedy and hopelessness of a people for whom disasters had become a way of life. "It is a sad situation, indeed," she wrote. "The families that are suffering now, or on the verge of it, are not singled out as by flood or tornado or fire, but are just in their homes, with gardens ruined, sweet potatoes not making a crop, the prospect of being in debt to the landlord when the pitiable cotton crop is gathered instead of having money with which to buy food and clothing for the winter." Ignorance and limited resources added to their helplessness, she continued. "At best, their lives are hard enough under present circumstances. Hunger, and probably sickness now will mean real suffering."[14]

Reports from other Arkansas groups supported Red Cross predictions of famine. A Methodist minister from Glenwood, near the Ouachita Forest, wrote that "it would be hard to over estimate conditions. If something is not done soon, if there is not help for us, there will be great suffering among the people."[15] A county agent in Conway noted that, because crops had reached only 10 percent of normal production, 1,000 of the county's 2,000 farm families lacked food for families and feed for livestock.[16]

Surveys from Kentucky revealed equally dire circumstances. In the western part of the state 50 to 80 percent of the corn, hay, and garden production had been destroyed. Farmers had already suffered five successive failures, and the drought threatened total economic collapse for many. The southeastern section lost 75 percent of its corn and all of its potatoes and hay. Cattle, sheep, and pigs were being sold at low prices

7

due to the lack of feed and water. In Carlisle nine carloads of cattle, purchased at 12¢ per pound, were shipped out and sold for 3¢ or 4¢.[17] Polluted streams had quadrupled the typhoid rate, and several counties reported an increase in dysentery.[18] "There is actually suffering now," stated the study. "It is too late to replant and there are no better prospects for the fall and winter." A field representative in the eastern section was certain that the agency would eventually administer relief to the entire mountain population, for the people were so poor that the counties had no funds to help their own.[19]

Another representative, Marion Rust, described circumstances in central Kentucky that resembled those depicted by Laptad in Arkansas. According to her, the drought was the greatest disaster that had ever occurred in the area. While floods were always more spectacular and attracted more sympathy and attention, all floods combined would not produce one-half the losses that would result from the drought. "The disaster is insidious," she argued. "The people must see their stock and crops go for naught."[20]

The Department of Agriculture surveys also revealed grim circumstances, especially in Arkansas and Kentucky. Wholesale stealing of food by poor tenants was noted in Poinsett County, Arkansas. Two thousand families in Carroll County, Mississippi, and 3,000 in Webster Parish, Louisiana, could not afford to buy food, and many in Estill County, Kentucky, were "at the point of starvation."[21]

As these studies showed, the drought came as a final blow to a section that had experienced a depression long before the rest of America did. Due to continual disasters and crop failures, few counties possessed the resources to meet the needs of their communities. As agents predicted, only an outside organization like the Red Cross could feed the hungry. When it became clear that the dry weather might persist indefinitely, the stricken states looked increasingly to Washington for salvation. There they found no inviting hand; rather they received sermons from the prophets of self-help and voluntary cooperation.

The drought presented a perplexing problem for the American Red Cross. According to its 1905 charter, Congress delegated the organization to administer relief for "mitigating the sufferings caused by pestilence, famine, fire, floods, and other national calamities."[22] Usually aid was given when catastrophes occurred that produced suffering, death, and widespread destruction of property. While the drought clearly qualified as a calamity, it was mainly viewed as one of the many hazards of farming—like the boll weevil or a bad harvest. Agency officials argued that farmers had traditionally accepted, like any other business-man, the risks of their enterprise. If crop yields were low one year, they must absorb the losses and look for a better income the next season. Mere loss did not justify an appeal for assistance. However, the Red Cross *Disaster Relief Handbook* did provide that should a famine develop, then the organization might be required under the provisions of its charter to carry out a relief program.[23]

Disagreements emerged among victims, politicians, and Red Cross officials over the interpretation of the charter and handbook. Some argued that people were suffering and help should be immediately forthcoming. Others insisted that a famine had yet to develop and thus the organization was not compelled to act until the disaster had completed its course. The controversy centered around the nature of the drought. It did not strike suddenly, like a tornado, leaving instant and obvious destruction. Nor did it occur dramatically like a flood, engulfing thousands of acres and creating clearly defined refugees. Instead, the drought developed gradually and persisted indefinitely. Inhabitants were not driven from their land, nor was there evidence of extensive property damage. People simply remained in their homes while crops slowly burned and blew away into dust.

Another source of conflict concerned the distinction between loss due to economic collapse rather than due to drought. Red Cross officials insisted that help could only be given to those whose hunger resulted from a national disaster. In the plantation South, where the economy was based on a one-crop system, who could determine if farmers were starving because of an economic or a natural misfortune? Although one farmer might miraculously escape the dry spell, he was nevertheless affected by its economic consequences. This distinction thus represented a nearsighted view of the complex southern economic structure.

By early August Red Cross and Department of Agriculture officials had received the county reports and formulated a relief policy. A. L. Schafer, director of Red Cross Disaster Relief, ordered field agents to work with local groups like the Farm Bureau, Home Demonstration Agents, and welfare and poor relief organizations. He stressed that crop failures would not be financed and that self-help would be the major relief policy.[24]

Self-help and voluntary cooperation became the basis for both governmental and private aid, perhaps because one of the world's

greatest relief administrators was president. Herbert Hoover personified the American work and success ethics. After organizing his own
successful engineering firm, he retired from private business and devoted
his remaining years to public service. He served as food administrator
during Woodrow Wilson's administration, fed the starving Belgians in
World War I and the famine-stricken Russians in 1921–23, organized a
conference on unemployment in 1921, and directed flood relief in
1927.[25] Americans felt secure and grateful that the "Great Humanitarian" sat in the White House when the stock market crashed in 1929.
Who better knew how to feed and clothe the needy?

Hoover intended to administer a relief program that would preserve the cherished values of individualism and self-reliance and that
would bolster cooperation. Farmers could retain these seemingly contra-
dictory virtues by forming cooperatives and applying for loans through
the Agricultural Marketing Act of 1929. Co-ops encouraged growers to
join capital and other resources to market and regulate their own
production. They could be used as a basis for credit and for monitoring
crop yields, thus preventing the need for federal intervention. By working together, farmers could preserve their independence.[26]

The president looked to the Red Cross to help those who, lacking
collateral, could not obtain loans. For him, this agency represented the
ideal method for dispensing relief. Local chapters formed the heart of
the organization. Composed of the leaders of the communities, they
raised funds and administered assistance. National headquarters in Washington served a function similar to Hoover's concept of the federal
government—it encouraged and coordinated the activities of its members,
only offering help after all local reserves had been exhausted. It
represented the legitimate and just method for helping Americans in
distress, for as long as the Red Cross existed, the national government
would never be forced to assume responsibility for disaster or unemployment relief—a fear that haunted Hoover. If anywhere, voluntary cooperation should have succeeded in the agrarian setting of the rural
South. Hoover's own values sprang from a small community in Iowa;
however, as the drought demonstrated, the country in 1930 was not the
West Branch of his youth, and his application of self-help through
mutual support did not meet the needs of rural southerners.[27]

With these ideas in mind, Hoover proceeded to erect an elaborate
system of committees to handle the disaster. On August 8 he issued an
invitation to the governors of the stricken states to attend a conference at

the White House. Three days later he met with Red Cross chairman, Judge John Barton Payne, who was an admirer and colleague of the president. Payne had served as secretary of interior in the Wilson administration when Hoover was food administrator, and the men had worked together in 1927 on the Mississippi flood operation.[28] The president told Payne that his organization would be responsible for those families who could not help themselves; although he did not envision a major task as in 1927, Hoover thought it was best that no Red Cross official attend the governors' conference, since the emphasis would be on local responsibility. The availability of outside help would not be stressed.[29] After the meeting, the judge informed his chapters of the possibility of extensive involvement in the South, though he continued to express publicly the view that each state would take care of its own problems.[30]

When the governors visited the White House on August 14, Hoover ordered them to form both a local and a state drought committee to consist of a banker, a state agricultural official, a member of the Red Cross, a railway representative, and a farmer. When counties exhausted their resources, they could appeal to the state committee, which, if lacking funds, could apply to the national organization for help. The major outside source of assistance, the president argued, would come from already existing credit facilities like the Federal Farm Board or the Intermediate Credit system. Although the Red Cross had a reserve fund of $5 million, it would not be tapped unless a disaster developed. Railroads had also reduced their freight rates to allow for cheaper transportation of feed, seed, and livestock.[31]

Hoover drew also from his experience as secretary of commerce in organizing the Conference on Unemployment in 1921.[32] As before, he sought to stimulate the economy with a limited amount of public works. On August 15 Secretary of Agriculture Arthur Hyde announced that the $125 million allotment for federal roads, originally designated to be released to the states on January 1, would instead be given on September 1. This would provide alternative work for the farmers by creating jobs on public roads.[33]

A National Drought Committee was formed with Hyde as chairman. The secretary of agriculture, a self-made man who had been an automobile salesman and an insurance executive in Missouri, strongly supported the president's philosophy of relief. At a meeting on August 21 Hoover informed the committee that, with the exception of Arkansas and one or two other states, most areas could handle their own problems. However, he considered that Arkansas would be the responsibility of the Red Cross, for the Mississippi flood and other calamities had destroyed that state's resources, and credit facilities would aid Arkansas very little. After discussing the various available agricultural credit measures, Hoover stressed that no one would receive loans without sufficient collateral, for it would be "schooling people to disregard their obligations."[34] Each state and county was to appoint a drought committee to survey conditions and to coordinate existing relief programs.

Hoover's voluntaristic and decentralized approach to relief would never work in the plantation South. A major flaw in the measures designed in August was the issue of credit. Despite a statement issued by the banker members of the various state and local committees and a National Bankers' Conference that banks were solvent, in reality they had gone bankrupt. The financial structure in the plantation region rested on the cotton economy and the credit had dried up as the bolls had.[35] Further, cooperatives depended upon capital—a rare commodity in the South of 1930. As Seymour Jones, a Mississippi farmer noted, it took from $1,000 to $2,500 to organize a cooperative and farmers simply lacked that kind of money. "There are so many strings attached to the several agencies being spoken of that the small fellow will starve along with his stock before any aid can be given."[36] And if Hoover's efforts at assistance were inadequate for landowners, they were useless for tenants and sharecroppers. Some of the hardest-hit counties were in the plantation country, where the tenancy rate was as high as 80 percent.[37] No sharecropper or tenant would be eligible for federal credit. These individuals would be totally at the mercy of the Red Cross and would receive aid only after the agency had declared the existence of a disaster—an action it was reluctant to take.

Another serious problem was the composition of the local drought committees. In the Delta they consisted of a banker, a merchant, a planter, and a county judge; they decided the eligibility for credit. None of these men would approve a loan to someone they believed lacked character or collateral. They would also be the ones to determine when and how much Red Cross aid would be given. As was revealed during the Mississippi flood relief program in 1927, when planters used Red Cross rations to retain their labor force, black sharecroppers would have difficulty in receiving their fair share from such a committee.[38]

Even the attempt at public works depended upon the ability of individual states to match federal allocations for highways, a proposal once again reflecting Hoover's insistence that government programs must be self-liquidating. The chief engineer of the Kentucky Highway Commission confessed that his state could at most match $2 million of the $2.5 million allocated it.[39] For states facing bankruptcy and suffering from high bonded indebtedness, these measures offered very little.[40] Feeding animals and offering credit for future crops would not alleviate the immediate human distress that some areas were experiencing.

And nothing could explain away Red Cross field reports that human suffering existed. Yet Payne, Hoover, and others insisted that the disaster was not serious enough to require extensive aid and that consequently localities should finance their own relief measures. Indeed, some agricultural experts argued that the drought appeared as the salvation they had been pleading for since the 1920s. Overproduction had plagued the South for some time; with crops destroyed, prices would rise. Perhaps the landowner would finally realize that planting his entire acreage in cotton was poor planning and bad business.[41]

It was not that Hoover lacked compassion and sympathy for the victims, but he approached the drought as he had other disasters — using surveys and reports to determine the seriousness of a problem and then forming a network of committees to deal with it. His heart may well have been in the right place, but his methodology and execution were in error. As Joan Hoff Wilson has noted, Hoover's aid to the Belgians, Russians, and others alleviated the suffering of an inestimable number of humans, yet he never referred privately or publicly to the suffering of any of the victims. "They all became statistics by the same impersonal, scientific engineering approach and temperament that was to shock and dismay his fellow Americans during the Great Depression and erode his political credibility with them."[42] Only when statistics grew to constitute what he considered a disaster would he support an extensive relief program, and even then it would not be adequate.

The plan not only reflected the engineer's scientific desire for facts and efficiency, but it also exposed the limitations of progressivism itself. Believing that technology and planning could solve any social problem, provided the correct information existed, Hoover personified the progressivism of the "New Era." Unfortunately, once the data had been collected, he disregarded its implications. Rather than viewing the accounts of widespread destitution and the breakdown of the southern credit system as symptomatic of the total collapse of its economic structure,

13

the president chose to ignore the obvious by imposing his own assumptions about the way things should operate. By calling upon the victims to help themselves through charity, voluntarism, and cooperatives, he showed he did not understand the problems in the region. And yet he knew from his experience in the 1927 flood that poverty, racism, and peonage would pose unique problems for any relief program. The discrepancy between the assumptions, values, and perceptions of Hoover and his advisors and the actual plight of the sufferers presented one of the major problems for the drought program. He was indeed a product of his era, for like progressives generally he sought to apply his values and programs to a problem totally at odds with his conception of reality. His approach rested on a society of abundance, not scarcity.

Reaction to the proposed measures varied. A number of newspapers and members of the drought committees supported them, while letters from farmers criticized the limitations of offering credit to a people unable to obtain collateral. Newspapers in Arkansas and Kentucky expressed a preference for work rather than charity. According to the Mena (Arkansas) *Star,* "What real men want is a chance to earn their own way, a chance to work, honest employment."[43] The *Sentinel-Record* in Hot Springs agreed that the major problem was providing credit for next year's crop. Denying there were hungry mouths to feed, the paper concluded that the "farmer isn't yet in a position to be fed in a soup line."[44]

In Little Rock the state's leading newspaper urged its readers not to rely on outside help. The Arkansas *Gazette* quoted A. G. Little of Blytheville, who said that "acceptance of Red Cross aid in 1927 and 1929 cost us more in the loss of self-respect and manhood than anything before experienced and I hope we shall never see it again." The editor supported this view and counseled Arkansans to "worry through on their own resources." Although some individuals would suffer in the short run, it would profit the majority in the end to preserve its independence by not accepting a handout.[45]

Kentucky's major newspaper, the Louisville *Courier-Journal,* echoed the opinion of the Arkansans. Praising the emphasis on local and state responsibility, the editor realized that many would be dissatisfied that no direct aid would be forthcoming. "Of course there are those who are disappointed that the flood-gates of Federal largess will not at once be opened for the benefit of drought-stricken regions," he chided, "but self-help represented the logical alternative."[46]

Newspaper editors did not reflect the opinion of everyone. Self-help and loans were irrelevant for many. A banker from Mountain Park, Oklahoma, expressed the exasperation that some felt. "That Drought committee that met yesterday was a brilliant bunch," he wired. "Where do they suppose these drought sufferers are going to get bankable security after two short crops and a total failure and prices down to nothing. If people had bankable security, local banks could take care of them."[47]

In a letter to the editor of the *Courier-Journal*, T. L. Bush seemed certain that the policy formulators did not understand the problem in Kentucky. "People here in Grayson and surrounding counties haven't had much in farms for four years and especially last year," he wrote. "A vast number of people need food and clothing and aren't able to make a government note, or they would have borrowed from the local bank." He did not think enough public works existed to help all of the needy.[48] Another Kentuckian accused authorities of soft-pedaling the facts on the desperate condition of his state. "Drought is a disaster, not a disgrace," he began. "Of what use is it to offer drought loans for payment of taxes to people who are now stripped of all means of paying interest? Why pile up burdens on backs that are already bent?" Most farmers needed bread, not credit or reduced freight rates.[49]

Small farmers were not the only ones who found the measures insufficient. A mass meeting of 1,000 Arkansas and Missouri planters, bankers, and businessmen agreed to pay no more than 50¢ per 100 pounds for cotton picking in the coming season. They found the president's program insufficient, for few planters could meet the criteria required to qualify for loans. In the 1927 flood, for example, only twenty farmers in Mississippi County, Arkansas, qualified for crop loans and, with the security they were required to offer, could not have borrowed from any other agency. All agreed, however, that acute suffering in northeast Arkansas and southeast Missouri could be expected from January 1 to March 1 when planters would not furnish their tenants. Although none of the men wanted the Red Cross to feed their work force, they feared that it might be the only alternative unless looser credit were offered.[50]

A reporter for the Arkansas *Gazette* in Washington criticized the Pollyanna attitude of officials. "Today there is a steady stream of optimistic propaganda pouring from the Department of Agriculture relative to the drouth," observed the correspondent. "A few months ago, a similar flow was streaming from the Department of Commerce pertaining to business." Hoover's drought committees reminded him of the National

Business Conference that insisted the economy was sound and that the Depression was only a minor affair. Governmental agencies had downplayed the extent of suffering and economic collapse, he concluded, "in the hope that the public will realize there is no more drouth than there is business depression."[51]

Conflicting descriptions of the disaster also appeared from other sources. Since Hoover had cited Arkansas as the state with the most serious problem, that state's committee and the Red Cross initiated surveys to determine the extent of destruction and need. Official accounts minimized suffering while letters from the victims described widespread destitution and helplessness. Arkansas's State Drought Committee, under the leadership of utility magnate Harvey C. Couch, conducted surveys and urged the planting of fall vegetable gardens. Recognizing that acute conditions existed in some counties, the chairman was certain citizens could meet their own needs. "The fighting spirit of the pioneer people in the hills will carry them through if they are assured an opportunity to help themselves," he said. "That will be the keynote of the campaign—help the drouth sufferers to help themselves."[52]

The Arkansas Bankers' Association appointed one banker to each county committee and conducted its own study, discovering that conditions were not as severe as many believed. "I was much relieved and encouraged," wrote President Joe H. Stanley, "to note that the situation, while unfortunate and quite serious in spots, by no means justifies the hysteria which some of our people seem to be exhibiting."[53]

The assistant director of the State Extension Service, T. Roy Reid, took issue with the optimists, estimating that 110,000 families would be totally without food and feed in four months. "This means that practically one-half of the farm population of the state will be destitute if measures are not taken for relief." Reid concluded that every county was affected and that only one possessed enough food to survive the winter.[54] Despite Reid's observations, Albert Evans, assistant director for Red Cross Disaster Relief, said that he agreed with the bankers' assessment. "The major suffering at the present time is the mental anguish and alarm at what the winter may bring." He did not assure families of help should their communities be unable to provide for them and stressed that no major relief program was envisioned. At the most 100 to 200 families would need food in the winter. "Thousands of families, of course, will need to skimp."[55]

When the results of the relief committee surveys were compiled, they revealed that many were experiencing more than mere anxiety about their predicament. In Montgomery County, with 95 percent of its crops destroyed, hundreds lacked food and some did not have enough to provide a single meal. A local minister observed that in the past farmers could kill a deer or turkey. With the woods cut over and the destruction of forage, no wildlife existed and immediate relief was in order.[56]

Rather than hunting turkeys, the hungry searched directly for sustenance. In Lonoke County, Arkansas, Mrs. Ellis Robinson wrote that "the people in this locality are in distress and there is not a day but some one's by at my door." Predictions from Pope County estimated 2,000 families would starve in the winter while 300 required immediate food. Pellagra was rapidly increasing. The committee concluded proudly that its citizens wanted work and not charity.[57] While Couch voiced optimism and the virtues of individualism, his own committee reports offered evidence to the contrary.

Accounts from Kentucky reflected similar variations. On August 23 Secretary Hyde visited the state and found "conditions were not so bad as had been predicted." He was certain that rain and the governmental credit facilities would alleviate the distressed state.[58] The chairman of the State Drought Committee, however, argued that preliminary investigations had convinced him that the farmers' plight had not been exaggerated.[59] Others challenged Hyde's assessment of the state. Reversing its earlier view, the *Courier-Journal* questioned the effectiveness of lower freight rates and loans to co-ops. These measures, "though laudable in intent, can't feed hungry mouths when the food supply has been cut off, nor clothe children this winter. . . . What many poor farmers need now," continued the editor, "and will need all winter is food and shoes, and most of them are too proud to ask alms."[60]

A representative to the state legislature agreed with the newspaper and questioned the secretary of agriculture. "Because a few sprigs of green grass have sprung up in parched pastures does not mean that the drought situation has been relieved in Kentucky. The slowly greening grass cannot bring back the blighted corn, the burned tobacco or the livestock sacrificed for a pittance." The State Board of Health and the State College of Agriculture had both argued that conditions could not be worse. "Destitution and hunger are present now, and a winter famine is just around the corner."[61]

Ben Kilgore, editor of the *Progressive Farmer,* wrote Hyde after traveling across the state. Recalling how the government had aided the

17

flood refugees in 1927, Kilgore argued that an even greater calamity confronted the region. Although the drought was not as spectacular as the flood, it had been more deadly and far reaching. He predicted that many independent farmers would lose their land to the Federal Land Bank, insurance companies, or banks unless cheaper credit were offered. As for the poorer and tenant farmers, he urged Red Cross help immediately and the extension of some form of federal credit. Unless these measures were taken, he warned that starvation, sickness, suffering, and death would surely follow.[62]

By late August the Red Cross confronted difficult choices. Kentucky and Arkansas had emerged as the two hardest-hit states and both would undoubtedly require a relief program. The questions were when and how much. According to William Baxter, manager of the midwestern branch, all of Arkansas was "relief minded" because it had been accustomed to Red Cross aid. He also noted the impossibility of determining need due to drought or depression.[63] DeWitt Smith, assistant national director of Domestic Operations, agreed with Baxter and recognized that neither Arkansas nor Kentucky could possibly raise enough money to help their own people. Yet he thought a massive relief operation would bankrupt the agency. During the Mississippi flood the Red Cross operated in 170 counties but at least 200 and possibly 300 counties would need help with the current crisis. All estimates predicted that in Arkansas and Kentucky alone a program would cost $75,000 to $250,000 per county. Smith urged national headquarters to formulate a definite plan lest it be saddled with "a job of such magnitude as to dwarf by comparison everything else the Red Cross has done since the war."[64]

National headquarters faced grim prospects in late August—the fall and winter months would provide a task greater than any domestic effort it had ever undertaken. As a result, it would become involved, without calculation, in a program that was not always directly due to a disaster—at least as defined in traditional Red Cross terms. As human distress increased in the fall, representatives found it increasingly more difficult to deny relief to people whose suffering did not result directly from the drought. In late August and early fall the agency simply marked time, awaiting the winter's challenge and persistently denying that a major food program would be needed for fear the victims would increase their demands for help.

In the fall of 1930, while Hoover and the Red Cross continued to support a limited relief program, to conserve resources in anticipation of the certain famine they expected in the winter, farmers and their families desperately needed food and medical attention. They, too, awaited the winter, but these people knew better than Hoover or the Red Cross what lay ahead, for rural southerners were accustomed to natural and human misfortunes, as well as the hardship that usually resulted from the inadequate aid that they were given. For them, hunger and want in the winter would simply be a matter of degree. Many surely felt as J. Newt Brandt, a Kentucky farmer, who wrote to Hoover, "We are in the most critical condition with the most serious problems confronting us that we have ever faced. How many of us are to get by without suffering to humanity and also to our stock is beyond our comprehension. This is not a tale for sympathy," he insisted. "It is nothing but cold facts."[65]

Notes

1. For a discussion of life as a sharecropper, see Harry Crews, *A Childhood: The Biography of a Place* (New York, 1978); Jane Maguire, *On Shares: Ed Brown's Story* (New York, 1975); H. L. Mitchell, *Mean Things Happening in This Land: The Life and Times of H. L. Mitchell, Cofounder of the Southern Tenant Farmers Union* (Montclair, N.J., 1979); Theodore Rosengarten, *All God's Dangers: The Life of Nate Shaw* (New York, 1975).

2. American National Red Cross, *Relief Work in the Drought of 1930–31* (Washington, D.C., 1931), 9.

3. Arkansas *Gazette,* July 28, 1930.

4. Ibid., Aug. 21, 1930.

5. Louisville *Courier-Journal,* Aug. 9, 1930.

6. New York *Times,* Aug. 7, 1930.

7. Arkansas *Gazette,* Aug. 3, 1930.

8. Ibid., July 31, 1930.

9. Memphis *Commercial-Appeal,* Aug. 24, 1930.

10. Louisville *Courier-Journal,* Aug. 9, 1930.

11. Arkansas *Gazette,* Aug. 10, 1930.

12. Ibid., July 20, 1930.

13. Ibid., July 14, 1930.

14. Laptad to Edith Butler, Aug. 9, 1930, American Red Cross Papers, (hereafter ARC), DR-401. 11/08. These papers are now located in the National Archives, Washington, D.C.

15. Methodist Minister to Hoover, Aug. 15, 1930, Secretary of Agriculture Papers, Acc. 234, Dr. 191, Record Group 16, National Archives.

16. Arkansas *Gazette,* Aug. 10, 1930.

17. "Summary of Reports from Red Cross Field Representatives Related to the Drought Situation as of August 8, 1930," ARC, DR-401.11.

18. Brown to Bondy, July 31, 1930, Hayes to Bondy, July 26, 1930, ibid.

19. "Summary of Reports," ibid.

20. Rust to Bondy, Aug. 7, 1930, ibid.

21. Memphis *Commercial-Appeal,* Aug. 15, 1930.

22. Red Cross, *Relief Work in the Drought,* 17.

23. Ibid.

24. Schafer to Walter Davidson, Aug. 2, 1930, ARC, DR-401.02.

25. Hoover has been the subject of several recent studies. For biographies, see Joan Hoff Wilson, *Herbert Hoover: The Forgotten Progressive* (Boston, 1975), and David Burner, *Herbert Hoover: A Public Life* (New York, 1979). Two articles reflecting Hoover's attitude toward relief and unemployment are Carolyn Grin's "The Unemployment Conference of 1921: An Experiment in National Cooperative Planning," *Mid-America* 55 (1973), 83–107, and Ellis W. Hawley's "Herbert Hoover, the Commerce Secretariat, and the Vision of an 'Associative State.'" *Journal of American History* 61 (1974), 116–40. For Hoover's involvement in the Russian famine-relief program, see Benjamin M. Weissman, *Herbert Hoover and Famine Relief to Soviet Russia, 1921-23* (Stanford, 1974). For Hoover's role in the drought, see Robert Cowley, "The Drought and the Dole," *American Heritage* 23 (1972), 16–19, and David E. Hamilton, "Herbert Hoover and the Great Drought of 1930," *Journal of American History* 68 (1982), 850–75. See also Robert H. Zieger, "Herbert Hoover: A Reinterpretation," *American Historical Review* 81 (1976), 800–810.

26. Romasco, *Poverty of Abundance,* 111.

27. Ibid., 97–124.

28. This brief biographical information was obtained from an American Red Cross news release of Payne's death, Jan. 24, 1925. No biography exists.

29. Payne to members of the Central Committee, Aug. 13, 1930, ARC, DR-401.02.

30. Payne to Chapter Chairmen, Aug. 13, 1930, ibid.

31. William Starr Meyers, ed., *The State Papers and Other Public Writings of Herbert Hoover* (New York, 1934), 1:563.

32. Grin, "Unemployment Conference of 1921."

33. Arkansas *Gazette,* Aug. 16, 1930.

34. Memorandum on the Conference on the Drought Committee at the White House, Aug. 21, 1930, ARC, DR-401.02.

35. "Report submitted to the Hon. Henry M. Robinson," Aug. 27, 1930, ibid.

36. Jones to Hoover, Aug. 8, 1930, Secretary of Agriculture Papers, Acc. 234, Dr. 192. Jones was president of a farm loan association consisting of 500 members, many of whom were black.

37. J. A. Baker and J. G. McNeely, *Land Tenure in Arkansas: I, The Farm Tenancy Situation,* Arkansas Agricultural Experimental Station Bulletin No. 384 (Fayetteville, 1940).

38. Pete Daniel, *The Shadow of Slavery: Peonage in the South, 1901-1969* (Urbana, 1972), 158–66; Daniel, *Deep'n As It Come.*

39. Louisville *Courier-Journal,* Aug. 16, 1930.

40. Gail S. Murray, "Forty Years Ago: The Great Depression in Arkansas,"

Arkansas Historical Quarterly 29 (1970), 293. The following data, prepared by the Department of Agriculture in 1928, reveal the extent of farm mortgages and indebtedness by farmers in the drought states.

State	Farm mortgages	Ratio of debt to total value	Bank Failures 1928-29	
Ark.	$103,464,000	20.8	14	11
Ky.	103,789,000	13.2	7	2
Va.	87,117,000	11.0	—	—
W. Va.	20,155,000	6.2	5	14
Ala.	69,488,000	17.8	0	11
La.	61,760,000	20.3	2	0
Miss.	111,500,000	26.9	4	1
Tenn.	96,711,000	13.7	4	12

(Aug. 15, 1930. ARC, DR-401.08).

41. See the statements of Bernard W. Snow, former assistant secretary in the Department of Agriculture, Alexander Legge of the Federal Farm Board, and former Secretary of Agriculture Henry C. Wallace, in "The Great Drought of 1930," *Literary Digest*, Aug. 16, 1930, 6.

42. Wilson, *Herbert Hoover,* 46–47.

43. Mena (Ark.) *Star,* Aug. 29, 1930.

44. Hot Springs (Ark.) *Sentinel-Record,* Aug. 17, 1930.

45. Arkansas *Gazette,* Aug. 23, 1930.

46. Louisville *Courier-Journal,* Aug. 16, 1930.

47. William A. Capps to Carl Williams, Aug. 28, 1930, Secretary of Agriculture Papers, Acc. 234, Dr. 191.

48. Louisville *Courier-Journal,* Aug. 25, 1930.

49. Ibid., Aug. 26, 1930.

50. Arkansas *Gazette,* Aug. 22, 1930.

51. Ibid., Aug. 21, 1930.

52. Ibid., Aug. 22, 1930.

53. Ibid., Aug. 23, 1930.

54. Ibid., Aug. 21, 1930.

55. Ibid., Aug. 24, 1930.

56. Ibid.

57. Ibid.

58. Louisville *Courier-Journal,* Aug. 24, 1930.

59. Ibid.

60. Ibid., Aug. 29, 1930.

61. Ibid.

62. Kilgore to Hyde, Sept. 3, 1930, Secretary of Agriculture Papers, Acc. 234, DR. 191.

63. Baxter to Fieser, Aug. 22, 1930, ARC, DR-401.01.

64. Smith to Fieser, Aug. 24, 1930, ibid.

65. Brandt to Hoover, Aug. 31, 1930, Secretary of Agriculture Papers, Acc. 234, Dr. 191.

2
The Harvest

The seeds of disaster sown by the summer drought reaped a harvest of hunger and destitution in the fall and winter of 1930. Herbert Hoover's agricultural program proved inadequate—as many had predicted. Few farmers possessed collateral to obtain credit or the needed funds to purchase feed at reduced rates, and local grain dealers and wholesalers were accused of profiteering. According to C. E. Brehm of the University of Tennessee Extension Service, almost all the feed shipments had been consigned to dealers or wholesalers who sold to consumers in small lots. Since the average farmer did not need an entire car lot of feed, the dealers did not confine themselves to distributing to the needy drought farmers, but sold the surplus feed at higher prices to big farmers.[1]

At the same time the Red Cross's fall seed distribution program did not help the many who needed food now. Conflicting reports continued to appear concerning the extent of hunger, as both political and economic leaders in the plantation region insisted that conditions were not as bad as had been predicted. They called upon the victims to persevere, shrouding their arguments in the veneer of the work ethic by saying that those who were hungry had not labored enough. Letters from the sufferers, while taking issue with the optimistic reports of their plight, did not challenge the work ethic. The drought perplexed them and challenged their ideology, for they had worked hard and long, yet their families were starving. Many finally sought outside aid, while others, like the sharecroppers, accustomed to being fed by the landowners, looked immediately to the Red Cross for food.

These conflicting reports led Vice-Chairman James L. Fieser to observe, "Editorials are coming out saying that help is not needed, and yet the people themselves are asking for help." He urged the agency either to withdraw from the scene or begin a program. Fieser warned, however, that once the organization began feeding, it would not be able to stop until spring. "There no doubt is suffering now, and what we are to do about it is one of the most serious problems ever facing the organization."[2]

DeWitt Smith agreed that "the pressing problem now is food for human beings" and estimated that from 100,000 to 200,000 families would need to be fed—an effort that could cost as much as $5 million.[3] Most all of the officials questioned whether or not they could raise enough funds in the fall when America was in the midst of a depression and when other charitable groups would also try to solicit contributions. They finally decided to aid silently needy local chapters and to prevent any publicity regarding the extent of privation. Fieser made this clear to Hoover in a meeting on September 26, when he assured the president that states and localities would be encouraged to care for their own cases, while the increase in numbers of hungry would be downplayed.[4]

Fieser's plan was apparently successful, for at least one journal, *The Nation,* voiced skepticism over the sudden disappearance of the drought in the media. The optimistic outpourings from the region's leaders and newspapers did not suggest the "appalling calamity for which Mr. Hoover gave up his vacation and summoned the governors of a dozen states, worked out a great scheme of state and county committees and called on the Red Cross to stand by."[5]

The drought persisted, oblivious to the bureaucratic maneuverings in Washington, where officials played possum with the disaster. Letters from the sufferers continued to describe the hunger and disease that stalked their land, while the county and state committees argued that they could care for their own. The Red Cross chose to listen to the latter.

The agency's policy was influenced strongly by the plantation county committees that consisted of a planter, merchant, banker, and county judge. In September and October such committees denied fervently the existence of suffering, most agreeing with former Governor George W. Donaghey that conditions had been exaggerated. "I do not believe any honest man in Arkansas who wants to work and has done his best to make a living is actually facing starvation."[6] That nature nullified the Protestant work ethic was incomprehensible to Donaghey and others like him. In reality their major concern was less ideology and more a fear that a prospective free ration would encourage croppers not to pick cotton at a 50 percent wage reduction. Empty bellies served as an excellent motivation to work.

In September the state and local drought committees filed reports,

the majority arguing against Red Cross help. They expressed the traditional attitude toward the poor, viewing those who sought relief as the
usual residue of the southern agricultural system—the poor white trash
and the black sharecroppers who lazily awaited the dole. Those who
sought work, they believed, could find it. Harvey C. Couch of the
Arkansas committee warned that the drought should not be a "prosperous"
disaster like the 1927 flood, when blacks received enormous quantities
of free rations. "When this becomes generally known, many who are in
distress now will suddenly realize they are not so badly off after all."
He described an incident in southeastern Arkansas where hundreds of
blacks had descended upon a town after hearing a rumor that food
was available. "Nothing of this kind is contemplated by any relief
agency, and the quicker it is generally understood the better."[7] Apparently
he had forgotten that the major abuses in 1927 had come from the
planter community.[8]

In a similar vein E. P. Krick of the Louisiana Red Cross indicated
an indifference to the poor. Commenting on reports about families
unable to send their children to school for lack of clothing, Krick
responded, "I venture to say that in many of the rural sections it is
immaterial to almost 50 percent of the parents as to whether or not their
children go to school." Instead, they were simply using the disaster as an
excuse not to send them. "It is also a fact," he continued, "that during
the winter months of a normal year much suffering is evident on the
part of the poor white people and negroes, so I see no reason at this
time for all the hysteria on the subject."[9]

The American dream of success, the belief that anyone who worked
hard enough could survive and succeed, did not crash in 1929 or dry up
during the drought of 1930. The ideas of hard work, self-reliance,
independence, and individualism persisted, at least in theory, during
the difficult fall of 1930. Political and economic leaders refused to admit
that the system had collapsed and that they lacked the resources to care
for their own. The success myth declared that every individual could
make it if he or she tried hard enough. People asking the committees for
aid did not represent obvious examples of the economy's failure; rather,
they admitted a weakness of character. Men like Krick possessed a
callous acceptance of suffering among certain classes of people—an
almost Darwinian view that poor whites and blacks had always suffered
and always would, due to their innate inferiority and indolence. Croppers and the white trash of the hills or sandy pine areas represented

the unfit in society, the wasted people who lived beyond the pale of respectability. Since they exemplified the poor that "always ye have with you," many community leaders saw no reason to worry about them. They had been poor prior to the drought and depression, and there was no need to get hysterical about them during a famine.

The validity of the work ethic depended upon a society of abundance rather than one of scarcity. No provisions existed in the network of beliefs to deal with a drought or a depression. In any case, the American dream assumed continuing progress, and, if an occasional disaster occurred, it merely represented a temporary deviation from the norm. If people could just hold on long enough and have sufficient faith and endurance, they would survive until the inevitable times of prosperity returned. Because of this ideology, individuals were forced to accept the major responsibility for their condition in the fall of 1930. In the face of a destroyed credit system, ruined crops, and no food or clothing, they were expected to survive largely on their own or with the aid of their neighbors. For these reasons, when victims wrote to the Red Cross requesting help, they argued their case within the framework of these old American values.

Letters from the sufferers expressed more than a mere affirmation of faith in traditional values. Some disclosed bewilderment and frustration at the meager results produced by hard work, while others reflected anger at a system that refused to recognize the absurdity of trying to live on nonexistent resources. Still others revealed an honest humility when confronted with an inability to provide food for their families. All of these reactions reflected the complexities and contradictions of American ideology. In a democratic capitalistic society individuals were supposedly free to pursue their own goals. Hard work was the vehicle that propelled them along the road through the vast American garden of abundance, but when the garden shriveled no alternative cornucopias existed. Despite years of hard work, rural southerners in 1930 had reached, not the Garden of Eden, but a dry and arid desert. Self-reliance, thrift, and hard work would not produce crops from dust. Nor would the continued belief in the American dream substitute for food on the table. As people realized the bankruptcy of their resources, they looked first to the Red Cross and, finally, by December, to the federal government. Their letters revealed frustration, pathos, anger, but most of all guilt, for they questioned whether they had failed as Americans.

From the hills of Arkansas came letters indicating the failure of community efforts to meet the crisis. A Presbyterian minister from Montgomery County, John T. Barr, wrote that his county was unable to help itself. "We have no well-to-do-people. Our merchants are nearly all practically insolvent. All of us have been helping the destitute about us to the extent of our ability, and it is useless to attempt to raise money among people who do not have it." He had visited one family who had been, like many others, living on corn, bread, and grease for some time. According to Barr, people had planted some turnips, but he emphasized the immediate need for food to feed the starving. In a line that Erskine Caldwell might have used in *Tobacco Road,* Barr said, "We are *all* hard hit here, and we know we cannot raise any appreciable amount in this county."[10]

A local committeeman in Sevier County reported that 200 families required instant help. Pleading that the agency not be misled by newspaper accounts minimizing conditions, J. R. Hooten observed that "the failure of every bank in the county but three has finished the job. There are several fellows (well to do) who live in DeQueen who said we are Americans and not beggars. If you will investigate," he insisted, "you will find honest Americans here in Sevier County almost upon starvation."[11] John Penney corroborated Hooten's observations. Farmers in Sevier County "made crops and banks went broke with their savings. None can get credit for a sack of flour, picture a man with a family of 6 or 7, no money, no credit, no work."[12]

An angry lawyer from Russellville, Arkansas, Oliver Moore, was certain that starvation had already produced disease and death. Challenging the optimism of national officials and the millionaire ex-Governor Donaghey, he argued that "to say that people are not suffering of hunger and actually starving in Arkansas is a blind denial of plain facts." Although the dole was undesirable, it would be better than no relief at all. "The American people, however poor and wretched they may be, are a proud people. . . . Americans do not want to be beggars, nor indeed do they want to be hungry."[13]

Writing from the Ozarks, Mrs. Effie Shelton expressed her frustration at not being able to work and feed her family. She did not see how she would be able to make her land payments in December, "If I had the means to go I could go to pick cotton and take the children to help." She questioned her failure in spite of hard efforts. "I can't see why it is that we farmers work from 5 to 9 at night and can't have anything to go on when our merchants can have big new cars every year." Although she had raised 150 pullets, the merchants refused to sell her anymore feed on credit—just when the chickens were ready to produce. Somewhat bitterly, Shelton added that she had bought only feed for her chickens and food for her five children, yet her bill amounted to $350. "I can't pay it or the payment on my house."[14]

Mrs. F. K. Fowler in east central Mississippi, unable to provide for her family, requested aid in sending her children to school. "I am a mother of six little ones," she wrote, "and my husband, an ex-soldier. We have worked hard this year, made a very good crop but it will take every bit of our cotton and corn to pay our furnish bill. I don't expect new clothes, just clothes that is laid aside. I am a worried mother."[15]

Pleas came also from the Arkansas Delta as croppers and tenants faced starvation and cold weather. Many resembled that of A. C. Blount, a renter and father of six in Lincoln County, whose thirty acres of cotton had yielded only one bale for which he had received nine and one-half cents per pound. After paying the bank and his landowner their shares, he bought groceries with the remainder. His children needed clothes and shoes for school. "If my mules don't die this winter and I can get something for them to eat I am going to try to make a crop next year." Blount had gone twelve miles into Star City to buy grain, but it was all gone. "I don't know what to do. I don't want the Red Cross to give me nothing. But if you will help me and give me time I will pay you for all that you do for me. I am in need now so I will quit for I no you are getting tired of reading this letter."[16]

Mrs. Ella Price of Monticello, the mother of three sons, inquired of the Arkansas Farmers Protective Bureau about possible employment in her area. "We can't make the winter are all bare foot. The 13 years boy and the 7 years old is just naked, no shoes, nor clothes. We lost all we had three years ago and have made crop failure ever since. Now we surely would be glad to get some clothes and shoes for the winter or work." Price concluded that she had a sick child and no medicine for him. "I can't see how we will get by."[17]

Lillie Hughes, a widow in Shirley, Arkansas, asked the Red Cross for help in returning to England. "I wish if you will please send me some clothes. Just enough to wear to the cotton patch. I want to go to the Bottoms where I can get work to do. I haven't got a shoe are a dress are sweaters. Not a thing at all."[18] And in Magnolia Rena Brown wrote, "I am near at my row's end. I am asking you for help or advice some way." Neither she nor her children could find work and they lacked food and clothing. "I would hate to perries and suffer. I would hate to beg. The road looks dime to me."[19]

Things did not seem much brighter for A. S. Heath, a farmer near Pine Bluff, who could not find any work. Although he had sold everything to buy food, he still could not feed his family of eight. "The committee at Sheridan has turned me down twice and the way I have to go is in wagon while my mortgaged team is on the open range and quite a job to catch for a weak starving man and to be turned down." He asked the Red Cross for food and clothing.[20]

Some victims carried humility to great lengths, seeing themselves as sinners in the hands of an angry God. From the heart of the Delta, in Parkin, Arkansas, twenty-nine croppers, with families ranging from one to ten members, petitioned for assistance.

We sinners are asking the Red Cross for help. We are having rainey weather hear and can't get to pick cotton and just get 50 cents per 100, when we can pick and the landholders we are with will not advance any money or supplies only just as you pick the cotton and we can not support our families at the present price of cotton picking there are several of these sinners have children that kneeds to be in school, and can not go because their parents can not git the money to buy clothese for them to waire and pick cotton for 50¢ per 100, and we urged that you will give this prompt attention as we sinners or in kneed cessity for supplies.[21]

All of these letters and petitions, whether they came from community leaders, poor subsistence farmers in the hills, or Delta croppers, expressed similar concerns. All of the correspondents asked for help because their efforts had proved useless in the face of the drought. No matter how desperately they sought employment, jobs simply did not exist. A far cry from the indolent and shiftless described by the relief committees, they hardly represented people who complacently awaited Red Cross rations. The victims' letters clearly revealed that they had asked for help only after exhausting all other possibilities. Lacking food, clothes, and jobs, they faced two choices—either they could seek outside aid, or they could watch their families slowly starve to death. In September and October hundreds chose to ask for Red Cross support, but the agency listened to the planters. By November many had starved in cold cabins. Few letters from the destitute arrived at Red Cross headquarters after mid-October, for the organization had turned its ears to other voices.

The large landowners, who dominated the relief committees in the cotton-growing counties, denied the existence of suffering and refused to participate in the Red Cross seed distribution program. They feared that even a suggestion of outside aid would encourage their croppers to leave the fields and refuse to work at a wage reduction of 50 percent. Planters were pushing the workers past the threshold of endurance. With no gardens, no prospect of other furnishings, and no other source of work, croppers had no choice but to work for less wages, even as they were hungry and weak. By late November, however, after the cotton had been gathered, planters greedily accepted rations to furnish their workers. If croppers starved in the winter, they would not be able to plant in the spring.

On September 15, in the Delta city of Helena, Arkansas, twenty growers announced that Phillips County would not solicit outside aid. They argued that if black sharecroppers, who comprised 80 percent of the population, suspected a free ration they would refuse to work.[22] Despite this refusal of aid, a Red Cross report estimated that at least from 750 to 1,000 families would need food by November.[23]

Having similar apprehensions, Blytheville planters informed the Red Cross that Mississippi County would not participate in the seed distribution, insisting that the 1927 flood experience had ruined their labor force. Cotton-picking season had begun, and they feared croppers would refuse to pick for a 50¢ wage.[24]

In nearby Monroe County, a committee chairman questioned the wisdom of a fall operation. According to R. F. Milwee, if a Red Cross program were started, the workers would refuse to pick. "Some you know, are ready to let the Red Cross do it all, we think after the cotton is out we can raise some money, and as the worst is to come in the cold winter months, we think it best to postpone doing only what is absolutely necessary at this time, knowing that a person can get along on very little during warm weather."[25] The Pulaski County chairman agreed: "A food program at this time is, I think, not to be considered; would be extremely harmful to the participants, and disturb economic conditions. Such a program is a constant fear in the minds of many of our people. Of that we speak advisedly.[26]

Milwee's fears were justified, for many workers did as croppers in Cotton Plant, who, angry over the planters unwillingness to participate in the garden seed distribution, were reluctant to pick cotton at the reduced wage. According to a local committee member, "The Negroes have been holding meetings and I am sure they have written everybody from Hoover down. They are not in as good humor as I would like to see them. They do not like to pick cotton at 50¢."[27] Similar incidents occurred elsewhere. Jefferson County had a black population of 85 percent and, as described by a Red Cross agent, was an area where "the old traditions of the southern plantation hold more strongly" than in any other community.[28] Thus, it was understandable that when croppers refused to work, the Pine Bluff *Daily Graphic* attributed their unacceptable behavior to outside forces. "Belief that agitation of a communistic nature from some outside source is being fostered among the negro and 'poor white' farmers of Jefferson County was expressed here yesterday when plantation owners reported a flat refusal on the part of tenants to start picking cotton." Rumors had spread that the Red Cross would feed them and many had decided to await their rations.[29] In response to the incident, the local Red Cross chapter made a list of those refusing to work to insure they did not receive any benefits.[30]

A letter from a Jefferson County cropper revealed an awareness that the planters intended to prevent a feeding program until after picking season had ended. Annie Whitehead wrote in September that "some people in here are scarsley living in here and the white people here some of them grumbling about giving us something to eat and say they can no give us any work to do because they have not any money to pay for work." When she asked the planter how they were to eat, he replied that the Red Cross did not have any money. Whitehead had sought work, but the owners had told her that they had only enough cotton to pick for themselves. "We are in a poor state for living," she told the Red Cross, "if you can give us any aid please do so. We have our ground work well but no result."[31]

The Jefferson County incident exemplified the fear and hysteria produced by the drought. Planters, afraid of losing their work force and hence their crops, fought desperately to prevent any relief measures in the fall. Croppers, already weakened by hunger, saw no reason to work for reduced wages and no assurance of food for the winter, when the Red Cross would supposedly feed them. They knew from their previous experience in the 1927 flood that the organization could help if it wanted. Others, like Whitehead, desired earnestly to work but lacked opportunity. The Red Cross represented the only alternative. All of these responses were to be expected in the plantation counties where the landowners had always dictated the lives of their workers and where the laborers themselves were accustomed to the remnants of a paternalistic system that cared for their needs—though often inadequately and always at a dear price—not only in monetary, but in human terms as well.[32]

Officials at national headquarters realized that no relief would be administered except within the confines of the plantation system. A. L. Schafer observed in October that the planters would refuse aid in the fall but would plead for it in the winter. Ideally, he thought a work program the best form of relief.[33] Charles Carr of the Mississippi Red Cross committee agreed and suggested that planters be made beneficiaries, using the rations to hire croppers to clear plantations.[34] E. P. Krick of Louisiana, however, reminded Shafer of the fallacy of such an approach, saying that the planters would easily violate the plan, using the food to hold their workers.[35]

The Red Cross never adopted officially any of the suggested ideas, although some local organizations did. Abuses similar to those of 1927 occurred also. As early as December 4 President James P. Davis of the National Federation of Colored Farmers wrote DeWitt Smith that blacks in Tallahatchie, Mississippi, had complained about planter abuses of the relief operation. In their settlements with tenants landlords had allegedly deducted food which the tenants understood had been furnished by the Red Cross.[36]

By November all of the conditions predicted by agency workers had materialized. Cases of widespread suffering and increases in pellagra appeared with greater frequency. Finally even planters cried out for relief, inasmuch as their laborers lacked food and clothing. A letter from a black farmer in Moscow, Jefferson County, Arkansas, where planters had so adamantly refused aid until after picking season, expressed the hopeless plight of the workers. "There is thousands of collard farmers in Jefferson and Lincoln counties that has not bread," wrote W. R. Walker. "They are Bairfooted and thin closed many has went to the County Judge and to the local Red Cross they Both say that they has no Funds We are planning on sending a Collard men to Washington to lay our Trubles more clearly before you."[37]

Matters worsened on November 17, when forty-three Arkansas banks failed. The American Exchange Trust Company of Little Rock suspended operations and carried with it member institutions through-out the state with deposits totaling $27 million; a large number of these were planter-merchant banks in the Delta.[38] Even if the plantation counties had possessed sufficient resources prior to these failures, they certainly had none after the catastrophic events of mid-November.

Stories of needy families filled the newspapers and poured into the state Red Cross office during late November and early December. On November 29 the Arkansas *Gazette* reported "scores of school children in Pulaski County who have no shoes, no clothes, and little food." While many had lacked these necessities in the fall, they found it harder to get by in the cold winter months.[39] State Extension Director T. Roy Reid surveyed forty-three counties and discovered that 12,450 rural children could not attend school for lack of books and clothing.[40]

By December privation had reached extreme proportions. In Eudora, Arkansas, a township of 2,000 people, 1,069 registered for food, while Red Cross workers announced that 600 more would soon apply. A county chapter telegram to the national office described the situation as "grave and relief imperative," for many cases of actual slow starvation existed.[41] Despite requests from other Delta counties, agency officials still denied that plantation workers constituted a Red Cross responsibility. They recognized, however, that hunger had developed to the point where the organization was obliged to act, for the landowners could not assume the responsibility.[42] A report from St. Francis County finally convinced them of the need to help the victims.[43]

When the St. Francis County, Arkansas, chapter received over 3,774 requests for aid, the organization invited the state Red Cross director, Albert Evans, to visit cropper homes on Christmas day. Evans assumed that even in a drought families would struggle to have food for the holiday and, if not, the planters would "most assuredly supply them with the necessities over Christmas." What he found did not exactly fulfill his expectations, for in the thirty-seven homes he called upon, only six had received rations; one of them had shared their provisions with another family. None had coffee or butter, two had milk, and one sugar. A widow and seven children exemplified the plight. Their cupboard held a pint of flour and a few scraps of chicken bones, evidently the remains of the previous evening's meal. The only other food in the house consisted of twenty cans of fruit and vegetables the mother had put up during the summer. Their neighbors fared no better, living in cold cabins pasted with newspapers and eating remnants of lard and meal. One family of ten lived on a few pounds of rice, flour, beans, and lard, but all of the children were almost naked. Perhaps the most destitute he visited was a white family who had just eaten the last of their flour. Despite these conditions, Evans found no hysteria; instead, people just sat around their fires uncomplaining.[44] This listlessness probably represented the early stages of pellagra, for the cycle of the disease begins with an insufficient diet which manifests itself by sapping the energy from its victims.[45]

According to Evans, the landowners were just as incapable of helping themselves. One planter, Ed Belcher, frankly admitted he could not furnish his fifty-six families because he could no longer obtain credit. He carried a $75,000 mortgage on his land, and his crops had cost him $13,000 more than he had expected. In addition, his tenants owed over $12,000 in furnishings. Unless he could get a loan, Belcher doubted whether he could feed his croppers in the future.[46] What Evans did not recognize was that Belcher, though certainly in dire economic straits, could, unlike his croppers, still eat.

In nearby Lee County Evans talked with local chapter officials who told him that he had visited the accessible homes in St. Francis. If he had gone to the more isolated ones, he would have seen even worse conditions. The trip convinced him that there was a "condition not only of suffering but actual starvation in Arkansas." In almost all instances he had seen members of the families barefoot and inadequately clothed. These findings, he argued, questioned the adequacy of Red Cross relief, and he urged prompt and drastic action. "Had a newspaperman without Red Cross background gone into these homes, publicity of the most damaging character could result." Citing a plantation whose total crop returns had dropped from $33,000 in 1929 to $7,800 in 1930, he said that absolutely no local resources existed to meet the crisis.[47]

Evans's report represented the inadequacy of the Red Cross's and Hoover's approach to the drought. Officials had known since early August that people were hungry and ill and that conditions would certainly worsen in the winter. Instead of aiding the needy directly, the Red Cross followed the wishes of the planters. Although letters from the victims and some of their own representatives described suffering, the national headquarters chose to acknowledge only the most optimistic views of the local and state committees. On September 27 DeWitt Smith had observed improved morale in the stricken region and, especially, a desire among the Arkansas drought committee to have the Red Cross withdraw completely.[48] He noted again on October 2 that "pressure for a food program has lessened and most, if not all of our state directors now feel that even if they remain in the field they can withstand the demands until late November or early December." However, he stated that the agency would undoubtedly have to offer food during the winter at which time it would be easier to describe destitution to the public and to raise more funds.[49] Yet Smith had said only a few days earlier that the "most pressing problem now is food for human beings."[50] Red Cross policy in the fall revealed a greater concern for bureaucratic details than for the needs of the hungry. It knew from the flood experience that the planters would seek to control relief, and yet the agency accepted their estimation of the drought's impact on the poor. When in December thousands starved, the Red Cross shoved the drought back to the front pages. Surely a bewildered public wondered where all of the hungry people had come from after being told for so long that all was well in the dry land.

Had the Red Cross acted earlier, some of the problems (like pellagra) could have been prevented. In late September Arkansas State Health Commissioner Dr. C. W. Garrison had predicted a large increase in pellagra and warned that, unless early relief measures were instituted and pure yeast distributed, the incidence and death rate due to the disease would be higher in the spring than ever before. Garrison also informed Evans that many deaths would occur during the next twelve months that would never be recorded as having any relationship to the drought. He was convinced that the drought and inadequate relief measures would be responsible for the increased mortality, especially among those dying of malnutrition. Noting how he had received requests from numerous counties for yeasts to combat pellagra, Garrison urged Evans to begin yeast distribution immediately. However, Dr. William DeKleine, who was visiting the area on behalf of the agency, suggested that such a program not be initiated unless a ration operation was started in January and February. Unfortunately, DeKleine had talked only to drought county chairmen and had apparently adopted their viewpoint, for he said in his report that "the croppers would not work if they expected to be fed later by the Red Cross. Apparently the only way to get negroes to exert themselves as much as they should is to let them feel that they will not receive any help."[51]

National headquarters agreed with DeKleine and the regional leaders, for they led the croppers, through the planters, to believe no aid would be forthcoming, forcing them to work when many suffered from hunger and disease and lacked proper clothing. Furthermore, had the agency started yeast distribution in the fall, the increase in pellagra could have been prevented long before it reached serious proportions in the winter. The Red Cross knew from the Mississippi flood that, unless food was provided during the early winter months, the increase in the disease would be enormous. Yet nothing was done. The Red Cross ignored Garrison's advice and that of Reid, who insisted that reports on the states' conditions had been "overly optimistic" and who warned it would be disastrous should the agency withdraw from the scene.[52] By December A. L. Schafer was forced to admit that "in a considerable part of the drought territory actual suffering from want of food and warm clothing exists in greater intensity and to a greater extent than many of us at Headquarters, who are far removed from it, appreciate." That Red Cross records did not reflect this condition in requests received from its chapters for financial assistance, he continued, did not deny the facts. Many field workers had gone into their counties "feeling that national headquarters would prefer to close its eyes to the actual situation just as long as possible." Expressing the usual concern about the agency's public image, he concluded that "we must not lay ourselves open to the charge of inactivity or inefficiency on the part of our organization, nor of obstructing relief that might be administered through other agencies."[53]

From September through mid-October national headquarters had agreed publicly to help only those chapters that shared a part of the burden, expecting each to pay at least one-third of the seed distribution program.[54] Then by closing all relief offices, it created a public impression that the crisis had ended. Like Hoover and the state and local officials, organization personnel sought to instill confidence in the economic system, despite its total collapse. Their optimism was not warranted, for in December all of the forecasts made by both the sufferers and individuals like Garrison and Reid were realized. As thousands of croppers languished in their cabins, planters begged the Red Cross to feed their work force.[55] Relief procedures during the fall of 1930 revealed the absurdity of Red Cross policy. In an attempt to conserve its $5 million fund for the winter, when it would have to aid more people, it withheld in the fall—when starvation and deprivation actually existed—the food, clothing, and yeast that could have prevented widespread suffering and disease. It was as if statistics were all that mattered. As long as only a few hundred people starved, the problem was not considered serious. Even when the Red Cross provided relief, as in St. Francis County, administrative hold-ups often stalled relief.

In spite of local and state agency reports of extensive suffering in December, no relief program was forthcoming. As demands for help increased, Congress proposed its own plan. Due to his own inaction,

Hoover's nightmare of a dole system now loomed as a possibility as congressmen urged greater federal involvement with the needy.

Notes

1. C. E. Brehm to C. W. Warburton, Oct. 18, 1930, Secretary of Agriculture Papers, National Drought Relief Committee, 1930–31, Freight B–F, Box 4, RG 16. Letters poured into the office of Warburton, director of the U.S. Extension Service, complaining about the abuses of the reduced freight rate system. Kentucky State Drought Chairman Harry Volz wrote that "our dealers and millers in this territory are complaining that their competitors aren't passing on to the farmer consumer the freight rate reduction." In Volz's opinion the farmer consumer had not taken advantage of the reduction; rather, the dealers had used the reduction to increase their business. (Volz to Warburton, Sept. 20, 1930, ibid.) Other letters reported that wealthy farmers had benefited from the reduced rates when they obviously had not suffered the losses that smaller farmers had experienced. See A. Lane Cricher to County Agent of McAlester, Okla., Nov. 17, 1930, Cricher to County Agent of Rustberg, Va., Nov. 12, 1930, Cricher to County Agent in Quanah, Tex., Oct. 24, 1930, all in ibid., Box 5. The letters concerning these abuses are obviously too numerous to cite; however, the evidence strongly suggests that large farmers and grain dealers benefited most from the reduced rates.

Another complaint centered on the failure to grant extensions for farmers who had mortgages with the Federal Land Bank and could not meet their payments. Again these letters are numerous; for example, see Chester Morril to Hyde, Nov. 12, 1930, ibid., Box 4; Harvey G. Fields to Warburton, Dec. 3, 1930, ibid., Box 7; Leland Bunch to Joseph T. Robinson, Oct. 30, 1930, Robinson Papers, private collection of Grady Miller, Little Rock, Ark. Robinson received several letters requesting that he seek extensions for farmers with loans with the Federal Land Bank.

2. Minutes of the Staff Council Meeting, Sept. 23, 1930, ARC, No. 140.04, 1–2.

3. Ibid.

4. Fieser to Hoover, Sept. 26, 1930, ARC, DR-401.08.

5. *Nation,* Sept. 10, 1930, 257.

6. Arkansas *Gazette,* Sept. 4, 1930.

7. Ibid., Sept. 7, 1930.

8. Daniel, *Shadow of Slavery,* 158–66.

9. Krick, "Report of Louisiana Drought Relief as of October 11, 1930," ARC, DR-401.02.

10. Barr to Evans, Sept. 3, 6, 1930, ARC, DR-401.08.

11. Hooten to Evans, Sept. 3, 1930, ibid.

12. Penney to Gov. Harvey Parnell, Sept. 10, 1930, ibid.

13. Oliver Moore, an open letter to President Hoover and George W. Donaghey, Sept. 1, 1930, Secretary of Agriculture Papers, Acc. 234, Dr. 191.

14. Shelton to former President Calvin Coolidge, Sept. 10, 1930, ibid., Dr. 192.

15. Fowler to American Red Cross, Oct. 4, 1930, ARC, DR-401.08.

16. Blount to American Red Cross, Oct. 9, 1930, ibid.

17. Price to Arkansas Farmers Protective Bureau, Oct. 17, 1930, ibid.

18. Hughes to Red Cross, Sept. 9, 1930, ibid.

19. Brown to Harvey Couch, Aug. 26, 1930, ibid.

20. Heath to Arkansas Red Cross, Sept. 12, 1930, ibid.

21. Parkin, Ark., Sept. 11, 1930, ibid.

22. Memphis *Commercial-Appeal,* Sept. 6, 1930.

23. Confidential drought questionnaire, Phillips County, Ark., Sept. 10, 1930, ARC, DR-401.11.

24. Arkansas *Gazette,* Sept. 15, 1930. See A. G. Little's speech on the "cost of self-respect" in ibid., Aug. 23, 1930, and the report of a meeting held by planters, ginners, and merchants that resulted in the 50¢ wage reduction in ibid., Aug. 22, 1930.

25. Milwee to Evans, Sept. 3, 1930, ARC, DR-401.08.

26. Thompson to Couch, Sept. 25, 1930, ibid.

27. W. R. Jones to Evans, Sept. 18, 1930, ibid.

28. Drought Report, Jefferson County, Ark., Sept. 12, 1930, ARC, DR-401.11.

29. Pine Bluff *Daily Graphic,* Sept. 30, 1930.

30. Arkansas *Gazette,* Oct. 1, 1930.

31. Whitehead to Red Cross, Sept. 4, 1930, ARC, DR-401.08.

32. Accounts of similar fears and incidents came from other states. See narrative reports for Mississippi for the week ending Oct. 4, 1930, ibid., and Thompson to Warburton, Oct. 13, 1930, Secretary of Agriculture Papers, National Drought Committee, 1930–31, Box 3.

33. Schafer to Dewitt Smith, Oct. 8, 1930, ARC, DR-401.02.

34. Carr to Red Cross, Oct. 9, 1930, ARC, DR-401.63.

35. Krick to Schafer, Oct. 20, 1930, ibid. See also Evans to Schafer, Oct. 20, 1930, ibid.

36. Smith to Bondy, Dec. 4, 1930, ARC, DR-401.91.

37. Walker to Hyde, Nov. 15, 1930, Secretary of Agriculture Papers, National Drought Committee, Box 1.

38. Arkansas *Gazette,* Nov. 18, 19, 1930. This was part of a larger series of bank failures in the southern and central states. By November 22, 115 such banks had closed their doors—Indiana, 4; North Carolina, 11; Kentucky, 16; Tennessee, 3; Arkansas, 64; Kansas, 1; Illinois and Missouri, 16 total; Charleston (W. Va.) *Gazette,* Nov. 22, 1930.

39. Arkansas *Gazette,* Nov. 29, 1930.

40. Reid to Warburton, Nov. 11, 1930, ARC, DR-401.02.

41. Telegram to National Headquarters from Eudora, Ark., local chapter, Dec. 19, 1930, ARC, DR-401.11.

42. William Baxter to Smith, Dec. 22, 1930, ARC, DR-401.06.

43. Smith to Baxter, Jan. 3, 1931, ibid.

44. Evans to Baxter, "Conditions among the Sharecroppers of Arkansas with

Particular Reference to St. Francis and Lee Counties," Dec. 25, 1930, 1, ARC, DR-401.11.

45. See Joseph Goldberger, "Pellagra in the Mississippi Flood Area," in Milton Terris, ed., *Goldberger on Pellagra* (Baton Rouge, 1964), 271–94.

46. Evans, "Conditions among the Sharecroppers," 4.

47. Ibid., 5.

48. Smith to Fieser, Sept. 27, 1930, ARC, DR-401.031.

49. Smith to Fieser, Oct. 2, 1930, ibid.

50. See Minutes of the Staff Council Meeting, Sept. 23, 1930, ARC, DR-140.04, 1–2.

51. DeKleine, "Report of Visit to Little Rock, Arkansas, and Louisville, Kentucky," Sept. 29, 1930, ibid.

52. Reid to Charles Thompson, Sept. 30, 1930, ARC, DR-401.08.

53. Schafer to Fieser, Dec. 16, 1930, ibid.

54. Red Cross *Courier,* Oct. 15, 1930, 18.

55. Baxter to Smith, Dec. 22, 1930, ARC, DR-401.6.

3

Of Mules and Men

While families in the Delta shivered in the cold and wondered where their next meal would come from, bureaucrats in Washington continued debating the best means for administering relief. Herbert Hoover persisted in his determination to treat the natural and economic catastrophes as he had other such crises. The Red Cross fretted over the increasing numbers who appeared on their rolls and questioned how much longer they could stall a major operation. State drought chairmen looked increasingly to the federal government for help. In December these three groups clashed and, when the New Year dawned, the nation was engulfed in a major debate over unemployment assistance and drought relief.

Drought was only one aspect of the relief controversy in late 1930. With the country in the midst of a depression, millions of Americans were unemployed. Faced with ever-growing demands for aid from all over the nation, Hoover decided in December to coordinate both drought and unemployment assistance through one agency. He drew from his past experiences, especially the Unemployment Conference he had organized in 1921. As before he wanted local governmental and private agencies to coordinate relief to the idle workers. On October 17, 1930, he created the president's Committee for Employment. Under the direction of Colonel Arthur Woods, who had coordinated the 1921 plan, the committee was to encourage the cooperation of federal, state, and local governmental and charitable organizations with industry to increase employment opportunities. Only after these sources had been exhausted would federal intervention be recommended.[1]

The Committee for Employment reflected Hoover's ideology of self-help and local voluntarism and his desire to avoid the introduction of federal measures. His approach to drought and unemployment assistance resembled the techniques he had utilized when feeding the Belgians and Russians and as food administrator during World War I. Rather than working with Congress to devise methods of meeting the depression, he played the role of administrator. Thus, he formed the Woods committee without consulting either party in Congress. For several reasons Hoover viewed unemployment—indeed, the entire depression—as a job for disaster relief. First, he maintained that the depression represented merely a stage in the usual economic cycle and if left alone it would eventually correct itself. Until then the immediate task was to feed those who could not care for themselves. Second, to alleviate human suffering, disaster aid could be initiated by a nongovernmental agency like the Red Cross. By treating unemployment like a natural catastrophe, relief could be short-lived; it would not alter the fundamental social and economic structure; and it would certainly not entail any reforms, much less the beginning of a welfare state. Finally, his years as a relief executive had convinced him of the efficacy of nongovernmental aid. Consulting Congress on the matter could mean compromise, vast expenditures, and delay. For example, a few years earlier, when Hoover was secretary of commerce, President Calvin Coolidge had given Congress a free hand in the Mississippi Valley Flood Control Project, and greedy legislators had indulged in pork-barrel programs. This experience convinced him that relief belonged to the executive, not the legislative, branch.[2]

Even had the president consulted Congress, his chances of cooperation would have been slim. The Republican-dominated Seventy-first Congress had begun in unity only to end in discord. In the spring of 1930 it had overridden Hoover's tariff request and balked at a U.S. Supreme Court appointment. Many Republicans blamed the president for not providing leadership and for his reluctance to speak out on significant issues. But Hoover had never been a politician. As an engineer, an administrator, and as secretary of commerce, he had dictated orders, rarely considering the wishes of others. He lacked an understanding of how the political process worked, refusing to play the games that were so common on Capitol Hill or to compromise.[3] When directing aid to the Belgians and Russians, he had displayed a similar inability to cooperate. Refusing to work with other agencies in 1919, he urged President Woodrow Wilson to form an independent organization, the American Relief Administration, to provide food and supplies in postwar Europe. From 1921 through 1923 as secretary of commerce he directed a $20-million operation to aid famine-stricken Russians. He conducted the program singlehandedly, denying the American Friends

Service Committee and the Red Cross an opportunity to participate.[4] Thus, he had clearly defined ideas as to how relief should be carried out; private organizations, independent of governmental control, could best deal with a crisis. In the winter of 1930–31 the Red Cross—at least as far as Hoover was concerned—became the American Relief Administration for the nation.

As the depression deepened and more Americans searched for work and food, the need for help increased. By the fall of 1930 Hoover and his advisors were convinced that efforts would be made to pressure the federal government into providing aid. Fearing that Congress would soon initiate its own program, Hoover looked for an alternative to meet the needs of the idle. He decided to ask the Red Cross to conduct a fund-raising campaign for both drought and unemployment relief. James Fieser, when approached by Undersecretary of the Treasury Ogden Mills in October about the proposal, argued strongly that the Red Cross could not accept such a responsibility.[5] A few days later, the Committee for Employment urged the Red Cross to coordinate all relief measures rather than to launch a national unemployment fund drive.[6]

Hoover's efforts to place the responsibility of all assistance on the Red Cross failed. The agency's central committee did not want to deviate that far from its charter. Nor did it want such a tremendous duty. On December 5, however, the organization did agree to determine through its field representatives and local chapters whether misfortunes in the drought counties were due to natural disasters or economic collapse. Where drought was the main cause, the Red Cross would assume the task for both disaster and unemployment aid. Judge John Barton Payne also decided that no fund drive would be launched until local Community Chests and other charitable groups could raise their quotas.[7]

National headquarters had accepted the burden for both types of relief in the drought states, although it continued to avoid publicity concerning its program, fearing thousands would flock to their doors. Although agency officials feared a dole as much as Hoover, they dreaded even more the prospect of providing all forms of aid. That the president sought to make the Red Cross the sole administrator of assistance attested to his desire to keep the methods of confronting the depression and the drought outside of government. However, as the disaster worsened, the drought states looked increasingly to Congress for legislative action.

Since its creation in August, the National Drought Committee had functioned as coordinator of the local and state committees created by the president. It had encouraged the formation of agricultural credit cooperatives and had established the machinery to administer reduced freight rates. But events moved rapidly. By early September regional drought relief committees pointed to the need for federal feed and seed loans to allow farmers to plant their next year's crops. In mid-October Chairman Arthur Hyde requested Congress to release immediately the 1932 highway appropriation of $125 million to provide jobs for farmers.[8] Unfortunately, the states had to match the federal grant, and many lacked the funds. When the National Drought Conference met in November, the various chairmen came prepared to ask for more federal aid.[9]

On the day preceeding the start of the national conference, state chairmen met and suggested that a $60-million-crop-loan bill be introduced at the next congressional session. The loans could be repaid after the 1931 harvest. They also requested $40 million to be expended by the Red Cross for farm relief. Once again, the agency was pressured to exceed its traditional boundaries.[10] When the meeting convened on November 20, the states had a definite plan in mind.

Reports made at the conference revealed the toll of human suffering produced by the disaster. The Alabama delegate counted 50,000 families unable to obtain credit and estimated that it would take $10 million to finance the state's farmers. According to Harvey Couch of Arkansas, one-third of the state's 243,000 farmers would need credit that the banks could not furnish. He estimated that at least $12 million were required to help the growers.[11] B. F. Thompson of Louisiana expressed concern for the hill farmers in the north central region. Excluding the croppers, he asserted that $6 million would be needed to aid 30,000 hill families. A Mississippi delegate reported that the planters could furnish their croppers, but from 20,000 to 25,000 families would need loans.[12] Dean Cooper of the Kentucky Extension Service predicted extensive distress and suffering in the bluegrass state if the Red Cross failed to supply relief and assistance. At least $10 million would be required just for crop loans.[13] All representatives agreed to the necessity for federal crop loans, though they continued to support the establishment of credit corporations and expressed disappointment in the states' failure to respond to the previously proposed credit opportunities.[14]

James Fieser detailed Red Cross activities and explained the agency's efforts to minimize its role while allowing state and local committees to conduct their own operations. When asked to estimate the requirements for the winter, Fieser replied that it depended upon the nature of the winter and the level of unemployment. If relief needs and other demands were handled quietly, much less aid would be required. For these reasons he found it difficult to "hazard even a guess," for national headquarters simply had not reached a clear decision about its actions in the drought region. "It might be one thing and it might be seven times that."[15]

The national conference concluded by offering proposals for further measures and urged Congress to enact an appropriation for feed and seed loans and an additional road subsidy of $50 million for states unable to match the grant.[16] Hyde had appointed a committee to formulate a relief plan, and it recommended a seed and feed loan bill to be administered by the secretary of agriculture and the Agriculture Department. According to Oklahoma State Drought Relief Chairman J. G. Puterbaugh, all of the states unanimously agreed that the bill should allow farmers to use $50 or $60 of their loan for food. State representatives denounced the absurdity of a farmer borrowing money for his crops and then driving into town to ask the Red Cross for food. The national conference urged Congress to pass legislation to authorize loans for "crop production in 1931, seed for suitable crops, fertilizer, feed for livestock, and for such other purposes of production as may be prescribed by the Secretary of Agriculture." According to Puterbaugh, "such other purposes" referred to food loans. He also noted that all of the state chairmen had agreed to a $60-million appropriation as an adequate sum for the loans. Hyde and C. W. Warburton, however, advised against the specification of any amount.[17] Finally, the conference urged the American people to contribute liberally to the Red Cross so it could aid the stricken region.[18]

In actuality the national conference offered little in the way of innovative relief measures. The feed and seed loans aided only those farmers with substantial credit or community standing. Even while the conference met, Red Cross field reports had already shown that people were hungry. Fieser continued to express the organization's conservative policy when he offered his ambiguous reply concerning a projection of the winter's requirement. He had definite evidence to support the immediate need for an extensive operation, and yet he declined to discuss that information. A confidential report written in late November offered some explanation for his silence. It was "really the unemployment problem which accounts for us not knowing today where we are going," he explained. Neither Hoover nor his advisors had clearly defined their goals, although some had discussed the raising of from $15 to $200 million for relief during December, capitalizing on the Christmas spirit. "As things stand now we are still facing the drought problem with the utmost conservatism, placing the maximum effort on individual counties," Fieser concluded. Such a course would allow the agency to get by with from $2 million to $5 million.[19]

Fieser's report indicated both the conservative policy of national headquarters and the reluctance of officials toward adopting a massive operation. According to Fieser, some members of the central committee had stated in August that they did not want to commit the entire $5-million fund, and others argued that the agency should not spend over $1 million before January 1. This vacillation gave the organization the appearance of dragging its feet while people needed help.[20]

By late November the Red Cross faced pressure from both the National Drought Committee to administer drought relief and the Committee for Employment to provide unemployment assistance in small towns and rural areas. In one sense the Red Cross was simply marking time as its officials waited for either Hoover or Congress to initiate a relief and employment program. That it and other relief agencies, including local Community Chests and the Salvation Army, argued over the correct time for fund-raising drives and over whether or not a specific agency could raise funds in a large city, a small town, or in a county reveals how little officials understood the magnitude of the destitution that the depression and drought had created. The Red Cross decided against a fall fund-raising drive and allowed the other groups to raise their monies. In January, only one week after Judge Payne had announced that the Red Cross had sufficient funds to combat the crisis, he launched a national drive for additional money, as the enormous increase in requests for aid exceeded what was in the reserve fund. But by then Congress had become fully involved in the relief controversy.

Hoover had numerous problems with Congress during the winter of 1930–31. Since the summer Senator Robert Wagner of New York had sought to pass an employment relief bill. Although this measure resembled the public works program that Hoover had proposed in 1921, the president persistently refused to support it. In the November congressional elections the Republicans lost their majority in both houses, and many progressive members of the Republican party sided with the Democrats.[21] On December 2, in his second annual message to Congress, Hoover emphasized that the economic depression could not be cured by legislative action or executive pronouncement, for the "economic wounds must be healed by the action of the cells of the economic body—the producers and consumers themselves." He encouraged Americans to sustain their faith, courage, and self-reliance through voluntary cooperation in local communities.[22] To aid local and state agencies in creating jobs, he asked Congress to appropriate $100 to $150 million to be allocated among the various departments for public works projects.[23] The executive branch would administer these funds—an idea that did not please Congress. Throughout the last months of the Seventy-first Congress, Republicans and Democrats debated various relief measures with little success, while Hoover continued to insist that the executive branch should lead in relief matters.[24]

When Senators Joseph T. Robinson of Arkansas and Charles McNary of Oregon and Representative James B. Aswell of Louisiana introduced relief measures in early December, they entered the broader debate that had emerged concerning unemployment relief. Consequently, the proposed drought program became intermeshed with the debates concerning national unemployment relief. The drought relief controversy during the winter of 1930–31 revealed the frustration that many legislators had regarding Hoover's aloof attitude toward Congress. By December the degree of human suffering had increased in both urban and rural areas. Although Congress still remained conservative in its approach to relief, some members raised questions about the adequacy of voluntary cooperation and demanded a larger measure of federal intervention in the economic crisis.

Aswell's $60-million bill followed the resolution of the drought conference by providing for loans to cover "such other purposes of production as may be prescribed by the Secretary of Agriculture." It did not "undertake to deal with the general problem of unemployment, nor is it a step in the direction of a dole." That it required a first lien on the crop differentiated it from the general question of industrial unemployment.[25] McNary's proposal included loans for food, while Robinson's and Aswell's omitted any specific mention of food. All of the measures were referred to the respective committees on Agriculture and Forestry.[26]

While the committees considered the bills, the director of the budget reduced the request to $25 million, with the provision for food deleted.[27] This change presented a dilemma for the Republicans, for Hoover's secretary of agriculture had chaired the drought conference at which state representatives had unofficially recommended the sum of

$60 million after careful local and state surveys. That sum represented the estimates of the president's relief organization, yet, when the measure was introduced, Hoover pared the amount and eliminated the provision for food loans. Admittedly the conference proposal had not included a specified amount or the precise mention of food; however, as Puterbaugh had observed, the states had assumed that provisions would be included regardless of whether the word "food" was used.

Reducing the proposed relief sum became an inflammatory issue, as critics of food loans feared the establishment of a dole, while proponents argued that it was absurd to loan money to feed animals but not people. Arthur Hyde, who had chaired the National Drought Conference, supported the president's decision. The federal government, he stated, could no more justify granting food to farmers than it could to urban workers: "From a national point of view this latter class of loans approached perilously near the dole system and would be a move in the wrong direction."[28] In response to the secretary's qualms, Senator Robinson angrily rejoined, "It is alright to put the mule on the dole, but it calls for condemnation to put the man on an equality with a mule." Loans for food would prevent Arkansans from seeking charity and would preserve their pride, he concluded.[29] Republican Senator McNary and his agriculture committee also disagreed with the reduction and recommended that the full sum be submitted to Congress.[30]

Letters from state drought relief chairmen demanded passage of the bill with the full sum. Couch doubted the adequacy of $25 million, and Governor Garland Pollard of Virginia argued that the entire amount must be approved.[31] Thompson did not understand how farmers could plant crops without adequate nourishment for themselves, while Harry Wilson of the state's extension service predicted several deaths from starvation before the harvest of the next year's crop if the proposed measure did not include food.[32] Still Warburton maintained that only the Red Cross could provide for such destitute cases.[33]

Hyde made his statement in support of the loan reduction aware of the sentiment among the state chairmen. In addition to their collective support for $60 million in November, they had submitted descriptive reports to Congress on December 1. Alabama Chairman Seth P. Storr's report proved typical. In his state the tenant "tries to find a new place of work but can not find it. He is without food and clothing, has no place to go and he begins to think 'red.' He feels that there is plenty of food and feed and he will just go out and take it."[34]

After heated debate the Senate finally passed the $60-million bill with food provisions on December 9. As Congress voted on the measure, Hoover issued a scathing attack on the spendthrifts in the legislature. Criticizing the relief measures before the House and Senate, including the drought bill, the president warned that passage of such legislation would increase the taxes of farmers and workers. "Prosperity," he predicted, "cannot be restored by raids upon the public Treasury." In proposing a federal relief program, some congressmen were simply "playing politics at the expense of human misery."[35]

Hoover's press statement provoked angry responses in the Senate, particularly among the representatives from the drought region. According to Pat Harrison of Mississippi, Hoover was playing politics with the miseries of the hungry and unemployed. "Is it an obsession with the President?" The Republican chairmen of both agriculture committees also disagreed with the loan reduction.[36] Senator Thaddeus Caraway of Arkansas castigated Hoover for refusing to recognize that people were suffering. Since Congress appreciated the gravity of the crisis, the Arkansas senator expressed bewilderment at why the president "had lost his usual equilibrium and should say that we are playing politics on human misery down here."[37] Hoover's ill-considered statement destroyed any chance of reaching an easy compromise.

On December 11 the drought proposal went to the House for debate. Republican floor leader James Q. Tilson described it as a "revolutionary proposal," for under its provisions the federal government would assume responsibility for dispensing charity. "The high principled and industrious among the distressed will insist on treating it as a loan and will cripple themselves and their families in an attempt to repay it," Tilson argued, "and the idle and shiftless will accept it as a gift, dismiss any attempt at repayment, and live off the Federal Government as long as the opportunity exists." Those who faced starvation could look to the Red Cross for aid. Tilson disagreed with those congressmen who argued that the federal government had established a precedent for relief legislation when it had loaned $20 million to feed the famine-stricken Russians in 1921–23. Here the United States had "succored a people who were prostrate from war, with its stable government wiped away, industries paralyzed, money valueless, and without means of a livelihood or even hope of the future." The South, on the other hand, merely presented a problem of "temporary relief to a sturdy class of Americans possessing an unbounded carriage and an indomitable will to overcome the vicissi-

47

tudes which have come to them in their relentless fight with the forces of nature." Behind these Americans stood a strong government with a stable currency, unimpaired resources, and established relief agencies ready to carry them through the winter. To bypass the Red Cross would "atrophy one of the noblest emotions of the human heart—that of a generous response to a call for succor to distressed peoples."[38]

Aswell countered Tilson's remarks, noting how small farmers faced starvation and total ruin without the prospect of federal aid. Rather than charity or a raid on the treasury, loans would be repaid in ten months. Nor would such a program conflict with the operations of the Red Cross, he concluded, for they were concerned with an entirely different class of people.[39]

The press in the two hardest-hit states, Kentucky and Arkansas, supported Hoover and Tilson. According to the Louisville *Courier-Journal,* "There would be no end to a policy of doles once adopted . . . only the sufferers from higher and higher taxes could expect no relief from the Government." Individual resourcefulness and institutional charity "would be killed and paternalistic bureaucracy would be supreme." The Arkansas *Gazette* expressed a similar view. "The more money the government spends, even for emergency relief and the aiding for prosperity, the more money the government must take in, not from some outside source, but from the pocket of every individual who sleeps under a roof, wears clothes, eats paid-for-food."[40]

When the House failed to reach an agreement, the debate returned to the Senate, where Robert La Follette of Wisconsin introduced the subject of urban unemployment. He questioned reports that state and local agencies were adequately equipped to care for either drought or unemployment needs. In support of his observation, he presented letters from several cities, which claimed they lacked the necessary resources to meet rapidly increasing unemployment. Congress must accept full responsibility for gathering accurate information concerning the extent of suffering and the ability of localities to meet the crisis, and La Follette urged the Senate to issue a resolution requiring the president to submit to Congress any reports made by the Committee for Employment concerning relief needs.[41] Hoover replied that no such report existed, for he had only received notes and verbal suggestions from Colonel Woods. Since the suggestions were tentative and were, to his mind, confidential reports between a president and his officers, Hoover refused to relay any of the information to Congress.[42] La Follette then demanded that

Woods, Payne, and other representatives of the relief agencies appear before the Senate Appropriations Committee, to determine the nature of information which the president insisted he held in confidence.[43]

In the heat of the controversy the House Agriculture Committee summoned Hyde to testify in an effort to determine the origins of the $60-million sum. Since Aswell insisted that the state drought chairmen had recommended the amount as the necessary appropriation to deal with the crisis, many congressmen wondered why the administration should have changed the measure. Members of the committee explained to the secretary that a large allocation did not compel him to spend the entire amount; rather it simply insured the existence of an adequate sum should it be needed. Hyde denied that there was such a need. "You merely throw the Budget out of balance; you merely make a larger temptation to increase loans beyond the needs of the situation."[44] He saw in such loans the establishment of a dangerous precedent. "I personally regard loans by the Federal Government upon security that is so thin, in many cases, that it approaches the vanishing point, as a dangerous step toward the dole system in this country. If we make loans to farmers for food and clothing, then by the same token we should make loans to laboring men who are unemployed or otherwise in distress."[45]

The secretary stressed that drought relief meant crop loans rather than food and insisted that the National Drought Conference had intended the bill to have such an interpretation. Those who lacked collateral to obtain a loan would be fed by the Red Cross. However, according to Aswell, Warburton had sent him a resolution calling for a $60-million bill with provisions for food. Aswell had then circulated it among the various state relief chairmen who had all approved it. But Hyde remained firm in his conviction and disagreed with Aswell.[46]

The hearing never resolved the origin of the $60-million figure. Warburton supported Hyde and denied that he had ever seen the resolution mentioned by Aswell. Nor did the Louisiana representative ever produce a copy of the alleged document. Chairman Gilbert N. Haugen finally decided that there was a misunderstanding among Department of Agriculture officials, Aswell, and the state chairmen. Previous evidence, however, pointed to the correctness of both points of view. According to Puterbaugh, the state chairmen had agreed on the $60-million sum, but Hyde and Warburton had disregarded their recommendations, encouraging the conferees to leave the actual amount open for future agreement.[47] Hyde's testimony clarified for the Congress his position on the proposal, and that afternoon the House agreed to a $30-million bill with the word "food" replaced by "for such other purposes of crop production as may be prescribed by the Secretary of Agriculture." As Congressman John C. Ketcham astutely noted, however, the secretary would be the administrator of the law under any circumstances, and, based on his testimony, food would not be included in his interpretation of the measure.[48]

The Senate refused to accept the House bill and continued to debate the appropriate amount. Eager to adjourn for the Christmas holidays, the congressmen finally reached a compromise on December 18, and a $45-million feed and seed measure passed both houses—with no mention of food. Instead, the plan authorized the secretary of agriculture to use the loans for the "purposes incident to crop production."[49] Hoover had won. However, by replacing any provisions for food with an ambiguous phrase, Congress was haunted by the question of feeding the sufferers. When legislators returned from yuletide celebrations, the issue emerged again.

While Congress discussed aid, Red Cross administrators wondered how the resulting legislative program would affect their operations. Several congressmen had pointed to the organization as the only available and legitimate medium to aid those who could not provide for themselves. Few at national headquarters appreciated the free publicity the controversy had given the organization. According to Fieser, statements by such leaders as Senator James Watson that the Red Cross had offered assurance of aid to all the destitute prevented them from conducting a "quiet" relief program.[50] Any suggestions regarding national headquarters' financial ability to handle an extensive relief operation must have appeared interesting to the public in view of the "poor mouth" which the agency had presented when raising funds during roll call time. The Red Cross, Fieser continued, had found itself in a "rather exposed position with the possibility of all guns turned upon us." Because Congress described the organization as wealthy enough to care for drought victims, local chapters became disillusioned, for they had been working exhaustively to raise adequate funds. Fieser could see no alternative but a large fund drive in the near future.[51]

He further pointed to the possibility of the Red Cross becoming involved in unemployment relief if legislative debates continued. "Personally, I think that is somewhat inescapable as the months go on. It is understandable for the cities to wonder why the agency chose to limit itself to dire circumstances in the rural areas when the organization raised its funds in the unemployed cities." He was convinced that the Red Cross could not avoid the unemployment issue in small towns and communities. Judge Payne should devise a transition plan from the current "publicly assured position that we can take care of the problem with our own funds to the normal position when disaster strikes in which we say we will spend for a given disaster such funds as are given us for a specific calamity."[52] At the staff council meeting on December 16 Payne suggested that, even if the $60-million bill passed, he did not see how the Department of Agriculture could aid the hungry, for, unlike the Red Cross, it had no means of reaching the people.[53]

Other Red Cross officials expressed a similar concern over the relief controversy. William Baxter wrote DeWitt Smith that should the food loan measure pass, the agency would face difficulties in its campaign efforts. An appeal could only be launched on the basis of human need, and the act would supposedly have taken care of those needs. If Caraway had painted a correct picture of the extreme conditions in Arkansas, then the Senate should move to make federal funds available there as quickly as possible.[54] Smith, however, had assumed a seed bill would be passed from the beginning, an assumption which had guided the organization's estimates of the funds necessary for a relief program. National headquarters had always understood, continued Smith, that it would deal with those unable to obtain loans. Therefore, the $45-million act should not affect relief operations to any extent. Judge Payne had firmly ordered all officials to preserve traditional policy in attempting to influence the legislation. Smith assured Baxter that Hyde could end any complications in administering the loans by stating clearly that food did not constitute part of the provision. Then the Red Cross could proceed to raise the needed funds.[55]

The seed loan bill also drew comments from officials in the drought states. B. F. Thompson assumed that with the deletion of food from the loan bill the Red Cross would feed the 30,000 families who needed aid. After farmers had obtained a lien against their crop, they would be unable to receive credit from local merchants. The banks would also refuse to lend money to farmers who had already mortgaged their crops. Feed and seed loans were not enough, he concluded, and thus some agency would have to feed the hungry.[56] His letter revealed the limitations of the congressional measure and the task that confronted the Red Cross.

Other state drought chairmen feared Hyde would refuse the $45 million and insist on the $25 million instead. Chairman Harry Byrd of the Virginia Drought Relief Committee urged Puterbaugh to select a group of state relief chairmen to appear before the upcoming Senate appropriations hearings in support of the $45-million bill.[57] Couch also urged Hyde to accept the pending measure. "I am not in favor of the Government giving our people one penny, but I know that this credit can be made very, very helpful, and that the Department of Agriculture has an opportunity to put over a diversified farm program they have never before had an opportunity of doing."[58] After receiving these requests, the secretary of agriculture announced his support of the $45-million bill, minus the food provision.[59]

The drought relief controversy was revealing of the president's approach not only to disaster but also to unemployment relief. Since the Red Cross had already entered the stricken region to administer relief, Hoover used the precedent as an opportunity to encumber the agency with the entire burden of assistance. His refusal to support loans for food convinced many that he lacked compassion. Feed would certainly save farm animals till the spring; however, seed for forage and crops could not be planted until that time. Meanwhile, how were people to live through the winter without any food? Hoover, like Representative Tilson, failed to recognize how totally bankrupt the southern economy was. Americans had always survived on their own resources, and they undoubtedly would weather this crisis with a minimum of outside help. The Red Cross could feed the croppers while loans would insure a spring crop and healthy work stock. By planting time the crisis would be passed and the inevitable good times would return. Unfortunately, the relief machinery did not operate fast enough. By early January some Arkansas farmers, wary of forms and rations, had decided to take more immediate action.

Notes

1. Grin, "Unemployment Conference of 1921," 93; E. P. Hayes, *Activities of the President's Committee for Employment, 1930–31* (New Haven, 1931), 96.

2. Jordan A. Schwarz, *Interregnum of Despair: Hoover, Congress, and the Depression* (New York, 1970), 5; Donald R. McCoy, *Calvin Coolidge: The Quiet President* (New York, 1967), 329–32.

3. Schwarz, *Interregnum of Despair,* 10–11, 48–49.

4. For Hoover's role in the Russian operation, see Weissman, *Herbert Hoover and Famine Relief.*

5. Fieser to Payne, Oct. 22, 1930, ARC, DR-401.21.

6. Fieser to Payne, Confidential Report on Conference at the Cosmos Club, Oct. 27, 1930, ibid.

7. Conference Report of Red Cross and President's Committee for Employment, Dec. 5, 1930, Smith to Fieser, ibid.

8. Louisville *Courier-Journal*, Oct. 19, 1930.

9. For preliminary statements concerning the need for a loan, see ibid., Sept. 18, 1930; "Oklahoma State Drought Relief Meeting," Nov. 7, 1930, ARC, DR-401.02; E. C. McGinnis, director of Mississippi State Agricultural Service Department, to Senator Pat Harrison, Oct. 22, 1930, Secretary of Agriculture Papers, Acc. 234, Dr. 190.

10. Fieser to Payne, "Report of National Drought Conference," Nov. 20, 1930, ARC, DR-401.02.

11. Ibid., 11.

12. Ibid., 13.

13. Ibid., 12. Oklahoma reported 17,763 farmers who needed aid, and Tennessee described at least 5,000 families in need with an estimated $3,500,000 required for loans (ibid., 15–17).

14. Ibid., 17.

15. Ibid., 9.

16. The states would repay the appropriation by an annual deduction from the normal federal road allocation over a period of ten years. Ibid., 19.

17. Puterbaugh to Rep. James E. Watson, Jan. 10, 1931, ibid.

18. The conference also urged that federal funds be provided to allow counties to maintain their county agents. An objective of the Department of Agriculture during the drought relief program was to encourage crop diversification. Due to the bankruptcy of local governments, the positions of many agents had been discontinued. ("Report of National Drought Conference," 19).

19. Fieser, "The Winter's Outlook," no date given but from the text it appears to have been written in November or early December. ARC, DR-401.08.

20. Ibid., 2.

21. For a discussion of the relationship between Hoover and Congress during the winter of 1930–31, see Schwarz, *Interregnum of Despair.*

22. Meyers, ed., *State Papers of Hoover,* 1: 429–30.

23. Ibid., 433.

24. For a discussion of relief measures from January to March, see Schwarz, *Interregnum of Despair,* 23–44.

25. U.S. Congress, *Congressional Record,* 71 Cong., 3 sess., Vol. 74, pt. 1, 7.

26. Senator Joseph T. Robinson, "A Bill for the Relief of Drouth-Stricken Areas." S 4786, Dec. 2, 1930, ARC, DR-401.001. For details concerning McNary's bill, see *Congressional Record* (hereafter *Cong. Record*), 71 Cong., 3 sess., vol. 74, pt. 1, 393.

27. For details of the Senate Committee, see McNary's remarks in ibid., 697.

28. Louisville *Courier-Journal,* Dec. 9, 1930.

29. *Cong. Record,* 71 Cong., 3 sess., vol. 74, pt. 1, 398.

30. Ibid., 393–94.

31. Couch to Hoover, Dec. 5, 1930, Pollard to Hoover, Dec. 4, 1930, Drought Correspondence, Box 118, Herbert Hoover Papers, Herbert Hoover Presidential Library, West Branch, Ia.

32. Thompson to Warburton, Dec. 6, 1930, Secretary of Agriculture Papers, National Drought Relief Committee, 1930–31, Box 3; Wilson to Hyde, Dec. 1 1930, Secretary of Agriculture Papers, Office of Agriculture, Incoming Correspondence, Acc. 234, Dr. 190.

33. Warburton to Wilson, Dec. 5, 1930, Secretary of Agriculture Papers, Acc. 234, Dr. 190.

34. Quoted in the *Cong. Record,* 71 Cong., 3 sess., vol. 74, pt. 1, 7.

35. Meyers, ed., *State Papers of Hoover,* 1:459–60.

36. *Cong. Record,* 71 Cong., 3 sess., vol. 74, pt. 1, 423–24.

37. Ibid., 407.

38. Ibid., 628–29.

39. Ibid., 630–31.

40. Louisville *Courier-Journal,* Dec. 16, 1930; Arkansas *Gazette,* Dec. 12, 1930.

41. For individual city reports, see *Cong. Record,* 71 Cong., 3 sess., vol. 74, pt. 1, 702–7.

42. Meyers, ed., *State Papers of Hoover,* 1:471. Colonel Woods had requested the Red Cross to conduct a survey of the small towns and rural areas to determine the extent of destitution and the ability of local agencies to carry the relief load. This was to be given to Hoover for his presidential address to Congress. (Fieser to Payne, Nov. 25, 1930, ARC, DR-401.02.)

43. Louisville *Courier-Journal,* Dec. 17, 1930.

44. U.S. Congress, House, Committee on Agriculture, *Drought and Storm Relief,* 71 Cong., 3 sess., Dec. 17, 1930, 56.

45. Ibid., 57.

46. Ibid., 67–68.

47. See Fieser to Payne, Nov. 20, 1930, ARC, DR-401.02. Actual estimates offered by the individual states for the required loans exceeded $60,000,000; Alabama—$10,000,000; Arkansas—$12,000,000; Kentucky—$10,000,000; Louisiana—$6,000,000; Texas—$5,000,000; Virginia—$5,000,000; and West Virginia—$3,500,000. Mississippi reported that 20,000 to 25,000 families needed loans; Missouri estimated that from 15,000 to 20,000 families required loans based on an average of $200 per family, and Tennessee reported 5,000 families needing aid. "Report of National Drought Conference," 11–17.

48. *Cong. Record,* 71 Cong., 3 sess., vol. 74, pt. 1, 969.

49. New York *Times,* Dec. 19, 1930.

50. See Watson's statement, *Cong. Record,* 71 Cong., 3 sess., vol. 74, pt. 1, 699.

51. Fieser to Payne, Dec. 16, 1930, ARC, DR-401.21.

52. Ibid.

53. Minutes of the Staff Council Meeting, Dec. 16, 1930, ARC, No. 140.40.

54. Baxter to Smith, Dec. 22, 1930, ARC, DR-401.001.

55. Smith to Baxter, Dec. 26, 1930, ibid.

56. Thompson to Fieser, Dec. 27, 1930, ARC, DR-401.11.

57. Puterbaugh to Rep. James V. McClintic, Dec. 28, 1930, ARC, DR-401.02.

58. Couch to Hyde, Dec. 22, 1930, Secretary of Agriculture Papers, Acc. 234, Dr. 190.

59. New York *Times,* Dec. 30, 1930.

4

In the Dry Land Dwell the Rebellious

H. C. Coney, a white tenant farmer, lived with his family on a forty-one-acre farm near England, Arkansas. A Memphis cotton broker owned the sprawling acres of rich land that lay on the level alluvial plains of the Arkansas River Valley. Renting the land for $8 an acre, the farmer planted corn and cotton. Like his neighbors, he did not produce a crop in 1930; the usually fecund soil turned to endurated clay during the hot summer months of the drought. Lacking a crop, Coney could not obtain furnishings to carry his family through the winter. Even an attempt to sell his truck for a deflated $25 proved unsuccessful. In December the seven Coneys lived in their shack, walls pasted with newspapers to shield them from the crisp winter wind, and endured the cold on empty stomachs. The cabin's scanty decor reflected the meager resources of the family—a cheap print of the Last Supper partially covered by an old cylinder gasket and a geography book and Bible on the mantlepiece. "We hain't got enough clothes in this house to wad a shotgun proper," Coney explained. "That pair o' rompers the kid's a-wearin' is the only clothes we bought in a year." Food proved just as scarce, for all "winter we've been a-feeden' on beans and a bit o' lard to kinda give it flavor." Although the Red Cross gave the family rations every two weeks, they had found it difficult to "squeeze through" on $12 a month.[1]

The Coneys were a typical Arkansas tenant family in the winter of 1930–31. While the Red Cross had publicly minimized the extent of human suffering in the drought region during the fall, destitution ran rampant by winter, and the relief lines rapidly increased. By December 31 the Red Cross was aiding 20,012 families in Arkansas.[2] All too often local chapters had discovered the inadequacy of their resources and then frantically appealed to state and national headquarters for instant financial assistance. Neither national headquarters, located in Washington, nor even the state offices could always respond quickly enough. Such a case occurred in Lonoke County in January 1931.

All of the local chapters in the townships of Lonoke County had used up their ration forms by December 31. C. E. Hankins, England banker and relief chairman, ordered more forms, but they had not arrived. The chapters, meanwhile, refused to assist applicants, explaining that the rations could not be issued without the proper forms. When the smaller villages of Pettus, Indian Bayou, Gundwood, and Lafayette declined to grant aid, the applicants journeyed to nearby England (population 2,408) in search of relief. But the town also lacked forms. Gradually farmers became suspicious of continued refusals and decided that the Red Cross had simply put them off. As food supplies dwindled, some people resolved that, if the agency refused them aid, they would demand or even take food, if necessary.

On January 3 a neighboring mother visited Coney and told him that her children had not eaten in two days. Grabbing him, she cried, "Coney, what are we a-goin' to do?" Reacting to her frantic plea, he immediately prepared to leave. "Lady, you wait here. I'm a-goin' to get some food." Pulling his wife along, he jumped into his truck and headed for the home of L. L. Bell, the Red Cross chairman in Pettus. At Bell's place he found a crowd of hungry men who were being refused aid due to the lack of forms. Recognizing the futility of the situation, he yelled, "All you that hain't yaller, climb on my truck. We-re a-goin' into England to get some grub." According to Coney, "Forty-seven clum on and there warn't a one among'em that had a gun of any sort." En route to England, he instructed his followers, "We'll ask for food quiet'like, and if they don't give it to us, we'll take it, also quiet like." The men just sat calmly, for they were a "right pathetic sight."[3]

When the farmers arrived in town, they visited the chief of police and the mayor, informing them that their families had no food. The officials instructed them to wait; the men decided to do their waiting in front of a grocery store. According to Coney, the storeowner became so frightened that he fainted and, when he regained consciousness, exclaimed, "I'll give a thousand dollars!"[4]

Meanwhile, a crowd of approximately 500 people gathered in support of Coney's men. Some began to shout angrily as officials continued to stall. "We are not going to let our children starve," cried one. "We want food and we want it now," demanded another. "We are not beggars," one pushed forward to explain. "We are willing to work for fifty cents a day, but we are not going to starve, and we are not going to let our families starve. Give us work and we'll not come back."[5] In response

G. E. Morris, a lawyer and Lonoke County drought chairman, stood up and promised the people immediate aid if they would be patient. Coney interrupted him, asking if it "warn't true that Congress in Washington wanted to vote relief, but that the Red Cross says they would handle it and no folks would starve." Morris agreed and assured the people they would soon be aided.[6]

While the crowd increased, Chairman Hankins frantically telephoned Albert Evans in Little Rock regarding the forms; the latter replied that seasonal congestion slowed the mail. He instructed Hankins to use merchants' invoices if the families were in serious need. The chairman expressed fear of a riot because the farmers had threatened to raid stores. In Evans's view, that was a police matter and not a problem for the Red Cross. The agency only administered assistance in an orderly way, and, while every effort should be made to supply the destitute with food, it should not appear as though they were receiving an unwarranted ration simply because they had become forceful. He consoled Hankins by sending representative Henry Baker to England that afternoon.[7]

Coming from nearby Brinkley, Baker arrived in England by noon and directed the relief program. By the end of the day, 500 families had received approximately $1,500 in rations to last them for the next two weeks.[8] When the Red Cross began its rationing, the people stood quietly in line, waiting their turn. According to Coney, "It wouldn't a' wanted but jest a little bit o' sass ter've had a showdown. But they doled out the feed and we all idled back here without nobody gettin' hurt."[9] The England riot had ended.

Newspapers quickly picked up the story of the angry farmers' march into England and reported wildly varying accounts of the event. Almost all portrayed the incident as a riot. *Outlook* viewed the event as "the first touch of violence" in the depression, while *Time* reported that 500 "half-starved" farmers and their wives raided the food stores. "Assembling in England with guns tucked in their clothes, they demanded Red Cross relief. When this was not forthcoming because the supply of Red Cross requisition blanks had been exhausted, they threatened to loot the stores."[10] The New York *Times* described the incident in similar terms, stressing the potential violence of the mob had the people not been fed. A reporter from the St. Louis *Post-Dispatch* described the storming and looting by hungry tenants and cotton pickers as the fourth such occurrence in Arkansas over the past few weeks. Similar demands for food had been reported in Lepanto, Crawfordsville, and Monett, and officials expected others in the cotton country if local chapters did not administer relief quickly and without interruption. The reporter also noted the serious economic conditions in the region, for tenants could not obtain the much needed credit and only six planters possessed funds to furnish their renters. The closing of one of England's two banks had further complicated the problem by freezing $250,000 in public and private assets.[11]

The numerical and racial composition of the crowd varied with the accounts, too. Of the 500, *Time* observed, most were white; the Louisville *Courier-Journal* claimed that there were only 200 in the gathering, most of whom were black.[12] The Red Cross report established the original number at forty-two farmers who initially demanded relief, with the number soon increasing to 500; it did not address the matter of racial composition.[13]

Although Coney and his men did not ransack England's merchants, the event did reveal that Arkansas farmers would no longer idly watch their families starve. Had the Red Cross not quickly disbursed rations, the quiet requests could have become louder and perhaps more violent. According to Morris, "The merchants of England either must move their goods or mount machine guns on their stores." He also criticized the local chapter for refusing aid to some who wore warm clothes. "These men may have been as hungry as the rest. I know many who until last year were fairly prosperous farmers, but they have been reduced to poverty in the last few months." Nor did Morris describe the crowd as violent. "These men and women who came here today just simply got hungry, that's all. . . . It was pathetic to hear these men and women crying for food, telling us their children actually were starving. The crowd was really not wild, considering everything, but they were in earnest."[14]

Local officials did not appreciate Morris's analysis and indicated he "had not been himself" and had lost his sense of perspective regarding the event. Chagrined at the newspaper accounts, England's mayor, W. O. Williams, wired Senator Thaddeus Caraway that the Red Cross could adequately care for everyone's needs. Hankins also informed Evans that the situation had been greatly exaggerated and expressed concern over press reports. According to Henry Baker, none of the town's leaders were apprehensive over a recurrence of the disorder. Yet England officials apparently did fear another incident, for on January 9 William Baxter received a confidential report that Governor Harvey Parnell, upon the request of the mayor, had alerted state troops for possible duty on the following day. According to Baxter, Charles Walls of the North Lonoke chapter had described the section as quiet and suggested that the merchants in the county were unduly disturbed; nevertheless, Baxter requested supplementary forms and a cash grant from national headquarters.[15]

On the state level the Arkansas *Gazette,* undaunted by the incident, encouraged the public to continue its efforts at self-help, while Governor Parnell insisted that conditions had been exaggerated. According to the *Gazette,* the reports of increasing destitution and predictions of an increase in the caseload from 21,000 to 50,000 by February 1 simply meant that the "long-drawn-out emergency created by drouth and crop failure is passing into its final and most critical stage." Authorities had known the previous fall that the "real pinch would come with the winter months." Arkansans now faced the task of feeding thousands of families through March, the editorial continued, and, given the widespread economic depression, "keeping our neighbors from starving and protecting them from the diseases that attend on want and anxiety is almost wholly up to us." Recognizing the continued generosity of Arkansans, the editor called upon the public to contribute further to the Red Cross. "Continuing and self-sacrificing support of the emergency relief agencies is the only way out of this crisis."[16] Two days later the editor once again urged the public to give its last dollar, "a small price to pay for the preservation of orderly social life, not to mention the relief of stark and abject want."[17]

Responding to critical newspaper reports concerning conditions in his state, Parnell informed the Baltimore *Sun* that "conditions in Arkansas are by no means alarming and no rioting or violence of any form has taken place nor is it contemplated that such will be the case." Although conditions were not the best due to the drought, neither "are they alarming and indications are that normalcy is being resumed." The people of Arkansas and the Red Cross had the situation in hand.[18] His letter created concern among Arkansas representatives in Washington who were attempting to secure federal drought relief. Senator Joseph Robinson asked Parnell if the state legislature would deal with the region's relief needs. "This message [letter] is being construed that you believe further measures here to be unnecessary and that the State with the assistance of the Red Cross can make adequate provisions." The governor immediately wired the senator that his letter had expressed his opinion only concerning the food riot. "You can appreciate the seriousness of having before the eastern public the idea our people were looting and otherwise committing depredations," Parnell explained. He certainly did not intend to leave the impression Arkansans did not need assistance. "The people in drought-stricken areas must have continued help from the Red Cross and the Federal Government, and additional appropriations for food and otherwise should be made to mitigate misery now growing worse with all food gone and no winter clothing." Revenues would not permit the state legislature to make an appropriation, he concluded.[19]

Not all state officials glossed over the affair. Charles L. Thompson, chairman of the Pulaski County chapter and the Red Cross representative on the state drought committee, expressed fear that England could be a prelude to the future.[20] Neither the midwestern branch nor national headquarters realized the gravity of the conditions in Arkansas. An attorney had affirmed his personal knowledge of deaths due to malnutrition and added that "unless something is done immediately the Red Cross will be called upon to purchase coffins instead of food."[21]

Some people immediately charged that the incident in England was Communist inspired. Chairman Will R. Wood of the House Appropriations Committee denounced the farmers as Communist instigators, provoking an angry response from Arkansas leaders. England Mayor Williams called the accusation preposterous, while another citizen described the people involved as 98 percent old Anglo-Saxon stock to whom radicalism seemed repugnant. At the request of an Arkansas congressman, the mayor of Little Rock and the city police conducted an investigation in the region and discovered no radicals.[22] Nor did Morris view the farmers as threatening, for they had merely asserted "that their wives and babies were on starvation, completely without food, and if the merchants refused them food they would take it." Morris insisted that no one in the crowd carried a gun. "I knew the crowd to whom I spoke. I have seen them for years. All of them were poor, illiterate Americans, having made share crops around England for years. They never heard that Russia had a revolution. Does Mr. Wood believe you can buy a 'red' for a sack of meal and a piece of meat?" Morris informed Arkansas Congressman D. D. Glover that he had warned the Red Cross two months prior to the incident that starvation threatened the cropper population, but the officials had ignored him.[23]

A report by Phillip Kinsley of the Chicago *Tribune* lent additional support to Morris's observations on the conservative nature of the group. Describing the hungry families as they stood in line for their rations, he was certain Communism represented an unknown element in Arkansas. "These are simple folk, with ordinary living standards marked by a farm labor wage of one dollar a day." Although he discovered no talk of radicalism, he did hear talk of sickness, starvation, and clothes made of gunny sacks. Despite stories of families of eight existing on a two-week ration of $1.50, he insisted that the people in the relief lines appeared "shy and ashamed." They would work for 50¢ a day, but no such jobs existed.[24]

Notwithstanding these denials of any Communist influence, the New York *Daily Worker,* the organ of the Communist party, acknowledged that a unit of party members had been working near England and had distributed copies of the newspaper. It explained that "by reading the *Daily Worker* these starving farmers learned that the best way out of starvation is mass action and in order to show their gratitude to the *Daily Worker* these starving farmers send contributions for the *Daily Worker* from their last pennies." According to this source, these destitute men had taken up the class struggle, and the party had pledged to support their cause.[25] Shortly after the England event, the Communist party issued leaflets in the drought region, calling on the croppers to organize their own relief councils. According to the handbill, the "Red Cross, headed by Hoover, is deliberately starving toiling people to death." Farmers should demand that all relief expenditures be turned over to their own control and require the already federally appropriated funds to be released immediately. It also questioned the adequacy of the Red Cross relief operation.[26]

The available evidence makes clear that no riot occurred in England, Communist inspired or otherwise. Once the Red Cross issued the expected rations, the farmers quietly assembled into a relief line. The biweekly ration of $2.75 per family hardly constituted an extensive amount of food; yet no reports of further disturbances appeared, since the agency continued to feed the farmers until March. The apparent willingness of the farmers to accept a meager amount did not suggest a revolutionary mentality, nor was it surprising. Croppers and tenants, accustomed to being furnished by planters and to subsistence living, insisted only that they be provided with their normal supply of food—little though it was. Once the Red Cross had issued enough rations for them to survive, the angry crowd dispersed. The agency's relief, no matter how inadequate, diffused a potentially radical situation.

American humorist and social critic Will Rogers suggested another reason for the failure of the angry families to become radicals. "There are lots of reports of the circulation of red propaganda. In this little town where I am going tomorrow there ain't no reds. A red can't live there because he can't eat, and therefore he can't holler," Rogers wryly observed. "He has to have something to eat before he can talk—and a lot of people to hear him." Congress could help, but Rogers doubted he would live to see it.[27]

The plight of Coney explained more poignantly the lack of further disruptions in 1931. In May a reporter found him sitting in his cabin, waiting for a government loan to be approved in Memphis. The landlord had tried to persuade Coney to sign the loan fund over to him, allowing him to spend it for the renter, but he had refused. Yet the winter of 1931 had not thwarted Coney's desire to plant another crop. Like Jeeter Lester in Erskine Caldwell's *Tobacco Road,* his determination to live on the land persisted. But unlike Jeeter, Coney neither passively accepted his predicament nor waited upon the graces of the good Lord to save him. "I don't know what's a-comin'. I hain't got no edjication to speak of, but I hain't yaller. Mebbe I'll be closed out next fall, but I tell you, I don't aim to leave a-runnin!" He did recognize one positive result of the drought experience: "The farmers are more sociable-like. Was a time when they would'a walked by you, without knowin' you was there." Three winters like the previous one would see farmers organized, he predicted. "I'll tell you that there's sure goin' to be somethin' tearin' loose 'round here some day."[28] No further disorders occurred in the Delta during the winter of 1931, but time would prove the accuracy of Coney's predictions.

The England incident had uncalculated repercussions. Locally, it revealed that the drought had pushed croppers and tenants below their normally low subsistence level. Farmers on January 3 refused to watch their families starve and freeze for another day. Although local and state officials continued to deny publicly the serious implications of the event, privately they acknowledged the reasons for the angry farmers' demands, and out of fear they sought more immediate relief. On a national level the England protest provoked a new round of drought legislative proposals and questions pertaining to the adequacy of Red Cross relief. The appeal of a destitute mother to an equally impoverished neighbor had initiated a chain of events that culminated in one of the most crucial debates in the history of American relief. The significance of England, as *Outlook* noted, was that it served "dramatic notice on the country that all public and private attempts to meet the present crisis have been strikingly insufficient."[29] It brought into national focus the contest between direct federal relief and Hoover's program of voluntarism and private charity. Speaking of the angry tenants from England, Will Rogers observed that "Paul Revere just woke up Concord, these birds woke up America."[30] The congressional debates of January and February testified to the accuracy of the humorist's observation.

Notes

1. "An Arkansas Farmer Speaks," *New Republic* 67 (May 27, 1931), 40–41.

2. St. Louis *Post-Dispatch,* Jan. 6, 1931.

3. "An Arkansas Farmer Speaks," 40.

4. Ibid.

5. Baltimore *Sun,* Jan. 4, 1931.

6. "An Arkansas Farmer Speaks," 41.

7. Memo on telephone conversation between Evans and Hankins, Jan. 3, 1931, ARC, DR-401.11.

8. Memo on telephone conversation between Baker and Fieser, Jan. 5, 1931, ibid.

9. "An Arkansas Farmer Speaks," 41.

10. *Outlook* 157 (Jan. 14, 1931), 43; *Time,* Jan. 12, 1931, 13.

11. *Outlook* 157 (Jan. 3, 1931), 1; St. Louis *Post-Dispatch,* Jan. 5, 1931.

12. *Time,* Jan. 12, 1931, 13; Louisville *Courier-Journal,* Jan. 6, 1931.

13. Memo on telephone conversation between Baker and Fieser, Jan. 5, 1931, ARC, DR-401.11.

14. New York *Times,* Jan. 3, 1931.

15. Emma V. Morentenson Report, South Lonoke, Arkansas Chapter, Jan. 5, 1931; memo on telephone conversation between Evans and Hankins, Jan. 5, 1931; Baxter to Fieser, Jan. 5, 1931, ARC, DR-401.11.

16. Arkansas *Gazette,* Jan. 3, 1931.

17. Ibid., Jan. 5, 1931.

18. Baltimore *Sun,* Jan. 6, 1931.

19. *Cong. Record,* 71 Cong., 3 sess., vol. 74, pt. 2, 1534.

20. New York *Times,* Jan. 4, 1931.

21. E. G. Bylander to Hyde, Jan. 6, 1931, Secretary of Agriculture Papers, Acc. 234, Dr. 370.

22. Arkansas *Gazette,* Jan. 11, 1931.

23. Morris to Glover, Jan. 14, 1931, ARC, DR-401.14.

24. Reprinted in the Arkansas *Gazette,* Jan. 13, 1931.

25. H. Puro, "Class Struggle Flares Up in Countryside," New York *Daily Worker,* Jan. 15, 1931.

26. Communist Handbill, "Starving farmers," ARC, DR-401.91. As a result of the England incident, the Alabama Communist party informed the state's farmers that the "farmers of Arkansas point the way. They were starving and they 'Refused to Starve.' . . . Every farming community in the South where there is hunger and want can and must do the same thing." ("Appeal by the Communist Party Farmers of the South: Fight Starvation," ibid.).

27. New York *Times,* Jan. 23, 1931.

28. "An Arkansas Farmer Speaks," 41.

29. *Outlook* 157 (Jan. 14, 1931), 43.

30. Arthur Schlesinger, Jr., *The Crisis of the Old Order, 1919–1933* (New York, 1957), 175.

5

"Let Them Eat Hay"

After the Christmas holidays Congressmen returned from the drought area with stories of widespread hunger and the inability of local agencies to meet the crisis. In Arkansas alone the Red Cross claimed to be feeding 100,000 people and estimated the figure would reach 250,000 by the beginning of February.[1] Following the England incident, many legislators questioned the ability of the feed and seed loans and the Red Cross to meet the needs of the sufferers. Convinced that the relief measures could not provide the necessary assistance the victims required, on January 5 Senator Thaddeus Caraway of Arkansas introduced an amendment to the previously passed $45-million loan bill, adding $15 million that specifically provided for food loans. Attacking the measure as a dole, administration supporters killed it. Undaunted, Senator Joseph T. Robinson sponsored—unsuccessfully—a bill providing for a $25-million allocation to the Red Cross to be administered for both drought and unemployment relief.

The introduction of drought relief legislation raised the more general issue of unemployment assistance. Congressmen such as Senator Robert Wagner and Representative Fiorello La Guardia of New York argued persistently that the federal government had the responsibility of aiding all those who suffered from the depression, not just drought victims. Measures were introduced providing additional funds to the Red Cross, allowing it to administer unemployment relief. John Barton Payne insisted the organization could handle only disaster relief and refused the appropriation.

Herbert Hoover, terrified at the prospect of a dole, refused to support the measures adding food to the feed and seed loan bill. As pleas poured into his office and that of the Red Cross for further aid, the president insisted publicly that the Red Cross could provide for all the needy while he sought privately to persuade the Red Cross to accept responsibility for unemployment relief. His refusal to support further congressional relief measures won for the Great Humanitarian a reputation for callousness and indifference to human suffering.

The debates that ensued in January and February were crucial to the history of American relief, for the issue to be decided was whether or not the federal government had the responsibility to provide for its citizens in the midst of natural disaster and economic ruin. Hoover and his followers persisted in their nineteenth-century liberal view that self-help and private charity were the solutions, while Republican Insurgents, urban Democrats in the North, and many southern congressmen argued strongly for federal intervention. It was one of the last triumphs of the old view before Franklin D. Roosevelt and the New Deal transformed both the concept of relief and the federal government's role in the economy and society.

During January and February the last session of the Seventy-first Congress and the president debated the proper method for helping the drought victims and the unemployed. Although the Republicans possessed a majority — 56 to 39 in the Senate and 267 to 167 in the House — by the fall of 1930 Hoover had alienated a sufficient number to prevent the passage of his programs without a struggle.[2] Congressional leaders gave Hoover support, however. In the Senate James Watson was the Republican majority leader. He represented, as historian Jordan A. Schwarz observes, the "nadir" of Republicanism in Congress. A Gilded Age politician whose career extended from Benjamin Harrison to Hoover, the Indianan had been in the Senate since 1917 and, during the prosperous and xenophobic decade of the 1920s, had courted the support of such groups as the Ku Klux Klan. According to Schwarz, "He never attached his name to any noticeable piece of legislation, but he always made certain that Indiana got what it wanted." He represented the kind of selfish and incompetent politician that Hoover despised.[3] But Watson led the Senate fight to save America from the dole. In the House the venerable Nicholas Longworth led the Grand Old Party as Speaker with the support of James Q. Tilson as majority leader. Tilson, a Connecticut lawyer with a "bland personality whose greatest attributes were organizational ability and steadfastness," staunchly supported the president's programs to combat the economic collapse, claiming that Hoover had kept the "recent depression from being as bad as other depressions."[4]

While the Old Guard Republicans like Watson, Longworth, and Tilson controlled the party, their leadership was not without challenge. Since the early years of the progressive era, Insurgent Republicans from the Midwest, such as Robert M. La Follette, George W. Norris, William S. Borah, and Burton K. Wheeler, had insisted that the federal government provide greater assistance not only to farmers but also to labor and other disadvantaged classes in American society. Never able to wrest control of the party, they represented a continuation of the progressive tradition, demanding greater regulation of business and the end of privilege in government.[5] During the "New Era" of the 1920s, Insurgents bolted the party, forming the Progressive party in 1924 with Robert La Follette, Sr., as its unsuccessful presidential candidate. Throughout the decade they served as the conscience of an otherwise business-oriented Congress, proposing such programs as Norris's public utilities project and the McNary-Haugen agricultural plan. Although Charles L. McNary often sided with the Insurgents, he shrewdly avoided identification with either the Old Guard or the progressives, and he became one of the nation's ablest legislators.[6]

After the crash in 1929, the Insurgents became the most innovative group in proposing legislation to aid the farmers and unemployed. They were joined by Democratic sympathizers such as Senators Wagner of New York, Alben Barkley of Kentucky, and Hugo Black of Alabama. Wagner came to Washington in the 1920s and, with Representative La Guardia, the maverick Republican from East Harlem, became the spokesman for urban liberalism, persistently demanding federal assistance for the unemployed.[7] Barkley, a country lawyer from Graves County, Kentucky, who arrived in Washington in 1913 as a Wilsonian progressive, joined with Black to demand a greater degree of federal aid for the distressed.[8]

Except for these few lone progressive voices, the Seventy-first Congress was a conservative body. Despite the refusal of the majority of members to support alternatives to Hoover's proposals, the Insurgents and Democrats such as Wagner and Barkley forced Congress and the nation into a debate over the role of the federal government in the economy and the administration of relief. Young Robert La Follette, Jr., and the aging Borah lashed out at the administration and their colleagues for refusing to administer aid, while La Guardia and Wagner championed the cause of the urban unemployed, demanding a public works program and unemployment insurance. In the end Hoover won, for the feed and seed loan bill, combined with a farm rehabilitation program, were the only relief measures passed for the drought victims. Wagner's unemployment programs were defeated. The president consistently adhered to his plan of voluntary cooperation and local responsibility, viewing the proponents of federal expenditures as "radicals," who saw "great political grist in emotional appeals to presumed sympathy—or human greed."[9]

The debate over relief did not end when the feed and seed bill was passed in February; indeed, the conflict plagued the remainder of Hoover's term. The drought relief controversy did, however, represent the last major attempt by the president and his aides to solve the massive relief problem by private charity.

On January 5 senators from the most destitute states, Arkansas and Kentucky, presented evidence of widespread suffering. The angry demands of the farmers from Pettus had successfully questioned the adequacy of Red Cross relief efforts. Describing the rapidly increasing demands for assistance, Senator Caraway questioned the competence of the Red Cross to relieve all of the victims. By November 15 Arkansas had 86,450 families requiring aid, about 1.8 million people. Since the organization had administered assistance to only 100,000 people in January, Caraway did not see how all of the needy could be reached. He also doubted the adequacy of the monthly ration of $1.15 for three people. "That is no relief; that is an insult. The Red Cross is not in any position to care for the situation," he charged. "The Red Cross has never been able to visualize the wide extent of suffering in at least one of the states affected." Nor had the agency been able to meet the demands in England. According to Caraway, "The Red Cross undertook to take care of the situation by giving to 250 families $2.75 each. I do not think anybody would imagine that the distribution of $2.75 to a family without a bite to eat is taking care of the situation. We all know something of the cost of living," he concluded, "and we know that the necessity is so urgent that men are willing to band themselves together to go out and insist on their right to live."[10]

Senator Barkley read twenty reports from county relief chairmen, judges, and relief workers in Kentucky, describing the complete exhaustion of local resources and a tremendous increase in malnutrition, pellagra, and typhoid. A county judge in Butler County depicted a large number of families needing clothing and food and had informed the drought committee that the Red Cross would not enter the scene until spring. Two bank failures and a county debt of several thousand dollars had dried up emergency funds. The county judge estimated that at least 1,100 families needed immediate help. "For four years our farmers have suffered heavy losses. Conditions have grown worse every year, and as a result the farmers are unable to take care of themselves," he explained. "Our people as a whole do not ask for charity, but have gone to the end of our own strength, as it were, and if we do not get relief from some outside source many of our people will starve. Our people would work and in fact would rather work if they could get employment, but there is not work for them to do."[11] Crittenden County faced equally dire circumstances with delinquent taxes that amounted to $35,000, crippling local relief efforts. According to the county drought chairman, "The demands are too great and we can no longer meet their needs. In this regard, understand me, it is food and clothing that is needed, not seed and feed for stock."[12] All of the letters Barkley submitted painted a gloomy picture. County officials and prominent citizens, not the hungry, were pleading for aid.

To deal with the crisis, Caraway introduced a $15-million food loan bill as an amendment to the feed and seed act. Farmers would offer a lien on their tenants' crop. Only by adhering to this complex formula could those hardest hit obtain credit.[13] On January 6, the House began consideration of this proposal. Immediately Representative La Guardia of New York introduced the urban unemployment issue and threatened to block the bill unless it provided help for the idle workers in the cities. "But now the time has come when Congress will either make relief universal or this bill is not going to conference," he said. "You are either going to treat all needy American citizens alike or else we are going to know the reason why."[14] La Guardia focused on an issue that appeared throughout the debates, for he demanded that the federal government provide assistance for all Americans who suffered, whether from agricultural dislocation or the depression.

While Congress debated the amendment, John Barton Payne testified before the Senate Committee on Appropriations on January 6. La Follette had sponsored a resolution before Christmas demanding the appearance of Payne, Colonel Arthur Woods, and other representatives of the various relief agencies. The resolution required that Payne provide information regarding the drought region, the ability of his organization to provide for the needy in those states, and the current state of unemployment in the cities and towns.[15] In his testimony the judge read a statement outlining traditional Red Cross policy and explained that the agency firmly believed the individual could solve his own problem through normal banking and commercial channels. However, in December, he continued, the individual's ability to help himself had decreased as the cotton-picking season ended and families depleted their usual winter resources. Payne observed that relief rested upon need—not loss. "The Red Cross cannot provide a complete insurance against all the hazards of agriculture and industry."[16]

After his formal statement, Payne then answered questions pertaining to the adequacy of Red Cross funds. As of January 1 the Red Cross had spent $849,965.49 for drought relief; one-half of the sum had come from the $5-million drought fund and the other half had been raised by the local chapters. Thus $4.5 million remained to deal with the disaster. He expected the amount to cover any further relief needs, but, should it fall below $2.5 million, national headquarters would launch a fund drive. What constituted a sufficient grant of rations, he continued, was "left in the hands of the local chapters, and the local chapters, as I have explained, are composed of neighbors and friends of the sufferers, and I think it may be confidently stated that they do not treat people with a lack of consideration when they are their neighbors and their friends." As far as he knew, the allotments fulfilled the victim's needs. "When you come to feed people, who knows better how to feed them, and whether they are in need, than their neighbors?"[17]

Senator Royal S. Copeland of New York doubted that the organization's $4.5 million would be sufficient to aid all of the needy. In New York City alone $8 million had been raised for the unemployed. The current Red Cross amount would not be a "flea bonnet" when it came to meeting the crisis. Due to the extraordinary nature of the combined forces of disaster and depression, the senator felt the government should consider administering aid through Payne's agency by allocating the $15 million specifically for a Red Cross relief program. The judge disagreed, saying that national headquarters had never requested a cent from the government, nor did it intend to. However, he did concede that if Congress "should say that they want the Red Cross to do something, we would do it."[18]

The senators inquired as to the exact number currently receiving rations. Although the chairman could not answer the question, his director of disaster relief, DeWitt Smith, claimed the organization was feeding 25,000 families in Arkansas alone. When asked to estimate the possible needs in the winter, the judge refused, for due to the gradual nature of the drought people exhausted their resources at various rates, while employment and weather conditions also determined the extent of their ability to meet the crisis. Despite Payne's ambiguous reply,

71

Senator Copeland advised him to launch a fund drive immediately, for "you are in imminent danger of having some money thrust upon you by the Government." Payne promised to "yell" should his agency's reserves fall below an adequate level.[19]

His testimony did not satisfy the senators from Arkansas; in fact, it provoked further demands for a more accurate survey of the state. According to Senator Joseph Robinson, Payne's inability to state how many people had received aid in Arkansas was evidence of the agency's failure to estimate the degree of need. He quoted Red Cross official William Baxter, who had visited the state and had reported that the organization had fed 100,000 persons and expected the number to soon reach 250,000. The existing $4 million would at least be required for these victims alone. England had presented a perfect example of the organization's inability to handle relief, continued Robinson, nor was it the first incident that had occurred within the region. News regarding other episodes had been suppressed.[20]

Although Robinson and Caraway questioned the adequacy of the current plan, they clearly did not support an extensive direct relief program. Both sought to provide credit facilities for the farmers rather than a dole. A government loan for food, seed, and feed, Robinson confidently asserted, would solve the problem in Arkansas. The existing policy compelled anyone who did not possess credit "to secure food, to ask alms, to beg, and it is bad for the citizens and bad for the country and the institutions of the country." The federal government could distribute the Federal Farm Board's wheat surplus either through the Red Cross or credit corporations, thus providing an extensive relief measure to the needy. Yet the major goal of the Red Cross was to prevent starvation, not to undertake rehabilitation work or to furnish crop production supplies. Their operation represented charity rather than credit, making the passage of the $60 million food, feed, and seed act imperative.[21]

As the congressional debate continued, Payne decided to "yell" and on January 10 launched a $10-million national drive for drought funds. Increased demands since the first of the year, he announced, had necessitated an immediate campaign to prevent "untold suffering and actual starvation by thousands of families."[22] Hoover gave the program his blessing and called upon Americans to contribute to the Red Cross— "the nation's sole agency for relief in such a crisis." A few days later the president appointed a national committee to aid the organization in its appeal. "We are faced with a national emergency," he finally admitted. While the cities could care for their needy, he doubted that the rural areas could carry their burden and, hence, must look to their fellow citizens for assistance. "The American way of meeting such a relief problem has been through voluntary effort and for many years this effort has been centered in the American Red Cross, created by the people themselves to act in just such emergencies. . . . It is essential that we should maintain that sound American tradition and spirit of voluntary aid in such an emergency," he concluded, "and should not undermine the spirit which has made our Red Cross the outstanding guardian of our people in time of disaster."[23]

Payne's announcement added more fuel to a legislative debate that had already reached white-hot proportions. Some congressmen questioned the integrity of the organization for launching a national drive so soon after the chairman had testified to the adequacy of its resources. Urban representatives demanded relief for the unemployed and angrily expressed their resentment over the agency's conducting such an appeal in their cities. The judge's action, however, had the immediate impact of defeating Caraway's proposal and increasing the hostility between Hoover and a growing number of congressional leaders.

Angrily observing how national headquarters had designated the six largest states containing the major urban centers to raise $7,606,000 of the $10 million goal, La Guardia introduced an amendment to the food bill, eliminating all "classes, occupations, or residences of persons entitled to receive food" under the Senate measure. The House overwhelmingly adopted the resolution; however, Speaker Longworth overruled it on a parliamentary point of order. After this action, the body defeated Caraway's proposal by a 215 to 135 vote.[24] The representatives insisted that the measure threatened to establish a bad precedent for federal food appropriations. But, as Will Rogers accurately observed, while congressmen assumed that such an appropriation would encourage hunger, the "way things look, hunger don't need much encouragement, it's just coming around naturally."[25]

The following day, on January 14, Senate Democrats and Insurgent Republicans expressed their indignation over the House's decision. Senator Norris could not comprehend how Congress had justified its actions in view of the solid evidence of human suffering. "We will give relief to animals but not to people," for fear of establishing a dangerous precedent. "Suppose it does? Are we going to let people die of starvation because it may establish a precedent that will be difficult to overcome in the future?" he queried. "We ought to establish the precedent that we are not immune to appeals because of human suffering. We ought to establish the precedent that we are human beings and that the Government of the United States is human and is moved by the appeals of human suffering."[26]

Senator Borah questioned the feasibility of stalling the $45-million loan any longer: "We are keeping the farmer from preparing his crops, which is absolutely necessary." The Senate should pass the feed and seed provision and attach the food amendment to another bill. Barkley disagreed. Acknowledging the necessity of the crop loan, he noted that a food bill would encounter opposition no matter what legislation it became a part of. The pressure to prevent the appropriation of a dollar for food would be greater after the $45-million act had passed. "In other words, under the philosophy of the administration, if we provide feed for animals, the pressure will be greater to prevent the purchase of any food for humans." According to Borah, the farmers needed the crop loans immediately, or they would neither receive food nor plant crops. The Kentuckian then pointed out that in the extreme southern portions of the drought region crops could not be made for two more months. Although the work stock obviously required feed for the winter, the immediate need was food for humans rather than seed for crops. Norris supported Barkley, indignantly remarking, "We cannot get an appropriation for food for human beings because of the power and influence of the President of the United States." It would be impossible to pass a food proposal, for Hoover had forced Congress to choose between a feed and seed bill or no relief at all.[27]

After Norris's angry denunciation of the administration, Robinson suggested that the Senate approve the original measure and attach the food amendment to the appropriations bill. In recognition of the obstinate behavior of the House, he and other Democratic Senators decided to yield and adopt the $45-million loan proposal. But Norris, despite the obvious defeat, found it "humiliating on a great question that we have to yield and abandon relief when hourly and daily the suffering all over our country is increasing at a rapid rate." Outraged at the president's stubbornness, he remarked, "If we have reached the time when the United States Senate, right or wrong, cannot express itself in favor of the appropriation of public funds to relieve human suffering, then we ought to abandon our form of government."[28]

The sense of defeatism expressed by Norris found other outlets. Tom Connally of Texas decided also that the Senate had no choice but to submit to Hoover and the House or obtain no relief at all. Perhaps some consolation could be found, however. "As I recall, during the French Revolution one of the ministers when he heard the people crying for food said, 'Let them eat grass.' We are going to buy hay for animals," he noted, "and the attitude of the administration and the leaders undoubtedly is that if the people are really hungry, let them eat hay, because they will have hay when the $45 million appropriation shall finally be made."[29]

The Senate passed the feed bill but not without protest. Kenneth McKellar of Tennessee vowed to attach a relief provision to every appropriation proposal if necessary, for "when men become hungry in any country, there is a dangerous situation and I am pleading here now for our established institutions" to provide relief. Senators Black and Robinson decided to take immediate action and introduced a $25-million amendment to the Deficiency Appropriation bill to be expended by the Red Cross for drought and unemployment relief.[30] Thus the relief debate did not end when Congress approved the $45 million. Furthermore, the fears of the Red Cross had been fulfilled as the Senate now sought to allocate money to the agency for relief throughout the entire country— an action which called into question the traditional relief policy of the Red Cross.

Throughout the remainder of January, the Senate argued over the additional proposal and refused to pass the appropriation measure until the House accepted its amendment. Robinson continued to insist that the president should not expect local communities to bear the responsibility of assistance through their charitable institutions. As Black perceived it, Congress must confront the question of "who shall pay the amount which is needed to adequately take care of the suffering and the destitute" in America. If the responsibility lay with local official and charitable institutions, then increased land taxes would be necessary. So far the administration had merely sought to shield the large taxpayers from any increases.[31]

Although Hoover remained publicly aloof, he did respond to the accusations that he lacked adequate information on the extent of human suffering, sending his personal envoy, Colonel J. F. Lucey of the Committee for Employment, on a fact-finding mission. Not surprisingly, the colonel first visited England, Arkansas. Dr. William DeKleine of the

Red Cross medical staff guided him around Lonoke County. According to Lucey, $1.4 million of state and federal funds could be made available in Arkansas for road work to relieve the unemployed farmers. "That announcement did not meet with any great applause," noted DeKleine. The planters quickly informed the visitors that they needed their workers on the plantation to prepare for spring crops, and if their tenants worked on roads they would never plant the cotton. Credit to furnish spring crops and supplies would solve their problem. They urged the government to establish and finance a credit corporation independent of the depleted or bankrupt local banks, thus providing credit for both feed and food. According to the owners, this action would remove the necessity of Red Cross relief, for they could then furnish their croppers.

Visits to tenant homes had convinced DeKleine that the need for food and clothing had not been exaggerated. One school superintendent informed Lucey that Red Cross rations were often too scanty. Indeed, DeKleine seemed to feel that even with outside assistance most of the workers had less to eat than in normal times. Both he and Albert Evans had stressed to the local chapters the necessity of insuring a sufficient ration. DeKleine attributed the "economical attitude" of the relief committee to the planters' desire for tenants to be given less than they normally have.[32]

Despite the total economic collapse Lucey observed in England, his public statement denounced Arkansas's leaders as the major hindrance to any significant relief measures. "My report to the President will be that Arkansas alone of the states assigned to me, is not doing everything within its power to help its own people." Governor Parnell and the state Highway Commission had refused to release further funds for public roads because there were too many county roads that were already expensive to maintain. He accused the chairman of the governor's unemployment committee of failure to recognize the state's actual predicament, being more concerned with adverse publicity for Arkansas. Although he found no Communists residing in England, Lucey was convinced that croppers lacked adequate care. "But no request for help for those people had come to me. I didn't realize what the situation was and I doubt that the President realizes it."[33]

A few days later assistant director of Red Cross Disaster Relief, John D. Cremer, and field director Everett Dix talked to Lucey concerning his visit to Arkansas and the other southern states. As the colonel viewed it, the Red Cross would soon be forced to feed large numbers of tenants. According to Dix, the organization had just sent a $40,000 grant to the state. The $45-million act, continued Lucey, would only partially restore credit, forcing the organization to feed Arkansas tenants through September or October. He did feel that the agency had done a splendid job. He interpreted his own responsibility as protecting both the president and the Red Cross from any abuse.[34] Members of the Committee for Employment, however, had other ideas.

Once again the Woods committee urged the Red Cross to accept responsibility for unemployment relief. On the day of Lucey's visit to Arkansas Porter Lee, a member of the committee, presented a report to Woods, suggesting that more immediate steps be taken to aid state and local relief agencies. National Red Cross reports, state and local relief committee reports, and evidence gathered by Senator La Follette clearly indicated the inability of many local areas to deal with the unemployed. Although these reports did not appear to reveal a sudden acute phase of suffering occasioned by unemployment, he was convinced that matters had definitely moved from bad to worse—as the committee had predicted would happen. The large cities would probably be able to carry their burdens, but the time had come to urge the Red Cross to assume responsibility for the unorganized, smaller cities and rural sections. A previous conference with the agency's staff had indicated that the Red Cross had expected to have this responsibility placed upon it, and Hoover's letter to Payne on January 10 approving the relief appeal implied an expectation that the organization would handle unemployment needs in the drought region. "There is also difficulty in the smaller rural and industrial towns as a double reaction from the drought and depression," President Hoover explained. "I understand that those towns are unable to organize to effectively meet their problems as are the municipalities." Lee suggested that it might be unwise for the Red Cross to acknowledge responsibility for unemployment during the drought relief drive. In view of the increasing demands for help, however, he wanted the agency to offer definite assurance that it would accept the responsibility. Colonel Woods should ask Hoover to approach Payne and request the proposed action of his agency. Should the Red Cross undertake to include unemployment relief, an additional $15 million would be required. Perhaps some of the funds could be obtained from state treasuries. "It is clear to me that the assumption of unemployment relief by the Red Cross may necessitate a grant of federal funds for the purpose," Lee concluded.[35]

Lee also discussed the pending legislation, particularly La Follette's canvass to ascertain the degree of unemployment and needs of the idle workers. The Wisconsin senator seemed to move toward a federal appropriation to be expended through state and local poor law officials. However, the committee's findings, continued Lee, indicated the poor law machinery in most areas had proved totally unable to handle unemployment relief. An alternative would be a federal appropriation to the Red Cross for assistance outside the cities. Lee proposed a conference between La Follette and other proponents of federal relief and officials at the national headquarters to discuss the possibility of the plan. He recognized, however, that for political reasons such a meeting would be inexpedient at that time.[36]

Even Hoover's own Committee for Employment clearly expressed a desire for a federal appropriation to enable the Red Cross to aid both the victims and the unemployed. In late January the organization faced the possibility of accepting the entire burden of relief in all rural areas and small towns. Robinson's bill definitely placed the responsibility upon the agency, and Lee's report indicated that the members of the committee privately supported the plan. The continuing legislative debates in the latter part of January consistently questioned the sufficiency of Red Cross rations and placed the organization on the defensive. Consequently, national headquarters initiated its own studies of the drought operation.

Judge Payne, in his testimony before the Senate committee on January 6, had explained the procedure whereby each chapter determined the amount to be rationed to each family.[37] The policy represented the democratic and neighborly way of feeding people, for the local committee would best know the needs of their friends. The Delta relief organizations proved the naiveté of this assumption. The kinds of food and the amount issued varied from region to region, depending on local customs. In the plantation areas the diet consisted of corn meal, flour, beans, rice, salt meat, lard, and molasses.[38] Of all the Delta states, Arkansas had the lowest ration per family. According to the New York *Times,* the average individual in Marked Tree lived on $3^{1}/3$¢ per meal, provided he ate three times daily. A weekly ration of $2 per family plus 50¢ per child with a maximum of $4.50 constituted Red Cross relief. Since some families consisted of fifteen members, they received less proportionally than a family of five.[39]

The surveys conducted by local Arkansas chapters demonstrated

that local customs did indeed prevail. According to one county, sufficient assistance had been administered to prevent suffering. Although
the quantity represented a less than average figure, the committee
declared, "We do not believe we should give enough food to be comfortable for this would destroy the incentive of our negroes to work and
might even ruin our labor for years." According to another citizen,
"Our people don't expect normal conditions. They are satisfied with the
relief given."[40] If anything, large landowners felt the ration had been
too generous. In Pulaski County, adjacent to England, three planters
protested that the scale of relief given had created serious problems for
them due to the generous nature of rations.[41] As DeWitt Smith noted,
the general feeling appeared to be that "we are going too far rather than
not enough."[42]

Despite accusations by Robinson and others regarding the inadequacy of Red Cross relief in the Magnolia state, the agency's own
reports showed that assistance had been adequate. As Dr. DeKleine had
noted on Colonel Lucey's visit, too many of the planter-dominated
chapters had pursued an economically conservative policy, fearing the
ruin of their labor force. Apparently, the organization did not consider
this a problem for national headquarters. When it became obvious that
children suffered from malnutrition, however, the agency did conduct a
school lunch program. According to the assistant director of the Red
Cross Nutrition Service, the Red Cross had appropriated funds to be
used in Arkansas by the extension service and the health department
for lunch programs, but they must insure that the officials used the
money for the best advantage—meaning it should be made to stretch as
far as possible. In fact, officials had stated explicitly that the organization did not aim to improve nutritional conditions in the area, because
in an emergency the object was to prevent starvation. National headquarters advised nutritionists to stay out of the area, since no educa-
tional program would be undertaken in the region.[43]

In an effort to determine the impact of the feeding program, Dr.
DeKleine visited Louisiana parishes and found the need for food becoming more critical each day. Although rations exceeded those of Arkansas
by one-third in the small farm region, allowing from $7.50 to $10.70 per
month, respectively, for a family of two and five, the doctor thought
chapters in both states were too conservative in their programs. During
his visits to cropper homes, he observed a greater degree of child
malnutrition than in Arkansas. Because of planter pressure in the state,

many chapters hesitated to undertake a feeding program for tenants. The Red Cross had already fed 500 families—if tenants were to be included the number could reach 2,000 or 3,000. He recommended a school lunch program and a yeast distribution operation to prevent a larger increase of pellagra in the spring.[44]

Regions other than Arkansas also indicated the Red Cross program was a success. Greenville, Mississippi, reported 90 percent of the needy had been reached, and grants equaling one-third of the normal $16 monthly ration had been issued. The chapter warned, however, of the disastrous consequences should a feeding operation be continued after March 1. Not all local Mississippi officials agreed with the Greenville chapter. According to T. Y. Williford, county agent in Bolivar County, a biweekly grant of $4 for a family of seven could not possibly satisfy the proper dietary needs of the croppers; normally the planter's furnishings amount to from $16 to $20. Nor would credit measures solve the problem, and federal loans without a food provision would be worthless.[45]

The survey reports convinced James Fieser that many chapters had been too economical regarding the administration of assistance. He instructed Robert Bondy on the "absolute necessity now of making sure that none of our Field people or supervisors hold to the idea of conservatism in requesting appropriations where there is need." Hoover and Payne had insisted, he continued, that adequate relief be administered, and this goal must be made clear to the chapters. Bondy wired the chapters in the Delta region, ordering that food should be furnished to all the hungry, "whether they would normally be fed or could now be fed by planters or not."[46]

Apparently the Red Cross surveys and Fieser's orders to the plantation states did not stop abuses in Arkansas. On February 2 Harvey Couch wired Hoover's assistant, Lawrence Richey, that the issue of local relief had become "delicate and critical," and he urged the president to advise Payne or Fieser to visit the state immediately.[47] Hoover then called national headquarters and inquired about the adequacy of the program in the state. Fieser assured him that all of the victims' needs had been met. According to the national representative in Arkansas, William Baxter, more had been attempted there than in other disasters. The state had "sunk" into chaos not only as a result of the drought but also due to the depression. He could see no constructive efforts at long-range planning for recovery. Most people, added Baxter, simply did not know how the state would get back on its feet. Arkansans clung tenaciously to any free relief offered. Despite the severe economic problems in the state, Fieser maintained that the food program had improved significantly.[48]

From the beginning the Red Cross had merely sought to provide the normal standard of subsistence for the drought sufferers, always maintaining that individual chapters could best determine the needs of their constituents. Payne reiterated this position in response to Hoover's inquiry. Local committees made up of the "most public-spirited and helpful people, the neighbors and friends of the sufferers who know many of them personally, are sympathetic with them, had determined the needs and distributed orders to the local country store for rations. We know of no better method of helping them."[49] Reports of planter abuse through the committees had obviously not swayed the judge from his traditional position on local responsibility and self-help, even as surveys clearly revealed the limitations of this approach.

Despite reports that rations often fell below the minimum plantation standard, the Red Cross insisted its disaster operation did not "undertake to provide a more liberal standard of living than those existing in normal times," for the "economic condition of the States and the customs of the community are always the basis of the relief given." Whenever a family obtained a day's labor, then the ration could be reduced.[50] The organization recognized the difficulty of administering assistance in the Delta and acknowledged that local sentiment would not allow any relief to improve upon the customary standard of living. According to national headquarters, questions regarding the adequacy of the feeding operation came from those unfamiliar with the plantation economy. The credit structure must be fully understood, for in general it "is so low that a person not familiar with the system would scarcely believe a family could subsist upon it."[51] As one official observed, "It is practically impossible to convey to the public outside of the area concerned, an understanding of the standard of living which we are endeavoring to maintain in Arkansas."[52] Nevertheless, the Red Cross once again succumbed to the wishes of planters. National headquarters could demand that chapters administer adequate relief, but the determining factor of the amount continued to be local custom.

While the Red Cross conducted its surveys and Congress continued to debate the $25-million appropriation, the press and other groups in the drought region expressed opinions on the impending legislation and the Red Cross operation. In Memphis twelve prominent southern bankers, businessmen, and farmers appealed to Congress to pass all pending disaster measures. They expressed indignation over the slowness of legislative action and noted the complete exhaustion of economic resources and feed and food supplies. All available reserves had been deadlocked due to the bank failures in thousands of southern communities, producing a state of abject poverty in the South.[53]

The Memphis *Commercial-Appeal* supported the twelve leaders in an editorial advocating the immediate passage of the drought measures. Providing for the hungry far outweighed any worry over a dole, even though it ran contrary to the American spirit of thrift and initiative. "We have always opposed doles or indiscriminate charity, but we realize that either is much preferred to starvation. If starvation is such now that only doles can prevent disease, suffering and starvation, then let us have them." By his inaction, the president "may bring about the very thing he set out to avoid."[54]

The New York *Times* disagreed with any approach resembling that of the *Appeal.* Instead, it fully supported the Red Cross relief fund drive. "The nation's response through this channel will have a moral value which no outright congressional appropriation could have, for the generosity of such a response would make of a disaster a triumph of man's spirit over the material thing and give proof of the ideal that dwells in America's practical soul and write another golden chapter in the book of America's chronicles of Mercy." In a Hooverian tone the *Times* observed that "it is time for the American people, not for Congress, to provide for whatever may be needed to keep the victims of last summer's drought from the perils of destitution or actual starvation."[55]

Hoover continued his effort to save the drought victims through voluntarism, despite pleas from the disaster region. On January 23 in a national radio appeal he called upon the American people to protect "our greatest American institution of charity." He invited an array of prominent citizens and celebrities such as Al Smith, Calvin Coolidge, Mary Pickford, and Will Rogers to present radio addresses in an attempt to raise funds.[56] On the following day Payne predicted that by February 1 one million people would need relief.[57]

Red Cross efforts to convince the public to conduct a sufficient relief operation in the drought area and Hoover's constant support of the $10-million fund drive clearly represented both the president's and the judge's attempts to defeat the Robinson proposal. By late January they had succeeded. On January 29 Payne informed the House that the central committee had unanimously voted that it could adequately meet the needs of the drought, and thus it could not accept the appropriation.[58] This action was taken in spite of Payne's testimony on January 6 that the agency would do whatever the Congress requested.

This announcement immediately provoked angry responses in the Senate. Caraway questioned the political autonomy of the organization, saying it had ceased to be an "independent organization, controlled and dedicated to the relief of human suffering everywhere, but is now the political screen behind which the President of the United States is undertaking to shirk his responsibility to see that those who are suffering and the starving in this country are relieved."[59] Copeland expressed disbelief. "Everybody who knows anything about the situation realizes that $10,000,000 will hardly be a drop in the bucket in taking care of the situation that exists today." He questioned if the Red Cross could have deliberately taken this action; if it had, the time had come for an explanation of its stand on human suffering. The fund should be sent to Arkansas alone, he maintained, and a much larger sum allocated for the entire region.[60]

For Senator Robinson, the rejection meant that no general relief measure for the unemployed would be passed, "no matter how long the present condition continues or how great the disaster may become." Hoover's refusal to support further funding shocked the Arkansan. "When I hear it suggested that a man who did so much for the relief of starving people in other countries in any way whatever interfering with the relief of American citizens who are starving, I simply cannot believe it possible. There must be some mistake."[61] In a more combative tone, Senator McKellar announced his intention to fight for relief for the starving, because the president would not relinquish his stand under any circumstances. He pledged to block all appropriation bills until relief had been granted. "It would seem that the Red Cross has taken this present position for political reasons because that organization has come before the Congress time after time asking for appropriations."[62]

On January 28 a joint session of the House Deficiency and Interior Department Subcommittees of the Committee on Appropriations held hearings to consider both Robinson's bill and a measure to grant $3 million to county health departments to combat the increase in typhoid, pellagra, and other diseases resulting from the drought. Once again Secretary Arthur Hyde and Director of Extension Work C. W. Warburton testified to the efficacy of loans to aid the farmers. Both continued to deny the need for a food loan bill, saying the Red Cross could care for those not covered by the $45-million provision. Payne also appeared again, this time to refuse the proposed grant of federal funds. Claiming that the Robinson proposal had hindered the organization's drought fund-raising campaign, he insisted the Red Cross could raise an adequate sum to meet the crisis if Congress would stay out of the picture. A federal appropriation would destroy voluntary giving. "All we pray for is that you let us alone and let us do the job, and if we do not do it, kick us."[63] In his estimation the agency had taken care of the drought victims.

Dr. Hugh S. Cummings, the U.S. surgeon general, painted a bleaker picture. As a result of the drought, tremendous increases in typhoid and malnutrition had occurred; in Arkansas alone typhoid had increased 50 percent from July to November. There had been a significant increase in malnutrition among children. Representative Joseph Byrns of Tennessee observed that, unless food were provided, medical aid could do little to care for the other ills. Although Cummings refused openly to support the Robinson bill (which delegated the Red Cross to administer medical supplies), he did urge the immediate passage of $3 million to aid rural sanitation authorities.[64]

Obviously neither Hyde nor Payne had waivered on their former positions. The immediate result of their testimonies was the House's defeat of the Robinson amendment on the following day. Hoover's legislative spokesmen based their rejection on the judge's testimony that the Red Cross could meet the crisis with its current resources. The opposition presented several amendments in an effort to retain the $25 million, seeking to replace the Red Cross with the president; religious, charitable, or fraternal organizations; or even the War Department as the administrator of relief. House Majority Leader Tilson clearly stated the administration's position: "Once the door to the Federal Treasury for a dole to aid citizens in distress is opened, the appropriation used as the opening wedge, whatever its magnitude, will soon pale into insignificance in the wake of what will follow." There should be no compromise on so important a principle. "Once the Red Cross is destroyed, as it must inevitably be by a Federal dole," he observed, "and our local charities paralyzed, as they will be when the Federal Government takes over responsibility for charitable relief, the appropriations that must follow as a consequence of such a policy would now stagger belief. We are now at the cross-roads so far as our charities are concerned." The organization had always represented the heart of America. "Shall we stab it to death and make it a cold, lifeless thing, substituting for it a governmental bureaucracy, bound with red tape, administering a Federal dole?"[65] he queried. Hoover had once again triumphed in the House.

Meanwhile Robinson demanded the passage of a five-point relief plan that included the $45-million feed and seed bill, the Capper resolution providing for the distribution of 20 million bushels of surplus wheat, $5 million of the feed and seed bill to be used as capital stock for the Agricultural Credit Corporation, $3 million for rural sanitation, and a bill to reappropriate the money collected on the 1930 feed, seed, and fertilizer allocation to be used in 1931. He warned the House of certain defeat of the appropriation bill if it chose to reject these proposals. It did not matter which agency distributed the funds as long as the relief was administered.[66]

When the Senate learned of the House rejection, the battle intensified. Neither side expressed a willingness to compromise, for the argument had now been placed in absolute terms—either a $25-million bill or no measure at all. The House supported Hoover and refused to allocate any funds, regardless of the administrative agency. During the next few days Democratic senators and Insurgent Republicans castigated the president, the House, and the Red Cross. Borah did not understand the logic that an appropriation for relief would establish a dangerous precedent. Clearly, the southern drought had resulted from an "act of God," thus warranting Red Cross action. Questioning the ability of the agency to offer ample aid, he related a story of a worker in Tennessee who had visited a widow with four children. Their rations had been reduced to a dish of rancid grease and some sour meal. The children "were emaciated in the extreme." When asked why she had not sought assistance, the mother replied that all of her neighbors were in the same condition, despite their efforts to help each other. For Borah, this proved the self-reliant and proud nature of the victims, disproving any fears that relief would constitute a dole and produce shiftless people. "We will either feed these people, or we will stay here and tell the American people why we do not feed them," he declared.[67] Other senators, especially Pat Harrison, noted that, if anything, the Senate had expressed confidence in the president and had offered to grant relief funds for him to administer. Unless the House acted soon, the angry drought representatives threatened an extra session until a program was agreed upon.[68] They did not have to wait long for an executive reaction.

Hoover quickly responded to the barrage against his administration.

"This is not an issue as to whether people shall go hungry or cold in the United States. It is solely a question of the best method by which hunger and cold shall be prevented. It is a question as to whether the American people on the one hand will maintain the spirit of charity and mutual self help through voluntary giving and the responsibility of local government," he emphasized, "as distinguished on the other hand from appropriations out of the Federal Treasury for such purposes." The president feared the consequences should the government become involved in relief, bypassing the American spirit of generosity. He quoted President Grover Cleveland's famous speech when he faced a similar crisis in 1887. Confronted with demands for a feed and seed bill for the Texas drought sufferers, Cleveland vetoed it, observing that "the lesson should be constantly enforced that though the people support the Government, the Government should not support the people." Cleveland's approach proved inadequate in 1887; it was disastrous in 1931 when American society was even more interdependent than in the late nineteenth century. In a tone reminiscent of his earlier years as relief administrator, Hoover insisted the basis of successful assistance in national distress came from the mobilization and organization of the infinite number of charitable organizations. "That has been the American way of relieving distress among our own people and the country is successfully meeting its problem in the American way today." In conclusion, the president expressed bewilderment over the accusations that he lacked compassion. "I have indeed spent much of my life in fighting hardship and starvation both abroad and in the southern states. I do not feel that I should be charged with lack of human sympathy for those who suffer but I recall that in all the organizations with which I have been connected over these many years, the foundation has been to summon the maximum of self help."[69]

The press statement merely increased hostility. Several senators accused Hoover of presenting a picture of the legislative body as the destroyer of self-help and initiative. Out of desperation some offered to accept the original $15-million dollar proposal—anything to relieve their states. Somewhat optimistically, Harrison noted a more conciliatory spirit in the president's statement—that he would accredit to "those who advocate Federal charity a natural anxiety for the people of their states"—and hoped that Hoover might seek a compromise. The majority of Democrats and Insurgents, however, were angry at the president's response.[70]

Harrison's prediction proved accurate. On February 4 Hoover sent his personal envoy, Colonel Campbell Hodges, to Arkansas; on the fifth, through his close friend Harvey Couch, he initiated a conference with Robinson and Caraway. Couch had recently phoned Fieser, offering to ask the Arkansas senators to amend their bill to a loan basis, conditioned on lending the Red Cross such additional sums as might be needed beyond the amount collected from the public. Due to the crisis in Arkansas and his previous conversations with Robinson, Couch seemed certain the senator would not back down unless an acceptable alternative could be arranged. Fieser replied that the Red Cross "was not disposed to enter into this discussion," whereupon Couch indicated that he could handle the matter "indirectly" without involving the organization.[71] His confidence proved justified.

On February 5 Robinson met with Senate Majority Leader James Watson and Senator Charles L. McNary to draft a $20-million farm production and rehabilitation bill. Hyde also attended and lent his support. Still Hoover needed a congressional spokesman, and this created a problem. Tilson and others were maintaining an absolute position of no compromise, and McNary seemed inclined to allow the secretary of agriculture to accept the responsibility. Further, if the Red Cross campaign did not reach its goal soon, the Louisville *Courier-Journal* predicted that unidentified Old Guard Republicans threatened to bolt the administration and support a federal appropriation.[72] On February 6 Robinson added the $20-million dollar amendment to the feed and seed measure, excluding any mention of food. The loan would be used to strengthen credit banks and agricultural credit associations, enabling them to lend money for agricultural rehabilitation and crop production. Hyde had assured the compromisers that loans would be made to planters who could, in turn, extend credit to reliable farmers working for them to purchase food. Robinson and Watson agreed to interpret "farm rehabilitation" as meaning loans to purchase food or any other necessities in the drought area. Although presidential secretary Walter Newton had attended the meeting and supposedly represented the president's views, Hoover did not publicly support any such interpretation. If he agreed to this rendition, then he would have capitulated to the demands of representatives from the stricken states. Administration supporters, however, still rejected a compromise. Tilson told reporters on the afternoon of February 6, "We'll never yield to any subterfuge. We'll accept nothing containing provision for food in it."

Two hours later he stood by Speaker Longworth as the latter announced the amendment to the bill.[73] Robinson and Watson had triumphed, but other senators did not willingly submit.

Lacking knowledge as to how far the administration had been "pinned down," others refrained from supporting the Arkansan. According to Alben Barkley, "If it is intended to mean food, it is a cowardly evasion not to say so." He promised further "explosives" in the chamber until Hoover explicitly defined his interpretation of the measure. Nor did Robinson and Watson consult with the Insurgents, who had continually demanded direct federal relief. Senator Smith Brookhart of Iowa, reiterating his support for direct relief to all the hungry, remarked that Wall Street had "got hold of both parties." Others expressed concern over the attendance of New York financier Bernard Baruch, as giving the impression that Wall Street was seeking to influence senatorial action and prevent an extra legislative session. Senator Copeland described 1600 Pennsylvania Avenue as the "place where they juggle words."[74]

The following day's debates revealed the accuracy of some congressmen who attacked the compromise as a leaders' agreement. Although conferees in both houses reported the measure favorably, doubting Thomases continued to criticize the bill for not providing aid to the urban unemployed and for its obvious avoidance of the mention of food. Insurgents accused Robinson of having sold out to the administration and noted that the senator's law firm represented a number of utility companies also affiliated with Hoover's envoy, Arkansas utility magnate Couch. Burton K. Wheeler expressed disbelief over the Democratic leadership's capitulation. "It is not a creditable performance for the Senate or the President to agree to a face-saving proposition of this kind." The Montana senator reiterated the unfairness of not also offering aid to the urban idle. La Follette joined Wheeler in his attack and criticized the "vague" terminology used in the bill, which enabled Hoover to boast that he had not yielded to Congress and yet had somehow compromised.[75]

In a radio address that evening Robinson defended his position, asserting that the compromise would "fill the gap between the necessities of those who are properly recipients of Red Cross assistance and the requirements of those who are capable, if given credit, of carrying on their own farm operations." The rehabilitation loan combined with the feed and seed bill would certainly care for the farmers and the 1931 crop, he concluded, while the Red Cross could care for those who lacked collateral.[76] On the next day Robinson visited the White House and returned bearing a letter from Hoover that assured the Senate that the pending measure would be interpreted "fairly and sympathetically." Only Caraway supported his colleague in an endeavor to prove the Red Cross had sufficient means to care for the needy. No Republican voice emerged to support the two Democrats; however, the next day Insurgents vehemently attacked both Robinson and the administration.[77]

Both houses passed the compromise bill on February 14, but not until some Democrats and Insurgents explained their objections to the measure. Barkley observed that thousands of small Kentucky farmers did not qualify for the food loans because in 1931 they would have no crop to offer as a lien. According to Robinson, the Red Cross existed to relieve these people. The measure would also help tenants because the owners had security and thus would receive loans that enabled them to furnish their renters. As for the adequacy of the Red Cross's relief, the senator was now convinced that it had expanded its operation to meet the needs of the victims.[78] However, La Follette presented news dispatches from Arkansas clearly revealing that the local banks had refused to lend advances to farmers who had received seed loans, because the government took the first lien on the crop and banks refused to accept a second crop mortgage. In Lee County, for example, only twenty-two of 5,500 farmers qualified for the loans due to the "stringent inflexible" requirements. Further, most farmers received their food and supplies from furnishing merchants who also lacked credit. One merchant furnished $80,000 worth of credit to 400 farmers in 1930 and could not collect the debts; although he held mortgages on his debtors' livestock and land, foreclosures would be of small benefit. Under the feed and seed loan bill, the government required merchants to waive all liens before it extended any credit.[79] As far as the Wisconsin Insurgent could see, neither food nor seed loans would benefit many farmers.

La Follette also questioned the accuracy of Robinson's assessment of relief needs. Reading from various newspaper accounts, he argued that victims were still starving, particularly in the senator's own state. Recent reports revealed that the Red Cross had been frantically attempting to feed 600,000 sufferers for 7¢ a day in the state. A faculty member's wife from the College of the Ozarks in Clarkesville described extreme privation: "Whole families are homeless and are living in covered wagons." La Follette refused to accept Robinson's revised position that the agency could now meet the crisis. The entire drought relief program constituted a "humiliating surrender on the part of the Senate of a great principle, namely, the principle that the justification for government is that it will in emergencies protect its citizenship. We are permitting the precedent to be established," he concluded, "that the millions of working men and women in this country and the farmers who are the victims of this drought shall be required to bear the burden, the economic depression and the drought." He accurately predicted that the question of federal relief would continue to haunt the administration and would form the major issue in the election of 1932.[80]

In the waning days of the controversy Senator Wheeler asked Hyde to state clearly his interpretation of the amendment. In a wire from Louisville he replied that he understood the purpose of the loan was not to furnish food, but to go beyond the provisions of the seed loan bill. The Red Cross would provide charity for tenants and others unable to secure a lien. The major purpose of the new legislation, as he understood it, was the restoration of the weakened credit system. While loans under any part of the bill were to be made to those who had the securities for making the next crop and for rehabilitation from drought, "there could be no prohibition against the proceeds of such loans being used for food or other supplies if they were necessary to effect the purpose." Wheeler angrily submitted that the secretary had not changed from his previous position in December, for Hyde still maintained the restoration of the credit system presented the major problem. Wheeler summarized Hyde's remarks. "If you are hungry, you will have to go to charity. You will have to go to the Red Cross. You will have to take what the Red Cross gives."[81]

Despite these objections, the Senate passed the compromise with only fifteen dissenting votes. According to Senator Barkley, if Shakespeare could rewrite the *Merchant of Venice,* he would change the name of Shylock to Uncle Sam.[82] The debate that had originated in early December finally ended with the acceptance of a bill not too unlike the first $60-million measure submitted by Robinson. During those two and one-half months, however, the president, his administration, and Congress had confronted the issue of direct federal relief versus private charity. Both Hoover and Robinson won their original objectives—the president avoided the use of the word "food" and the Arkansan obtained credit for the plantation system in his region. And, those who could not secure loans relied on the Red Cross for their sole means of support.

After Robinson introduced the compromise bill, he suffered heavy abuse from his Democratic and Insurgent colleagues who claimed he had changed his position on drought relief. Actually he had pursued a consistent policy throughout the controversy. He never sought to accomplish other than the reestablishment of credit in his state, so that planters could furnish their renters and croppers. At first he had hoped to achieve this goal through credit corporations and seed and food loans. When the food issue provoked an intense response, however, he resorted to any means to furnish the planters, even a grant to the Red Cross. He had clearly stated his position to Hoover in a January 2 telegram. According to the senator, credit corporations would best solve the agricultural problem in Arkansas, and he urged the chief executive to support a congressional loan to the corporations, since Arkansas's financial system had collapsed. In his judgment such a measure would "stimulate and promote self-help to a greater extent than anything else now in contemplation."[83]

During the debates Robinson argued for food and seed loans as a means of helping the farmers who could offer collateral—the planters. Further, he had received letters from merchants and planters since the drought began, requesting him to introduce legislation to establish credit corporations and prevent foreclosures on the Federal Land Bank loans.[84]

Finally Robinson had been one of the senators who had signed in December an agreement that promised cooperation with Hoover in obtaining a relief program after the Christmas recess. He never wandered far from his conservative position. On November 29, 1930, he had written Bernard Baruch, expressing the need to "sit steady in the boat" regarding any unemployment relief measure. "I grow more and more impressed with the necessity of conservative action."[85] His detractors to the contrary, the Arkansan never proposed a radical measure; he simply wanted to refurbish the southern agricultural credit structure, a policy followed by both Hoover and Hyde. The $25-million allocation to the Red Cross represented a last-ditch effort to feed the tenants and save the plantation economy. England had exemplified the need to stabilize the cropper work force, and Robinson, a native of Lonoke County, understood this. When he did compromise with the president, he sacrificed very little, for the rehabilitation loans were to be funneled through the planters, who would then make grants to "dependable" farmers. No direct federal aid was offered the majority of agricultural workers. Once again the fairness of the program depended upon the discretion of the planters.

Several congressmen continued to question the adequacy of the loan program. If farmers suffered from indebtedness, they could hardly offer the government a first lien; indeed, Hoover's own envoy to Arkansas revealed the limitations of the plan. According to Colonel Hodges, the new rehabilitation amendment would include food to aid the planters; however, the feed and seed bill would not meet the state's needs because the first liens must go to the government and few banks would accept a second lien for the additional supplies not covered by the measure. The loans would be so small under the provision as to hinder any real relief.[86]

Red Cross reports also revealed the inadequacy of the loan plan. According to Robert Bondy, "There are a number of evidences of serious questioning in Louisiana and Mississippi of the efficacy of a Federal Feed, Seed, and Fertilizer Loan Act." At a local chapter meeting in Greenwood, Mississippi, members described the proposal as a "joke." The district's congressman admitted the effect of the appropriation "was that no relief would be given, at least in any extent that would meet the real need." J. M. Hamley, the chairman in Lake Providence, Louisiana, saw other limitations: "We had hoped that the forty-five million dollars relief voted by the Congress would be of some help, but it looks like the regulations are such that a very few of our people can take advantage of it." The only security a small farmer could offer was his first lien, but the Department of Agriculture demanded this for the few dollars it would loan for feed and seed; no collateral was left to obtain credit for food. "I have heard all along that the Department of Agriculture would make these regulations almost impossible so that very few farmers will be able to borrow any money voted for their relief," he despairingly concluded.[87]

Planters in Arkansas also expressed doubts over the ability of the federal loan program to alleviate their conditions. In Marianna bankers, merchants, and planters said the feed and seed bill would not help them, for the government would loan them only $30 per head of livestock; they needed at least $60. They also lacked food, and, with the government taking the first lien, they could not obtain it. "Parched corn, turnips, and walnuts have kept the wolf from the door for many sufferers."[88]

When Red Cross official J. D. Cremer informed Warburton of the doubts expressed in the Delta, the secretary replied that people in the region felt that way because they had never had any previous contact with this type of loan. His experience in administering such programs in Alabama in 1929 had convinced the extension director of the ability of the provision to meet the farmer's needs. He felt certain the owners would waive their liens on their tenants' crops and allow them to secure loans.[89] Despite Warburton's assurances, congressmen and the farmers in the region continued to question the feasibility of the loan program. Many demanded a larger degree of direct federal assistance.

Democrats like McKellar and Barkley and the Insurgent Republicans like La Follette and Wheeler were the innovative legislators during the debate. These senators accurately perceived the need for a relief program that went beyond extending credit to traditionally "respectable" farmers or simply the initiation of a Red Cross relief operation. As Barkley observed, the organization simply did not possess the resources to care adequately for the needy. Nor could drought relief be separated from unemployment assistance, for in a nation that suffered from an economic depression, human suffering was widespread. To have used federal funds to help one segment of the population without seeking to aid the other was a callous gesture by Congress. The Insurgents correctly insisted that direct federal relief be given to everyone whose suffering resulted from either the economic or the natural disaster. Members of both parties, however, chose to follow Hoover's conservative path.

The conflict during the winter of 1931 forced Congress, the administration, and the public to consider the most appropriate manner of dealing with relief. As the economic crisis deepened, some wondered if the existing governmental and charitable institutions could handle the emergency. By viewing both the drought and unemployment as problems for disaster relief, Hoover sought to administer assistance as he had done in previous emergencies. However, America in 1931 suffered from total collapse rather than from a temporary calamity. It was not enough to call upon Americans to conserve, for their problem was scarcity. Nor could one appeal to their generosity and ask them to give to charitable organizations, for they had nothing left to donate. Privately, the president wanted the organization to assume responsibility for all relief, but Payne declined. Hoover's refusal to allow food to be included in the loan bill made him appear uncaring and insensitive to human suffering. According to the Memphis *Commercial-Appeal,* "Nothing he has done has been so absolutely inexcusable as his cruel position in refusing food and other necessities to human victims of the drought. Of all men, he was the last who might be expected to turn a deaf ear to the agonized cry of human distress." The newspaper found it inexcusable that the president would use the Red Cross to buttress his position. Had Hoover been willing to cooperate with the Senate, a $20-million federal program could have been passed, rather than offering the sum to the

Red Cross. When Payne declined the Senate's offer, he appeared to represent the president's view. "It was bad enough to make a political issue of the hunger and distress of American citizens, but it is infinitely worse to make a political football out of the organization which was constituted for humanitarian work on any and all occasions," the editor charged. "If possible, the use of the Red Cross to bolster the position of any branch of Government in a political row is more infamous and insidious even than the creation of a political mix-up that may cause human suffering and anguish."[90]

The central issue confronting both Congress and the president was federal versus private relief. As the *Nation* observed, "Shall we have the anarchy Mr. Hoover and the Red Cross so clearly desire, or shall we have some sensible and responsible measure of social control in administering relief to the more unfortunate members of our society?" It insisted that "the issue goes straight to the heart of the meaning of government." The president and the business community denounced a federal program because they sought to retain government in the hands of elite managers. The Red Cross central committee, composed of a copper magnate, a multimillionaire steel man, a banker's widow, and eight other conservatives, reflected a similar desire.[91] The committee refused the Senate allocation because they feared people would discover that government could help them in times of distress; then they would realize that the government was really the servant of the people and should be used for their purposes. The grave problem confronting America centered on whether society should be allowed to control the solution to its own problems or whether the president and selected private organizations and advisors would choose the solution without being subject to public advice. "Either the organized state has certain duties and responsibilities to its individual members or it has not. If we agree that it has," asserted the *Nation*, "government is not only within its rights, but is morally and legally obligated to extend protection and relief to those of the individual members of the state who are suffering or in distress because of the faulty functioning or the unavoidable misfortunes of society as a whole."[92]

It was indeed ironic that Herbert Hoover should have been accused of indifference to human suffering, for he had spent much of his life in administering relief to victims of disasters. Admirable as such service was, it also convinced Hoover that all relief should be treated as disaster assistance. He believed strongly that communities should help themselves and that the consequences of federal intervention would be greater and more harmful than any suffering that might result from the limitations of voluntary cooperation. Thus, when the southern agricultural economy collapsed in 1930–31, the planters and the subsistence farmers had to save the system themselves. More than any other group, farmers personified the values Hoover believed in and sought to preserve. To have given to the tillers of the soil federal aid would have destroyed the heart of the American way of life, at least as he viewed it. Hoover would play his part in saving the system by seeing that neither dole nor threats to individualism emerged from Congress.

Hoover's view of agricultural life was that of an eighteenth-century Jeffersonian; however, that idyllic agrarian society never existed in the South, even in the Great Sage's time. From its inception southern society was based on the open exploitation of its agricultural labor force. The rural South by 1930 was dominated by a plantation system that rested on force and intimidation and that was characterized by extreme poverty and racism. To ask the leaders of such a community to administer relief ignored centuries of southern history, not to mention the more immediate realities of class relationships in that society. Hoover totally disregarded the abuses that his decentralized form of relief invited in the rural South, even though he knew from his experiences in the 1927 flood relief operation that planters had used rations to perpetuate peonage. A power greater than and independent of the planters was needed in the South to insure an adequate relief program for the croppers. But even Roosevelt's New Deal did not have that power.[93]

Notes

1. *Cong. Record,* 71 Cong., 3 sess., vol. 74, pt. 2, 1366.
2. Schwarz, *Interregnum of Despair,* 6.
3. Ibid., 55.
4. Ibid., 58–59.
5. Russell B. Nye, *Midwestern Progressive Politics: A Historical Study of Its Origins and Development, 1870–1950* (East Lansing, 1951), 273.
6. Schwarz, *Interregnum of Despair,* 58. For a discussion of the Insurgents during the 1920s, see Nye, *Midwestern Progressive Politics,* 310–86, and Ronald Fineman, *Twilight of Progressivism: The Western Republican Senator & the New Deal* (Baltimore, 1981), 1–33.

7. See Arthur Mann, *La Guardia: A Fighter against His Times, 1882–1933* (Chicago, 1959); Howard Zinn, *La Guardia in Congress* (Ithaca, 1959); J. Joseph Hutchmacher, *Senator Robert F. Wagner and the Rise of Urban Liberalism* (New York, 1968).

8. See Alben Barkley, *That Reminds Me* (New York, 1954).

9. Herbert Hoover, *The Memoirs of Herbert Hoover: The Great Depression, 1929–1941* (New York, 1952), 55.

10. *Cong. Record,* 71 Cong. 3 sess., vol. 74, pt. 2, 1368.

11. Ibid., 1336.

12. Ibid., 1335.

13. Ibid., 1366–67.

14. Ibid., 1477.

15. U.S. Congress, Senate, Committee on Appropriations, La Follette Resolution, *Drought Relief and Unemployment,* Hearings on S. Res. 376, 71 Cong., 3 sess., Jan. 6, 1931, 8.

16. Ibid., 9.

17. Ibid., 11, 12, 23, 13.

18. Ibid., 29, 25, 17, 24.

19. Ibid., 14, 11, 29.

20. *Cong. Record,* 71 Cong., 3 sess., vol. 74, pt. 2, 1534, 1533.

21. Ibid., 1536, 1538.

22. Payne to Chapters, Jan. 12, 1931, ARC, DR-401.21.

23. Meyers, ed., *State Papers of Hoover,* 1: 489–90, 491–92.

24. *Cong. Record,* 71 Cong., 3 sess., vol. 74, pt. 2, 2083, 2087.

25. Louisville *Courier-Journal,* Jan. 8, 1931.

26. *Cong. Record,* 71 Cong., 3 sess., vol. 74, pt. 2, 2141.

27. Ibid.

28. Ibid., 2141, 2142–43. Norris was referring to Hoover's December speech, in which he had accused his opponents of playing politics with human misery.

29. Ibid., 2143.

30. Ibid., 2145, 2147.

31. Ibid., 2359, 2361. For more on the debates, see ibid., 2358–65.

32. DeKleine to Fieser, Jan. 14, 1931, ARC, DR-401.11.

33. Arkansas *Gazette,* Jan. 14, 1931.

34. Memo on conversation between Lucey, Dix, and Cremer, Jan. 20, 1931, ARC, DR-401.02.

35. Lee to Woods, Jan. 14, 1931, PECE/POUR Papers-Central Files of the President's Emergency Committee on Employment, Committee Memo-Arthur Woods Folder, Box 1093, Hoover Papers.

36. Ibid.

37. U.S. Congress, Senate, Committee on Appropriations, La Follette Resolution, *Drought Relief and Unemployment,* 23.

38. Smith to Payne, Jan. 5, 1931, ARC, DR-401.63.

39. New York *Times,* Jan. 26, 1931.

40. "Survey taken in Arkansas from chapters on the adequacy of relief," Jan. 24, 1931, ARC, DR-401.08. The survey asked the following questions:

1. Is relief adequate in quantity?

> Yes. 33 counties—61%
> Fairly so. 10 counties—18.5%
> No. 8 counties—14.8%
> No answer. 3 counties—5.5%

2. How does it compare with normal years?

> Favorably. 17 counties—31.5%
> Fairly. 8 counties—14.8%
> Unfavorably. 11 counties—20.3%
> Unable to compare. 2 counties—3.7%

3. Is your chapter in touch with all needy families?

> Yes. 43 counties—79.6%
> No. 8 counties—14.8%

4. Are all needy cases taken care of?

> Yes. 36 counties—66.6%
> Fairly so. 3 counties—5.5%
> No. 6 counties—11.1%
> No answer. 9 counties—16.6%

41. DeKleine to Fieser, Jan. 14, 1931, ARC, DR-401.11.

42. Smith to Griesemer, Jan. 20, 1931, ARC, DR-401.63.

43. Dr. Marietta Eichelberger to Miss Clyde B. Schuman, Jan. 6, 1931, ibid.

44. DeKleine to Fieser, Jan. 16, 1931, ibid. County agents in Madison, Morehouse, and Webster parishes revealed the food allowance approximated one-half of the landlord's in normal times and predicted tremendous increases in relief demands in the next three months. Already Morehouse had aided 3,000 families with a monthly ration of $8.00 per family. "Telegrams from County Agents on the adequacy of relief," ibid.

45. "Telegrams from County Agents on the adequacy of relief," ibid.

46. Fieser to Bondy, Jan. 16, 1931, Bondy to Fieser, Jan. 20, 1931, ibid.

47. Couch to Richey, Feb. 2, 1931, Presidential Papers-Subject File-Container 61, American Red Cross Correspondence, Hoover Papers.

48. Fieser to Hoover, Feb. 3, 1931, ARC, DR-401.11/08.

49. Payne to Hoover, Feb. 3, 1931, ARC, DR-401.11.

50. "Adequacy of the Red Cross Feeding of the Drought Sufferers," Red Cross *Courier,* Feb. 16, 1931, 103.

51. "Report on the Adequacy of Red Cross Relief," no date, ARC, DR-401.63.

52. Mitchel to Baxter, Jan. 21, 1931, ARC, DR-401.08.

53. *Commercial and Financial Chronicle* 132 (Jan. 17, 1931), 418.

54. Memphis *Commercial-Appeal,* Jan. 17, 1931.

55. New York *Times,* Jan. 15, 17, 1931.

56. Ibid., Jan. 23, 1931.

57. Ibid., Jan. 24, 1931. Payne noted that the Red Cross was then feeding 587,034 families, close to the 600,000 figure aided during the Mississippi flood in 1927.

58. *Cong. Record,* 71 Cong., 3 sess., vol. 74, pt. 2, 3369.

59. Ibid., 3369–70.

60. Ibid., 3370.

61. Ibid., 3372.

62. Ibid., 3373–74. McKellar referred here to a previous request for a $10-million appropriation to aid Puerto Rico and a bill to construct an agency building.

63. U.S. Congress, House, Hearing before a Joint Session of the Deficiency and Interior Department Subcommittees of the House Committee on Appropriations, *Senate Amendments to the Interior Department Appropriation Bill for 1932* (HR 14675), 71 Cong., 3 sess., Jan. 28, 1931, 131. The Central Committee had voted against accepting the allocation on January 27 (103).

64. Ibid., 78, 86–87.

65. *Cong. Record,* 71 Cong., 3 sess., vol. 74, pt. 2, 3747.

66. Louisville *Courier-Journal,* Jan. 31, 1931.

67. *Cong. Record,* 71 Cong., 3 sess., vol. 74, pt. 2, 3760.

68. Ibid., 3849. For the Senate debate, see ibid., 3746–60, 3838–58.

69. Meyers, ed., *State Papers of Hoover, 1:* 496, 497, 499.

70. Louisville *Courier-Journal,* Feb. 4, 1931.

71. Memo of telephone conversation between Fieser, Winfrey, Baxter, and Couch, no date. It appears to have taken place on January 28 or 29. ARC, DR-401.08.

72. Louisville *Courier-Journal,* Feb. 6, 1931.

73. New York *Times,* Feb. 7, 1931.

74. Louisville *Courier-Journal,* Feb. 7, 1931.

75. Ibid., Feb. 8, 1931.

76. Ibid.

77. Ibid., Feb. 10, 1931. The letter read as follows: "Dear Mr. Senator: As to our conversation this morning, I am glad to confirm at once that the proposed additional drought-relief measure was suggested for the purpose of real aid to the weakened credit situation in the drought area and that in the administration of it the Secretary of Agriculture assures me he has no other intention and that he will interpret it fairly and sympathetically. Yours faithfully, Herbert Hoover." *Cong. Record,* 71 Cong., 3 sess., vol. 74, pt. 2, 4318.

78. *Cong. Record,* 71 Cong. 3 sess., vol. 74, pt. 2, 4316, 4318, 4320. Robinson stated that at first the Red Cross did not realize the magnitude of the situation, but, due to the Senate debates and extensive investigations, he believed the organization had acquired a full knowledge of the problem. Ibid., 4322.

79. Ibid., 4434–35.

80. La Follette further reasoned that it cost $8,000 to furnish a farm of 500 acres in Arkansas; yet no planter or his croppers could borrow over $2,000. Of the twenty-one stricken states, 24,725,000 acres produced crops that required at least $10 an acre. A $60-million relief program could hardly meet the needs, he insisted. Ibid., 4435–36, 4438.

81. Ibid., 4689.

82. The dissenting Republicans were William E. Borah, James Couzens, Bronson Cutting, Lynn J. Frazier, Hiram Johnson, Robert M. La Follette, Jr.,

George W. Norris, and Thomas D. Schall; the Democrats were Alben Barkley, Robert J. Bulkley, Thomas T. Connolly, Carter Glass, Elmer Thomas, and Burton K. Wheeler; there was also one Farm-Laborite, Henrik Shipstead. Louisville *Courier-Journal,* Feb. 15, 1931.

83. Robinson to Hoover, Jan. 2, 1931, Presidential Papers-Subject Files-Drought, Hoover Papers.

84. See Charles F. Scott to Robinson, Jan. 19, 1931, and Thomas G. Trimble, Jr., to Robinson, Dec. 1, 1930, Robinson Papers.

85. Quoted in Schwarz, *Interregnum of Despair,* 16.

86. Wesselius to Baxter, Feb. 9, 1931, ARC, DR-401.08.

87. Bondy to Fieser, Jan. 9, 1931, ARC, DR-401.001.

88. Arkansas *Gazette,* Jan. 28, 1931.

89. Cremer to Bondy, Jan. 16, 1931, ARC, DR-401.001.

90. Memphis *Commercial-Appeal,* Jan. 31, 1931.

91. "Anarchy and the Red Cross," *Nation* 132 (Feb. 11, 1931), 144. The article was probably referring to John D. Ryan of the Anaconda Copper Company, George E. Scott of the American Steel Foundries, and the wife of Henry P. Davidson, a prominent member of J. P. Morgan and Company. Dulles, *American Red Cross,* 146, 141. The other members of the central committee were Cornelius Bliss, Eliot Wadsworth, Mrs. Henry R. Rea, Mrs. Frank V. Hammer, Samuel Knight, Mrs. August Belmont, Gustavus Pope, and Henry Upson Sims. American National Red Cross, *Annual Report, 1930–31* (Washington, D.C., 1931), 11–12.

92. "Anarchy and the Red Cross," 144.

93. See Paul K. Conkin, *The New Deal* (New York, 1975), 40. For a discussion of the impact of the New Deal on blacks, see Raymond Wolters, *Negroes and the Great Depression: The Problem of Economic Recovery* (Greenwood, 1970); for the New Deal and sharecroppers, see David Conrad, *The Forgotten Farmers: The Story of the Sharecroppers in the New Deal* (Urbana, 1965), and Donald Grubbs, *Cry from Cotton: The Southern Tenant Farmers' Union and the New Deal* (Chapel Hill, 1971).

6

"We Are Sure Down Flat Now"

In Washington there was time to ponder the implications of direct federal assistance to the drought-stricken areas. But in those areas, where people were starving, the victims were not concerned with threats to their individualism. As Congress and the president debated and battled, the conditions in the South worsened. By the end of January 1931 the Red Cross had fed 275,000 families, more than the number fed in the Mississippi flood operation. And, as Table 2 indicates, by February 28, the Red Cross had aided 460,240 families (each family averaging four to five members). The greatest distress was evident in the home state of Senator Joseph T. Robinson: in this period 161,114 Arkansas families were being fed by the Red Cross.

Events in Arkansas during the winter of 1931 had proven the fallacy both of local voluntarism and of John Barton Payne's policy of relying on local officials to determine aid. National Red Cross officials and Herbert Hoover had known since August that Arkansas would need extensive help. However, despite reports in the fall from field representatives and state officials like T. Roy Reid of the Arkansas Extension Service and Dr. C. W. Garrison of the Health Department that people were suffering, national headquarters yielded to planter pressure, postponing a relief program until the cotton had been harvested. Consequently, by late December, thousands were starving, and the planters were begging for aid for their tenants. Faced with a totally bankrupt state and the possibility of a federal relief program, the Red Cross was compelled to initiate a major operation. National headquarters finally confronted the consequences of the policy it had adopted in August.

In an effort to raise funds and avoid federal intervention, the agency pushed the disaster back into the headlines, publicizing the horrible plight of Arkansans. As requests for help mounted rapidly, the Red Cross launched a media campaign to raise funds by eliciting sympathy for the bankrupt, helpless planters and their hungry, dependent sharecroppers. Once the program was initiated, however, the land-owners proved to be anything but helpless as they used the rations to control their labor force. The abuses that many critics of the Red Cross had predicted would happen now occurred.

TABLE 2

Families Aided during the Period of Peak Load

State	Number of Families
Alabama	22,752
Arkansas	161,114
Georgia	1,122
Illinois	4,785
Indiana	2,356
Kansas	26
Kentucky	40,903
Louisiana	51,251
Maryland	567
Mississippi	31,389
Missouri	22,626
Montana	569
New Mexico	——
North Carolina	2,120
North Dakota	280
Ohio	8,045
Oklahoma	52,616
Pennsylvania	549
Tennessee	16,467
Texas	26,519
Virginia	9,175
West Virginia	5,009
Total	460,240

SOURCE: American National Red Cross. *Relief Work in the Drought, 1930–31* (Washington, 1931), Appendix IX, 90.

The enormity of the task the Red Cross faced in Arkansas could be measured by the numbers requesting help. During the peak period in late February, over one-third of the families the organization provided for in the twenty-three drought states were living in Arkansas.[1] The highest relief load centered in the black Delta counties. On January 31, 100,000 people applied for aid within twenty-four hours, and three days later the total reached 165,518.[2] By February 8 White County, the second largest in the state, had fed 17,000 families; the following counties were also bearing heavy loads—Chico, 5,400 families; Desha, 3,800;

Marianna, 5,200; Crittenden, 5,750; and Phillips, 7,200.[3] Counties outside the Delta usually averaged much less, although in some hill sections the numbers increased by the thousands.[4]

Despite Hoover's demand that states assume responsibility for their relief needs, Arkansas proved unable to feed the thousands needing food. The failure of Little Rock's American Exchange and Trust Company in November affected the state's financial structure like an earthquake, as the tremors destroyed 100 other banks. In domino fashion over one-fourth of the state's banks had collapsed by mid-January, leaving many counties with no bank at all.[5] When a local institution closed its doors, it froze city and county relief expenditures and the funds of charitable organizations like the Red Cross or the Salvation Army. Nor could the bank finance the 1931 crops; credit simply did not exist.

Hoover's envoy, Colonel J. F. Lucey, had attacked the state government in mid-January for not utilizing the $5-million federal road appropriation to expand the county road program and for its failure to maintain industrial employment. J. B. Carter of the State Unemployment Commission countered that the factories and warehouses had remained in operation and had extended credit beyond the limits of good business. Former Governor C. M. Brough insisted that Arkansas could not accept responsibility for its problems, for they had resulted from a series of disasters and misfortunes—floods, tornadoes, drought, and crop failures.[6] The extent of the crisis could be measured by figures from the Federal Bureau of Crop Estimates that revealed the state's 1931 crop production amounted to only $91,964,000 as compared to $210,880,000 the previous year and $205,305,000 in 1928.[7]

State officials maintained that Arkansas could do very little to help its distressed. Indeed, Controller Harry Reed indicated that the state could not initiate any further financial activities for five years.[8] An investigative reporter from the Baltimore *Sun*, W. A. Douglas, proved the accuracy of this assessment when he found that Arkansas had spent all of its funds on schools and road building. In order to accomplish this, the state had committed itself heavily. For a relatively poor community, the 1,800,000 Arkansans paid exceedingly high sales taxes, a five-cent gasoline tax, and expensive automobile licenses. According to Douglas, the state could not possibly feed its hungry, for its total revenues for 1929–30 had amounted to only $23,354,721.84, while its total indebtedness amounted to $227,839,520.42. To make things worse, bank failures had produced a further loss of $1,900,000 in state fund deposits.[9] Nevertheless, the state legislature did approve a $15-million bond issue to relieve the drought sufferers. According to one report, Representative Charles Fleming of St. Francis County wept as he described the 4,200 people in his county on Red Cross assistance. Governor Harvey Parnell, however, threatened to veto the bill because the state could not possibly sell the bonds.[10]

Newspaper accounts confirmed the state's desperate plight. According to Russell Owens of the New York *Times*, a "more completely bankrupt territory could not be imagined," for horses and mules, farm implements, and land had been mortgaged to the hilt. Scores of livestock had perished—"thin, bony-ribbed creatures that weakly nosed through lands covered only by dead cotton plants and dead leaves." Even the natural game of the state had been hunted to extinction. Not a raccoon could be found anywhere, and rabbits had become so scarce the people had named them "Hoover Hogs."[11] Allowing for regional distinctions, Owens could have been describing any of the seventy-five counties that received aid during the winter.

In the face of economic ruin and mounting relief rolls, the Red Cross finally initiated a major program. However, national headquarters was confronted with a dilemma of its own making. Since August officials had minimized the drought, insisting that the crisis, such as it was, did not require a massive operation. After Congress sought to introduce its own federal relief program, however, Payne declared that a disaster did indeed exist, calling upon Americans to contribute to a $10-million drought fund. Both he and Hoover believed rations preferable to a dole. The problem was how best to convince Americans that giving to the Red Cross was safer than a federal program. With millions unemployed and with Senator Robert Wagner and Representative Fiorello La Guardia arguing for aid to the urban as well as the rural needy, how could the agency justify asking a depression-struck society to contribute its meager resources to aid only the drought victims?

The solution was a media campaign conducted by both the Red Cross and the press to convince Americans of the total bankruptcy of the drought region, especially Arkansas. Reports used traditional stereotypes to persuade the public that the victims had sought relief reluctantly. For example, some releases described the hill farmers who, because of their isolation, had never encountered relief before. The drought had seared their subsistence gardens and forced them to look to an outside source for help. In the Delta the agency utilized the usual racial and class stereotypes to portray paternalistic landowners who could no longer feed their shiftless labor force. All of the press releases were designed to evoke sympathy for the poverty-stricken region without questioning the social structure. Perhaps in a more subtle sense the Red Cross sought also to prove that Americans did believe in self-help and truly sought to avoid a dole at any cost.

Newspaper accounts of the Arkansas mountain and hill sections did, even with the stereotypes, offer an accurate depiction of conditions. For example, Faulkner County, located in a region of rolling hills northwest of Little Rock and between the Delta bottomlands and the Ozark Mountains, consisted of independent and normally prosperous farmers who faced disaster in 1931. Although cotton constituted the main crop, farmers also planted corn, potatoes, fruits, and vegetables. In the winter women usually canned large quantities of fruit, vegetables, and chickens and cured hams. Because these families had traditionally been thriftier than Delta planters or croppers, they had rationed their reserves and had been able to survive longer without outside aid. The drought had created an unexpected disruption in their well-planned and orderly lives, and the meager crop yields of 1930 had prevented these farmers from meeting their mortgage payments. As a result, after Christmas the Faulkner County Bank closed its doors, freezing $450,000. The bank had issued loans to farmers to buy over 2,000 head of cattle. When they could no longer meet their payments or feed the livestock, they brought the animals to the empty bank and tied them there. Despite its protestations, the bank had to feed the animals at a cost of fifteen cents a day per head.[12]

As the Faulkner County financial structure collapsed and the 1929 food reserves dwindled, the relief load increased. By February 3 the Red Cross had fed 6,000 of the county's 26,000 persons. Many resented having to ask for aid and viewed the federal loans as entirely inadequate to meet their needs. As one farmer observed, the government had offered feed and seed loans but had provided no means for obtaining food. In order to obtain a seed loan the crop had to be mortgaged, and that meant no collateral left to apply for credit to buy food. According to the farmer, the credit bank cost too much. "If we borrow $100 we have to give a mortgage of $124, and it cost $15 to enter the corporation, and $9 for the cost of preparing the papers." Confused, people simply did not know what to do, and many questioned the feasibility of planting anything but food for themselves. Thanks to the Red Cross seed that had been distributed during the fall, most all families had gardens of

This child, gazing out of the window from his cabin in the foothills of the Ozarks, was typical of the thousands of children left hungry by the drought. (American Red Cross, 56–66)

A mother and her two children, like many drought victims, lived in a drafty cabin with no running water or electricity. (Library of Congress)

This sharecropper family in Tennessee exemplified the thousands of rural families who sought drought relief. Their tattered clothing left little protection from the cold. (Library of Congress)

Hungry farmers stand in line to receive their Red Cross rations. (Library of Congress)

A country storekeeper in Arkansas fills a Red Cross food order for drought-stricken farmers. (American Red Cross, 56–69)

Schoolchildren in El Paso, Texas, stand in line to receive their lunches, which were part of the Red Cross school lunch program. (Library of Congress)

These farmers are carrying their Red Cross rations that were issued to them in Forrest City, Arkansas. (Library of Congress)

This farmer displays the garden seeds that were issued by the Red Cross.
(American Red Cross, 56–67)

These hungry farmers have lined up in Louisiana to receive their Red Cross rations. A clergyman discusses relief policy with them. (Library of Congress)

At this relief office in a parish in Louisiana, Red Cross workers fill out applications for assistance. (Library of Congress)

In many of the drought counties blacks comprised a majority of the
population. However, the planter-dominated relief committees did not
always provide them with fair and adequate help. Applying for aid
often meant harassment, intimidation, or both. (Library of Congress)

turnips—called "Hoover apples." According to some reports, all of the chickens in the county had been eaten, quail and rabbits had become a rarity, and only the opossum remained as the major delicacy to grace the farmer's dinner table.[13]

Cold weather and snow increased distress in the hill sections and complicated the Red Cross relief program. In Van Buren County, located in the Ozark foothills, relief chairman Sam Patten had issued rations for 1,200 persons, a relatively small figure when compared to those of the Delta. Yet figures told only a part of the story. Many families lived on the verge of starvation in the isolated hills but refused to come down to Clinton and ask for aid. "And as long as there is a scrap in the house which they can eat," he explained, "they won't come to the Red Cross looking for it." The snow had trapped the families in their shacks and prevented the Red Cross from visiting them or the people from coming down the mountains to Clinton. One of the storekeepers in the region had informed Patten that the "stuff's getting pretty short among them" and that he had given credit until he had depleted his supplies. "They know you are giving out food here, but I can't get them to come down till there's no chance of scraping it up in other ways. Now, what with the snow, it seems as though they are leaving it kind of late."[14]

After the storekeeper had left, a widow and her four children came into Patten's office. Alice Reese looked fifty years old—she was thirty-two—and she wore a "bedraggled skirt, worn shoes and a dirty sweater." Her four children wore rags, and all five rushed to the potbellied stove for warmth. Ever since her husband's death four years ago, Alice Reese had supported her family as a day laborer in the fields. Due to the short cotton-picking season, the mother had earned very little. For seven weeks they had lived on turnip greens, after her last bit of lard and flour had been used up. They had walked seven miles through the snow to seek aid. After receiving their rations, the Reeses trudged back up the mountains to their drafty shack.[15]

An interview with a Van Buren banker revealed the inadequacy of federal relief measures. While Congress debated the food loan bill, a local bank official, Brad Frazier, noted that his bank would allow the government to have the first lien and loaned each farmer up to $200. But he did not think bankers could be expected to grant a food loan in addition to having accepted a second mortgage. They simply did not have the necessary cash, he disclosed. Congress could call their bill a feed and seed loan if they desired, but, despite provisions which prevented the purchase of food, farmers would spend $50 of the $200 for food. People had to eat, he concluded, and gardens would not produce until June.[16]

By the end of January the relief load in Van Buren County had reached 2,500 people and was predicted to reach 5,000 out of the population of 13,000. Clothing presented a serious problem, and, even though townspeople had emptied their attics of old garments, children still lacked shoes, underwear, and stockings.[17] No hope for recovery appeared in sight, since the demand for timber had decreased and the possibility of outside employment had disappeared. Van Buren typified the other hill counties with its poor whites who lived in isolated, rickety shacks without sufficient clothing or food and no hope for employment.

The cut-over cedar slopes of the Ouachita River region harbored still another class of farmers who suffered from the drought. Even in normal times they performed back-breaking work in their efforts to grow crops in the stump-dotted fields long since gleaned of trees. This was a region of small farms and niggardly soil in narrow valleys that occasionally dipped down between the protruded rocky ribs of the Ouachita hills. Like the Ozark people, these farmers were self-reliant and independent. "We have always depended on our neighbors to help us out in a tight place," an old farmer apologized as he applied for assistance. "Its downright embarrassing to ask a stranger fer help, but we all are in the same boat out our way. I guess we will have to look to the Red Cross as our neighbor this winter."[18]

A country storeowner in the region expressed a neighborly concern and extended aid to all of the traditionally independent farmers. "I ain't turnin' any of my neighbors who are deservin' away hungry from my store. I'll carry them on my books as long as they ask for I know they will pay up in the end." He further observed the reluctance of many of the hill farmers to apply for aid. "Its them who never have had help who are holdin' back. There is one family I'm worried about. They ain't been buyin' nothin' fer quite a spell, although I tell them the bill can run, but they are as proud as Lucifer and I know must be about to the end of their rope." At the merchant's directions the agency located the family on an eighty-acre farm in the cedar woods. Their food supply had indeed dwindled to a half bushel of potatoes and a quart of meal; they had not eaten meat since July, sugar for a month, and lard for a week. Their cow had long since "dried up." According to the father, he had never asked a man for food in his entire life. He had produced only eight rows of potatoes and a load of corn in 1930. Asked why he had not

106

applied for aid, he replied that he had known the Red Cross during the war overseas and "God help me if I ever thought I'd have to ask them to feed me if I got home alive." His wife suggested that maybe "we have held our heads a little too high, but its hard to get down in the class of the shiftless." Apparently other farmers in the area held a similar opinion, for according to a Red Cross report, the farmers of Garland County had been the slowest section in seeking assistance. However, by late January necessity had gradually compelled more of them to seek aid.[19]

Unlike the Delta, Arkansas hill people did not have a tradition of relief, except for limited county assistance for the poor. Their traditional isolation and self-reliance had kept them from any significant contact with an outside world that had charitable agencies like the Salvation Army to help the needy. However, when confronted with starvation and the possibility of outside help, they did choose to accept the rations. If the Red Cross had not assumed the responsibility in 1931, more than likely these victims would have accepted their lot or moved to Little Rock in search of work.

The Delta croppers and planters did not share this resignation or self-reliance, as the England riot had indicated. They not only expected but demanded that the Red Cross administer relief to their hungry families. Hunger in the Arkansas Delta far exceeded any of the Red Cross's predictions. While human privation certainly existed in December, by January thousands of predominantly black croppers poured into the local relief offices. Banks continued to close their doors after Christmas, precluding any chance of obtaining credit for furnishings. Indeed, many planters had received rations. Newspapers described the destitution of the croppers, utilizing the traditional racial stereotypes without mentioning the exploitation that was clearly occurring.

The St. Francis Delta, formed by the St. Francis River as it runs parallel to and eventually empties into the Mississippi River near Helena, is one of the richest regions in the Arkansas Delta. Like the surrounding counties, however, its usual alluvial soil had turned to baked clay during the scorching summer of 1930. Black stalks had replaced green spears of cotton. The meager harvest bankrupted the plantation economy, and both croppers and planters appealed to the Red Cross for aid. Without forage the livestock had dwindled to skin and bones. Mules resembling quilting frames nibbled on the shriveled corn stalks. The Red Cross fed both man and beast.

In Forrest City, the major town in St. Francis County, black and

107

white passed through Uncle George Parker's furniture store to apply for assistance. Since December 10 he had granted aid to 12,838 of the 33,000 people in the county, and he predicted the number to double by spring. The black applicants represented the sharecroppers and small farmers who comprised 75 percent of the county's population, while most of the whites came from the owner class. In fact, many of the planters had driven their workers into the city to seek help. R. C. McNeil owned a plantation with thirty-four families to feed. Unable to pay the interest on his mortgages or to furnish his workers, he simply loaded the men onto two mule-drawn wagons and took them into town for the agency to feed. Another planter, Walter Draper, operated a 4,000-acre plantation with 370 black croppers who owed him over $15,000 for furnishings. Like McNeil, Draper owed several mortgages to a Memphis bank. He drove a newspaper reporter to his empty commissary, where idle workers sat around a potbellied stove. As he entered the store, Draper told his men, "You boys owe me around $15,000. We're pulling in the same boat. If the Red Cross will carry you till we go to work again I've told them I'll set you free." According to the reporter, "loud protestations of thanks" came from the black audience when told their slate would be wiped clean.[20] Ironically, the drought would improve the status of the work force by freeing them from the plantation system.

The black croppers in St. Francis County depended totally upon planters for aid. Unless the Red Cross agreed to feed them, they would continue to starve. The ration consisted of $5 for a family of five, for an entire month. This money purchased the following food:

36 lbs. of flour	$0.90
24 lbs. of split beans	0.70
12 lbs. of cracked rice	0.35
2 lbs. of coffee	0.30
24 lbs. of meal	0.55
1/2 gal. of molasses	0.35
lard and bacon	1.75
baking powder	0.10
Total	$5.00

"They'll get no Thanksgiving or Christmas dinners," observed the field representative in St. Francis County, "but at lease we'll keep the wrinkles out of their bellies." Most people seemed satisfied with the organization's wrinkle-removing formula and simply accepted food. An old black called "Granny" indicated that her condition seemed "toable fo an ole nigger woman" who was "jes livin' off what de white folks" sent her. However, Granny did express bewilderment over the Red Cross beans. "Ah never saw a bean what's been busted open befoh." Thinking in terms of economy, the agency had purchased the cheaper culls of crops and shipped them to the region.[21]

In nearby Lee County Colonel Elgan Robertson, vice-president of the Marianna bank and city Red Cross chairman, quickly disposed of hungry applicants. He had approved 12,000 requests, predicting 20,000 of the county's 28,000 people would soon need relief. According to Robertson, the federal government should allocate funds to the organization because their present resources simply could not meet the demands. He then related the story of a close friend who had applied for aid that morning. He owned 1,800 acres and kept forty-five families. Formerly a major depositor at the colonel's bank, the planter now tearfully asked the Red Cross to feed not only his workers but also his own family. All of the relief committees, he concluded, had underestimated the degree of destitution, for already 40 percent of the county's population depended upon relief.[22]

A Red Cross press release from Lee County depicted the helplessness of both owner and cropper. In a line that contradicted Payne's insistence that neighbors could help each other, the press release argued that during the drought more fortunate neighbors did not exist—all lived on an "economy level." Nor could families sell their few remaining head of stock since everything had been mortgaged. "Mortgagitis" described the local malady that prevented families from selling their puny mules and cows to eke out a few more weeks of existence. The merchants could not be blamed nor could they offer further credit, for they had been writing off their books each month almost as much as they had collected. "They can't look a hungry man in the face, one they've known for years and refuse him a few pounds of beans or rice." Thus planters, merchants, and croppers were trapped in a web of debt. In conclusion the press release described the routine of a few sufferers to impress upon the public mind that these people did not simply sit around and wait for handouts. For example, R. M. Kilgore, a forty-nine-year-old farmer, had died from causes that could not exactly be determined. Field workers did not think his death had resulted directly from starvation, but they found it difficult to "tell what ailed a man" who had not complained and did not have a doctor until after his death. According to his wife, Kilgore had "took sick with a chill on Saturday night and couldn't get warm all day Sunday." He had refused to ask for Red Cross aid until the family had "got clean out." When representatives visited the home, they found a four-month-old baby asleep under a pile of old coats. Only one fireplace heated the two-room shack that had "cracks between the siding wide enough to admit a finger."[23]

While in the area, representatives decided to visit neighboring homes. In one house they encountered a woman in a sleeveless gingham apron and her daughter who sat huddled around the stove in an old sweater. "We've only the one sweater between us," she explained, "and Molly isn't feeling good today." Her husband volunteered that next year "I'm raising corn instead of cotton. You can eat corn." The father then advised the Red Cross to visit his neighbors who had five children and a food supply consisting of a month's supply of pork, a half sack of flour, and honey from a wild bee tree. They lived in a "shot-gun" house — a long, drawn-out one-story structure with one room behind the other. None of the children could attend school for lack of shoes, and they wore stocking caps on their otherwise ill-clad bodies to keep their ears warm. Since the family had six mortgaged cows, they did have milk, unlike most families. According to the mother, "We hadn't expected to ask for help yet, but we do need beans and rice."

These press releases clearly made a distinction between the white and black cropper families. "It is the white families who are suffering mental anguish and worry over the future with weeks before they can make a crop, not the negroes who are willing to trust to luck and the Red Cross." A Red Cross official described the response of "one darkey we met on the road" who cheerfully stated that he "was on rations" and about ready for the next issue. Approximately 90 percent of relief work in Lee County focused on the black cropper, although white families had fast approached the bottom of their barrels and would soon demand aid.

In response to congressional accusations concerning the adequacy of relief, the Red Cross replied that to many people "the Lee County rations might seem a limited bill of fare, but to the crop sharers and the tenant farmers, who never know what real abundance and variety is, it is the regular diet. . . . The Red Cross does not hope to raise the standard of living, it is performing a herculean task in maintaining it under the present conditions." According to the agency, the recipients seemed satisfied with their grants. "Anyone who sees the patience and the resignation with which the people are bearing their adversities and the unquestioned acceptance of the relief as it is being administered cannot doubt it." The local committees consisted of the neighbors to whom the people have been accustomed to look for help. "They are extending it now in the name of the Red Cross." Another report described conditions in Phillips County. On January 19 the Red Cross had fed 23,000 of the county's 44,350 population (compared to the 16,000 in 1927). Each day more planters had to ask the chapter to feed their croppers. After the Helena bank closed on January 2, they could no longer furnish their workers.[24]

Dr. Henry Rightor personified the typical Delta planter, according to the release, and he offered to drive a Red Cross representative around the plantations to visit croppers. As they toured the rich alluvial bottoms, Dr. Rightor told the story of "his struggles for the crop sharers during the past year" which had ended in Red Cross rations. "Lord I hate to see my niggers (or negroes if you prefer) put on any kind of a free dole," he declared. "It's their salvation to have to work for what they get, but there is no work, and no money to pay for work. They can't be allowed to starve to death." His twenty families owed from $50 to $300 for 1930, and their half of the cotton would obviously not pay the bill. The Rightor plantation produced only 130 of its average yield of 300 bales, and the price of cotton had been one-half of the usual rate. Even after the blacks had picked the crop, they still owed the doctor and would have absolutely no reserves to live on until planting season in April. So he paid them to pick anyway and accepted the losses on their previous advances. The blacks had soon exhausted their scanty earnings and by January faced starvation. "But the doctor was still master of the situation," according to the field representative, for he put his blacks plowing for next year's crop for a daily wage of $1 for two days a week. This solution proved inadequate, however, for after Christmas the Helena bank closed, and the owners no longer had any credit. The Red Cross represented their last hope.[25]

Rightor then took the representative to the house of a "real negro farmer with a home that will make you open your eyes." According to the doctor, "There was a mistake made with Henry and his wife for its only the color of their skins which kept them from being born Scotchmen." Henry lived on the edge of a bayou and had to paddle out for the visitors. His wife invited the callers into "as clean and tidy a house as a woman ever kept" and then proudly showed her quilts that she had pieced, her chicken coops, and her three mules and a cow that she boarded for Rightor, her rose bushes and garden spot, and her three

111

children ready for school. "We need groceries," she admitted, "but we can get by better than our cow and mules without something to eat." Rightor proudly noted that when a "hard working, thrifty colored couple like Henry and his wife need help from the Red Cross, Lord help the rest of the niggers." As the party returned to the car Pete, a "black boy," strolled by and the doctor hailed him and asked where he was going. "Ah's jest takin' a little exercise. Exercise is the onliest thing left ah can get my fill of." Rightor advised him to hurry home because the Red Cross would soon be there to offer aid. The young boy "turned in his tracks and without further delay began to exercise rapidly toward home and possible rations."[26]

On the way back to Helena the representative reported that they saw "tiny pickaninnies blinking their eyes like little kittens in a number of cabins." Six-year-old Julia collected two small brothers and a sister and led them in the singing of Negro spirituals for the visitors. While their mother showed the field worker her empty meal keg, the children sang, "When I lay my burdens down, when I lay my burdens down."[27]

At a black school in the county Rightor and the representative found that few children had sufficient diets. "Twenty-five little darkies would have to fill up at the water bucket in the corner at noon," reported the field worker. Over half of them came from families who had been receiving rations. According to the black teacher, "I don't know what we-all will do till its time to make a crop. My husband is sick in bed, and our planter can't help us out." Yet she indicated they would survive. "I reckon if we can jest pull through to crop time, we-all will leap up again, but we are sure down flat now." The representative described the woman as having been dressed no better than her "flock, for she had tied her shoe sole with a string and wore an old white sweater with holes in the elbows. One eleven-year-old girl wore her father's knee-high rubber boots." Before leaving, Dr. Rightor asked the black children to sing for him. On request they sang, "I am waiting to go to that home above" with a "rousing chorus of 'wondrous glory, wondrous glory.'" According to the worker, they had left them singing, "thirty-seven little darkies, most of them half-starved, without any chances of lunch, singing as if Arkansas had raised a bumper crop and hunger was unknown to them."[28]

After their trip around Phillips County the Red Cross worker concluded that it had been weeks since the blacks had eaten generously. The rations of meal, flour, rice, beans, and canned tomatoes represented "luxury." The official found that chickens and pigs had long since been consumed, and the drought had left them with nothing but the "tattered" clothes on their backs. The plantation system had broken down, and owners could not feed black workers and would do well to assume the burden in April. As one "old darkey" expressed it, "It sure enough is goin' to be a long time till cotton plantin' time."[29]

Feeding humans constituted only one aspect of the Red Cross program. In a predominantly agricultural region the survival of live-stock was an equally serious problem. In Earle twelve prominent planters issued an appeal to the Red Cross for livestock feed for their 3,080 head of mules. During the week of January 13 they had lost 376 mules and more faced certain death. The planters also offered sworn statements that they could no longer care for their workers.

E. S. Morrison of Earle Supply Company owned 6,000 acres and had 250 families who had produced in 1930 only 1,100 bales of cotton as against the previous crop of 2,400 bales. Only a few of his tenants had any food and all needed clothing and livestock feed. Another planter, A. H. Graham, declared that he would not collect over $4,000 of the $15,000 owed him and that his tenants lived in "deplorable and in some cases critical" circumstances. In a stronger tone J. R. Chapman insisted his croppers had reached a starvation level and that if aid did not arrive soon many would "perish." His farm had yielded only one-sixth of its usual crop, and all of the mules had been turned loose to find their own forage. Finally, Floyd F. Roberts reported that his tenants, unable to pay their bills, lacked food, clothing, and fuel.[30] All of these men painted a desolate picture of southern tenancy.

The Red Cross press releases reflected, as did its relief program, the planters' viewpoint. Agency officials, by asking landowners like Dr. Rightor to lead them on visits to cropper homes, slanted the reports to depict the planters as kind, paternalistic masters made impotent by economic forces beyond their control. This view was partially correct, for the planters were trapped by the cotton economy and the total bankruptcy that the drought and depression had produced in the planta-tion region. However, the accounts did not tell the entire story, particu-larly the exploitative nature of the furnishing system; they focused on how landowners were in debt and could not feed their workers because croppers had not paid their annual supply bills. That the planters had always used the furnishing system to hold their labor force in economic bondage was never mentioned.

113

The racial stereotypes that permeated the releases also reflected the planters' view, especially as the field representatives referred to the blacks as "darkies." The images ranged from the shiftless black who merely sat and waited for his ration, to the happy-go-lucky Pete who skipped along the road "exercising," and to Henry and his wife who represented the "good nigger," adopting all of the middle-class values of thrift, hard work, and cleanliness. And certainly the "darkie" children singing spirituals conveyed an image of a benevolent planter dearly loved by his childlike subjects. The story would assure any donor having doubts about planter-dominated committees dispensing aid to their croppers.

In spite of this positive description of class relationships in the plantation South, field reports and newspaper accounts did describe the abuses that the local committees inflicted upon the sharecroppers, which national headquarters was also recognizing in early January. At a staff council meeting on January 7, Henry Baker reported that relief needs were "somewhat worse than had been pictured" and that the "figures given of the number needing aid was too conservative." Indeed, several plantations in both Arkansas and Louisiana had been abandoned.[31] Although he did not mention it, the conservative estimates had resulted from the refusal of local committees to admit the existence of hunger. Within a few days, however, owners poured into relief offices, for, as bank failures continued, any hope of further credit diminished. Planters desperately needed the agency to feed their labor force.

National headquarters had always demanded that local customs determine the amount and kind of relief to be given and that the individual committees decide the validity of the requests. Judge Payne and others maintained that neighbors knew the needs of their fellow sufferers best. Ideally this seemed a perfect expression of cooperation and brotherly love; in reality it served as a means for racial discrimination and human abuse. In the Arkansas Delta the dominant local leaders, all connected with the plantation system, made certain rations did not exceed normal living standards; indeed, they often issued substandard proportions to insure that the croppers did not become accustomed to a comfortable standard of living, fearing it could affect their work habits. A second abuse centered around work relief. Although national headquarters insisted local committees could not require work in return for rations, Delta committees often refused to issue rations until a plantation had been cleaned up or a town street tidied up. For a

114

cropper who had not eaten in a few days, such a policy could be harmful.

During the Mississippi flood numerous abuses had occurred in the Delta region, as planters stocked their commissaries with Red Cross supplies and charged their tenants for them.[32] People in the area had not forgotten these violations, and, when a Red Cross worker visited Desha County, he discovered a suspicious attitude among some of the citizens. Although he mentioned no names, people informed him that the organization had expended $1 million in the area in 1927, but that the local administrators had shown partiality in distributing the rations. Big planters received most of them, they complained, while the little man was overlooked. The representatives made it clear that such abuses would not recur.[33]

Despite efforts to prevent the recurrence of the offenses of 1927, owners did try to stock their commissaries. In Hughes a planter's committee, grown weary of red tape, decided to take matters into its own hands. Landowners marched into a butcher shop and angrily demanded that the proprietor issue large amounts of rations directly to them. Their croppers needed food, and they could not bother with formalities. Red Cross field worker Carl Meyers then informed the planters that either they must follow the correct procedure of direct rationing to the families or the agency would cease its operations entirely. "I should dump food in their commissaries and let each planter stock up his commissary for his own people," Meyers sarcastically commented. "Then I'd have to come in again and take over all the poor folks who are farming independently or who are living by their wits along the roadside."[34]

Merchants also managed to make their share of profit from the program. In Jefferson County Red Cross officials discovered certain merchants had made a 30 to 40 percent profit on food orders issued to sufferers. They had also supplied sugar, tobacco, and coffee—items which had not been on the approved ration list. Red Cross policy allowed no more than a 10 percent profit. The chapter had issued requisition forms for fixed amounts, and the merchants then returned them to the agency for reimbursement rather than directly issuing food to the people. This arrangement could easily have led to abuses if it was not closely monitored.[35]

The local customs policy also created serious problems regarding the amount of rations issued. On a national level, Thaddeus Caraway and Joseph Robinson questioned the adequacy of the operation after the England incident received public attention, but they did not object to the committees determining the amount of assistance. Instead, they merely doubted that the organization's overall reserve could sufficiently meet the crisis. On a local level, however, inadequacy resulted from the conservative policies of the township committees rather than a paucity of funds.

Ever since England had first raised the issue of the adequacy of relief in the public mind, the Red Cross had constantly surveyed the program in Lonoke County. Colonel Lucey visited the county in mid-January. Both he and Dr. William DeKleine discovered that the planter-dominated committees followed a "conservative" feeding program which allowed tenants less than their normal standard of living. DeKleine informed them of their responsibility to supply the hungry with sufficient rations.[36] However, his orders did not calm public apprehension over the program in Lonoke, for Robinson and Caraway continued to attack it throughout January, and, as a result, William Baxter of the midwestern branch requested statements from the largest planters and merchants in the county concerning their feeding operations. According to planter-merchant W. W. McCrary, all of the requests handled by his store had been adequately filled. The ordinary requisition ranged from a biweekly ration of $4.20 to a larger amount, depending upon the size of the family. When furnishing began on March 1, the food supply would obviously be increased as work started. The local merchants and planters intended to reduce the usual monthly allowance by 20 percent due to the reduction in prices and the low price of cotton and farm products. Another planter supported McCrary's assessment. R. G. Kirk served on the Richwoods township committee and allowed a monthly ration of $16 for a family of eight; according to him, the ration had sufficiently met the needs of the croppers.[37]

Despite the planters' statements, as relief loads rapidly increased England required more aid. On January 27 Mayor Walter O. Williams announced that unless the Red Cross donated more funds the local committees could no longer feed its 1,600 child recipients. The committee had refused as insufficient a Red Cross grant of $300. The agency agreed to feed the schoolchildren on January 16, but the mayor had not heard from it since then. Unless the organization assumed responsibility soon, Williams said, either all feeding would stop or some other outside agency would be consulted.[38]

The riot of January 3 had complicated England's program, for constant publicity had drawn numerous victims to the township in

116

search of aid. According to the local chapter, many "imposters" applied for help. They simply refused to work, preferring to live off the Red Cross. One planter near the town informed the committee that thirty of his blacks abandoned the plantation in search of a "utopia" where one did not have to work. The croppers informed him that they planned to move to England and live off the Red Cross. Local chairman C. E. Hankins warned the prospective pilgrims that, if they arrived, "we will bounce them right out again." All applicants, he said, must have a sworn statement from a planter explaining his inability to feed them.[39]

In England the chapter based its rations upon a minimum, barely enough to keep people alive. One cropper with a family of seven received $7 worth of food to last two weeks. According to one report, seven "soft-spoken" blacks whose yeas and nays consisted of "yassuhs and nawsuhs" applied for shoes and clothes to work in the fields. Though they obviously were not shirkers, the agency still refused the request, for it lacked clothing supplies. Nor did the planters consider themselves in a better condition. Even though Congress had passed a feed and seed loan bill, it would benefit them little, for planters could not find credit for food and furnishings. Still, chapters maintained that their resources had been sufficient.[40] By February 2 the North Lonoke County chapter had fed 1,015 families and predicted an increase to 1,250 by the end of the week. The rations ranged from a biweekly amount of $4.20 for a family of five to $8.65 for a family of thirteen. According to Chairman Charles Walls, clothing had been provided for all who had seriously needed it, and 3,000 families had received aid to date in England, more than had been listed on the 1930 census.[41]

The Red Cross investigated other Delta counties to insure that the local chapters had met their applicants' needs. According to Lee County Chairman R. S. McClintock, his county's relief program had sufficiently met the requirements, for the "negroes stay about as fat and slick looking as the average over the county."[42] He investigated the ledger of a merchant to determine how much money had been spent by certain recipients and for what items. Responding to the accusations that rations had been inadequate, he explained it would be incorrect to say a cropper required the $20.25 he had spent each month in 1930, for he had not only purchased food. Instead, the worker had a tendency to buy "trivials," particularly snuff and tobacco. Given the currently depressed prices, he concluded that the agency could easily offer a sufficient diet to a family for 5¢ or 10¢ per meal.[43]

117

All of the other county studies reflected the opinions of the committees that the agency had met the needs of the victims. According to one chapter, the beneficiaries did not expect normal conditions, and thus they were satisfied with the help offered. Numerous counties expressed their opinion that they did not "believe we should give enough food to be comfortable," for it would destroy the initiative of the croppers. In general most counties indicated that the Red Cross had offered too much in administering assistance rather than too little. According to James Fieser, his representatives in the state, Albert Evans and Henry Baker, had been strongly convinced that the "Red Cross has done too much rather than too little in many of the Arkansas situations." There "seems to be a little feeling that even the normally strong people of the state are now standing on the street corner, cup in hand, and waiting for the bounty of the nation to engulf them through the Red Cross as it has in the past." The agency had spent $4.5 million dollars in the state during the past four and one-half years, although Arkansas itself had contributed only $400,000.[44]

Despite the continual barrage of attacks that the senators launched against the organization regarding the adequacy of its feeding program, the Red Cross consistently maintained that the operation had met the necessary requirements. Local customs continued to determine the amount of each county's ration. Food, however, did not constitute the only problem among the local committees and chapters.

England became the focus of other controversies, too. Since the town rested in the plantation region of the Arkansas River Valley, black croppers constituted a majority of the recipients. The National Association for the Advancement of Colored People (NAACP) expressed a justifiable concern over the treatment given to blacks by relief administrators. The organization's field secretary, William Pickens, wrote to Luther Moore of the Little Rock branch, conveying his suspicion that blacks might have received a less than adequate share of rations. Observing how applicants obtained their grants from local merchants, Pickens recalled how experience had proved that the "ignorant" black had often been taken advantage of. "He may be requested to sign some paper which binds him to some of these local merchants or landowners when he is getting his supplies." Pickens wanted Moore to investigate quietly the situation in England to prevent any abuses which could result in peonage or debt.[45]

When the Red Cross published its rations policy in the Red Cross

Courier on February 15, Walter White of the NAACP wrote Judge Payne, expressing deep concern over the implications of the local customs policy. The article recognized that the majority of the needy in Arkansas came from the cropper class and that the organization did not undertake to provide a "more liberal standard of living than those existing in normal times." It reaffirmed Payne's view that the "economic conditions of the states and the customs of the community are always the basis of the relief given." White reminded the judge of the "well known fact" that southern whites did not believe blacks required the same living standards as other races. Referring to the existence of "debt-slavery" and peonage, he encouraged the organization to "rise above" the local customs in administering its program and insure that blacks received an equal share. The chairman reassured White "with entire confidence" that the relief program had not allowed discrimination in the southern states.[46]

After corresponding with Payne, White then wrote Moore and urged him to "keep a close tab" on the distribution of Red Cross supplies. "From our experiences in the Mississippi Flood Investigation there is every chance of possible discrimination against colored people creeping in during times of distress." The flood had been "used to perpetuate and to extend peonage," and the organization did not want a recurrence of the violation, concluded White.[47] Moore sent a committee to England to investigate alleged discrimination by a white man. The group discovered that the local relief committee had employed both discrimination and intimidation. The local committee had required blacks to work on streets or clean plantations before they were given a ration. When one black voiced the sentiment that he did not object to working as long as the Red Cross was the beneficiary rather than a planter, a white man on the committee immediately drew a gun and severely whipped the man, who then became a "fugitive from justice." Despite these abuses, the report revealed that blacks had fared well in some communities, although conditions appeared "spotty," indicating "that proper care was not used in the selection of the Red Cross representative."[48]

The NAACP investigatory group interviewed several blacks in the England area to determine the adequacy of the program. The Reverend John Gatling informed them that he had applied for aid and received a $2 ration, followed by another of $2.50 the second week. However, when he applied the third week, committeemen told him he must work one day on the streets for each dollar grant. Because he had protested, the chapter had not called him to work on the streets, nor had he received further aid. Another black, J. J. Nathaniel, promised to work six days on the streets when the committee had agreed to give him $6 of rations. After five and one-half days of work he had still not received the grant. About eighteen other blacks and four whites had been working on the streets under the same conditions. The rations rather than city wages supposedly constituted the pay for the street work.[49]

While the Red Cross did not require all of its beneficiaries to work on the streets, it sometimes asked the impossible. For example, local officials ordered Alvertes Mahomes to work on his rented farm for three days before he could receive a grant. Mahomes could not meet the requirement because his mules had no feed and thus could not plow. The black renter could not feed his family of three without some aid, but the chapter refused him.[50]

Black women also related stories of discrimination. Local officials ordered one black woman to clean a white woman's yard in order to obtain a ration. When she refused, the committee rejected her request. Another described an incident when several blacks and whites had gathered in front of the Red Cross office to ask for aid. The City Marshall forced all of them back, referring to them as "cows."[51]

Finally, the planters did not always support their croppers' efforts to obtain assistance. When black renter Robert Davis applied for help, the committee informed his landlord, who objected. When Davis applied a second time, the planter arrived with the city marshal and beat the applicant. According to the newspapers, the "impudent negro" struck the two men and as a result received a fine of $60 for disturbing the peace. Since he was unable to pay the fine, the city ordered him to work on the streets for $1 a day until he had paid the assessment.[52]

White referred Moore's report to Payne, who replied that national headquarters had not authorized any work relief program. The judge optimistically noted, "I think we are very fortunate not to have anything more serious in a relief operation involving so many people." White replied that he realized the difficulty facing the local communities and thanked the chairman for his consideration.[53]

Responding to the NAACP report, Payne ordered an investigation. Colonel Frank Allen, the field representative in Lonoke County, quietly looked into the matter and reported that no coerced labor had occurred. A voluntary work program did exist to preserve the pride of those seeking aid. Many would have refused assistance had the chapters not allowed them to perform some task for their rations. City and relief officials had confronted a serious problem in England, for after the riot 800 "floaters" had remained in the town expecting assistance. They had come to pick cotton, but the short season and the scarce wages had left them without any travel resources. "These people squat in any place that they can find available and remain just as long as they are able to procure sufficient food to live on and consequently become a charge on the community." They "are characteristically lazy and will never work more than is barely necessary to take care of their living." It "is well known that unless they are required to perform some class of labor in which their efforts would redound to the public good, they would live on the Red Cross in ease and idleness as long as they could." According to all of the officials concerned, such a program would encourage the unwanted lot to move on, an assumption that often proved correct. Allen concluded that the community, rather than the Red Cross, had created the operation.[54]

To supplement Allen's report, the Red Cross also sent a black field representative, C. C. Neal, to visit England and the surrounding territory. He found a "most favorable" attitude toward the Red Cross in the community and disclosed no criticism of the relief program. "Things have quieted down considerably and the previous unrest in that section among both the whites and negroes is fast settling itself."[55] He talked with both black and white leaders, all of whom praised the agency and pointed to the number of black applicants who had received approval for feed and seed loans. Most complaints concerned the slowness of the loans. In Dermott and Eudora farmers had applied for $60, and only one check had arrived. Of the communities' 40,000 people, the local committees had food for only 16,000 and needed aid until the loan checks had been issued.[56] Neal did discover that when the planters had not started their furnishings as usual on March 1, most croppers had simply refused to work without a guarantee of food and other necessities. Since the loans had been slow in arriving, the owners lacked credit to furnish their croppers. Both blacks and whites had become "a bit nervous" by mid-March.[57] Finally, Neal reported that around Blytheville white people had moved into tenant homes, and the owners could not easily evict them. Thus the Red Cross had to feed the new arrivals for the planting season. Still, the committee continued feeding many more blacks. He described the planters' attitude toward them as "sympathetic and cooperative."[58]

Despite these accounts, stories of forced labor and discrimination continued to appear not just in England, but in the region in general. A black lawyer representing the Little Rock firm of Booker and Booker reported that black school teachers from all of the Delta counties maintained the relief committees had not issued fair rations to their race. Through personal interviews with representatives from fifteen counties, the lawyer had found that in some exceptional cases black leadership had successfully gained representatives on the local committees. He seemed convinced that "a good many violations had occurred" and suggested a county-by-county study should be made to determine the extent of committee prejudice.[59]

Other black organizations complained and investigated conditions in Arkansas. For example, the National Negro Business League conducted a survey in St. Francis County after having received complaints of discrimination. In one case a renter, Tom Hall, had been denied relief because his landowner, with whom he had quarreled, refused to sign the required ration form.[60] Other inquiries revealed that violations had occurred within the thirty-mile region south of Little Rock. In all cases the committees had denied aid due to applicants' refusal to perform various work tasks. In one instance, a black farmer had between ten and twelve members in his family, most of whom were underage, and yet the chapter had refused him aid. The report concluded that the applicants had reluctantly offered their testimonies due to "fear, superstitution, and general distrust." Most all the injustices occurred at the hands of local distributors, "who ingeniously 'cover their tracks' of unfair play in sufficient time and manner to keep such occurences from the direct ears and views of higher officials on their inspection tours."[61]

Neal presented a different picture than had the NAACP or the Business League. Perhaps as a Red Cross representative he had indeed met only the white leaders and a few selected blacks who had been chosen for their cooperative attitude toward the white community. Previous reports by DeKleine and others had certainly shown the conservative attitude of the planters and their fears of a program too liberally administered. Due to the local customs policy, abuses could easily have occurred, for national representatives could not be in every county. When violations took place, blacks did not always complacently accept their predicament. In Magnolia Lindsay Sharp attacked a relief worker with a cant hook when the committee denied him help because he refused to work.[62]

122

Reports from other Red Cross officials and newspapers substantiated the existence of work relief programs. An official agency report described the various work programs undertaken by local chapters. In Marked Tree tenants and croppers labored for their planters for $1 a day, thereby reducing their debts while the Red Cross fed them. The field representative insisted no one had to work before receiving aid. In Blytheville the chapter asked all able-bodied men to work and expected that "self-respecting" persons should be willing to do so without coercion. In nearby Osceola all "able-bodied" beneficiaries had to perform tasks for their rations at the daily rate of $1.[63]

When the midwestern branch received information of these programs, it immediately issued a policy statement that the agency did not sponsor work programs. If such plans were instituted, they resulted from a community effort separate from the relief operation. Any tasks undertaken should be on a voluntary basis, for official policy did not restrict assistance to such a requirement.[64] This clarification did not satisfy local administrators. According to them, their labor programs formed a significant aspect of the community relief operation, and without them dire consequences might result. For example, A. L. Gray in Marked Tree had visited all of the major Delta counties in both Mississippi and Arkansas and became convinced of the necessity of the approach. Allowing recipients to perform tasks was a godsend. The Red Cross followed the policy of issuing ration slips to the needy and leaving the "details" of completing the order to the local committees. In order to eliminate "corner gossip and idleness," the committees decided to aid only those who accepted work assignments. After national headquarters' recent statement, however, Gray saw people "standing around in groups." Town officials informed him they had rather do without assistance than permit any further idleness.[65]

Further evidence of work programs came from a reporter sent to the state by *Labor,* the Washington, D.C., newspaper representing the opinion of organized labor in the railroad industry. According to his inquiries the mayor and Red Cross officials in Benton, a town of 3,000 located southwest of Little Rock, had devised a program paying $1.20 a day in rations as compared to the normal city wage of $2. Employed laborers objected that the scheme would eventually lower their wages or even destroy their jobs. In Clay County the chapter forced tenants to work on the plantations before receiving aid, and in Poinsett County the Red Cross agreed to clear and "grub" land for $6 an acre rather than

123

the usual $10—the workers received a daily ration of $1. No one tried to hide the operation; in fact, officials proudly stated they "ain't going to let those bums get into the habit of not working." Both white and black recipients reluctantly talked to outsiders. "I'm afraid, mister. If I say anything I'd most likely get taken off the list," one beneficiary confided. The plan resulted, concluded the correspondent, because a "Power Trust official" (Harvey Couch) ran the Arkansas relief operation. Nor did he find many victims satisfied with the situation. One merchant told him the "whole trouble with the Red Cross is that it is commercialized," and he insisted the "men who have something to sell should not be placed in control, either in the state or locally." The merchant admitted he had filled a $6 order for the brother of a Red Cross official who had not earned it while all other orders had never exceeded $3. Each county agent and physician should dispense the aid, for they know the actual needy and their requirements. Finally, he emphatically stated that the Red Cross hardly represented a charitable institution, for it had been used to cut wages and for political purposes, thereby making "destitution and misery a permanent condition."[66]

When William Baxter of the Red Cross read the *Labor* article, he immediately wrote John Buxton, the chairman in Poinsett County, who offered no apologies and expressed the hope that he might "convert someone to our way of thinking." When the chapter began its fund drive in Marked Tree, people only made donations with the stipulation that the beneficiaries would be required to earn their rations. They remembered "how hard it was to get labor after the '27 overflow, when people had been allowed to loaf and eat." At its peak the chapter had fed over 15,000 with only 100 case investigators. If they had agreed to offer sixty hours a week of their time to administer relief, then the recipients should agree to work for their grants. Besides, 20 percent of the applicants preferred to work, 65 percent had no preference and usually did as they were told, and the remainder never worked except when forced. "I consider that a person who will not work to support himself and family is nobody's charge." All of the jobs undertaken had helped the community, and, if an individual desired to work off a debt, then that was agreeable, too. "The root of most of our trouble down here was laziness. I don't mean that they won't work if they have a job. They will." But he added, "They will work just about enough to meet the immediate need. Some of them will work about all of the time if there is some one to tell them what to do." He did not think they had learned anything from the drought experience, and thus they would not save or plan for the future. Therefore, Buxton considered it wrong to "foster the very thing that has brought this situation about."[67]

Buxton expressed the prevalent idea that most planter-dominated committees held regarding relief. They feared the "demoralization of their work force." He noted, "If people get it into their head that when they have made a little cotton crop and tried to make a corn crop and failed and then expected charity to feed them the other five months, then the Red Cross had defeated the very thing that it should have promoted, self-reliance and initiative." For Buxton, the continued stress of these values equaled the importance of meeting the human needs of survival. If an individual had refused to work, either for the community or to pay off a debt, he would find it difficult to approve the application for assistance.[68] Undoubtedly, he and his fellow leaders in the Delta personified the hazards of Judge Payne's policy of local responsibility and local custom as the determinant of an adequate relief program.

From the beginning, the Red Cross had intended to support the plantation system only until furnishing time began on March 1. Both the planters and the chapters had agreed that this constituted the best policy. When Hoover sent Colonel Hodges to Arkansas in early February, he had reported that all of the hungry had been adequately cared for. He firmly suggested, however, that after March 1 the agency should "tighten up and greatly reduce the amount of relief now being given out" and encourage the communities to help themselves. The organization should be "pretty hard-boiled" about this, for the farmers, renters, croppers, planters, merchants, and the "agricultural set-up in all grades" must be encouraged to make their financial arrangements.[69]

Fieser had also visited the state during February and had clearly stated the opinion of the planters and relief committees that assistance should end by the time furnishings were to start.[70] An editorial in the Arkansas *Gazette* also voiced this viewpoint. "It behooves our public officials, our planters, and our community leaders to concern themselves with getting the subject matter of this general notification understood so that there will be no misunderstanding when, on March 1, further Red Cross assistance is withdrawn, save under exceptional circumstances." By then farming would be underway and employment would have returned.[71]

Once again the Red Cross had aided the planters in feeding and retaining control over their labor force. The agency knew that no relief could be administered except within the confines of the plantation. Trying to feed the needy in a system that was characterized by violence, intimidation, and racism was not easy for any organization. That relief was given at all was remarkable. Nevertheless, the Red Cross policy in the Delta did not always seek to be fair. By depicting the planters as benevolent masters who were bound to a shiftless and inefficient labor force that was never able to pay its debts, the Red Cross distorted the reality of class relationships in the South, even as it had evidence of the cruelty and inequities of the plantation system.

While thousands of people were aided, many others never received truly adequate amounts of food and clothing. Others, weakened by hunger, were forced to work for their meager rations. And for the croppers who challenged the planter-dominated relief committees, no help was forthcoming at all. Finally, although no deaths were attributed to the drought directly, an unrecorded number of people succumbed to malnutrition, pellagra, exposure, and other diseases related to substandard diets and limited care. These examples are testimony to the limitations of decentralized relief and local voluntarism.

Notes

1. Red Cross, *Relief Work in the Drought,* Appendix IX, 90.
2. Arkansas *Gazette,* Jan. 31, 1931.
3. Other counties with large relief loads were Arkansas—2,737 families; Craighead—2,200 and predicted to reach 2,500; Lawrence—2,737 and predicted to reach 3,000; Drew—2,000; Woodruff—2,850 and predicted to reach 3,000; Monroe—3,000; Union—3,000. James Fieser, "Arkansas Trip Report," Feb. 16–18, 1931, 3–6, ARC, DR-401.08.
4. Ibid., 6–8.
5. Of 400 banks in the state more than 130 failed. Of these, thirty-eight reorganized but remained under withdrawal restrictions for depositors. Baltimore *Sun,* Jan. 9, 1931.
6. Arkansas *Gazette,* Jan. 15, 1931.
7. Baltimore *Sun,* Jan. 9, 1931. T. Roy Reid of the Arkansas State Extension Service observed that $51,420,000 of the 1930 crop consisted of cotton which had lost more than it would bring in. This left a residue crop production of $40,524,000 for a population of 1,800,000, averaging $22 per head without computing labor or seed costs. Arkansas *Gazette,* Jan. 10, 1931.
8. W. A. Douglas, "Arkansas Officials Blamed by Hoover's Representative," Baltimore *Sun,* Jan. 15, 1931.
9. Ibid. Douglas also observed that the state's assessed value was $614,000,000. The general revenue fund came from a 2 percent tax on insurance premiums; a

1 percent tax on the capital stock of corporations; a tax on inheritance; an annual license for cigarette dealers; charter fees for corporations; interest on state funds in depositors and inspection fees. One-third of the common school fund derived from a three mill tax placed on each one dollar of the assessed value of all property and two-thirds came from a severance tax and the first $750,000 received from cigar and cigarette taxes and all income tax collected above $500,000. The state's total revenue in 1929–30 amounted to $22,354,721.84. Its indebtedness on the road program was $213,930,353.75; on education— $2,434,166.67; Confederate soldiers' pensions—$9,447,000; state penal and mental institutions—$1,028,000; revenue-loan sinking fund—$1,000,000. Total indebtedness was $227,839,520.42.

10. New York *Times,* Jan. 30, 1931.

11. *Time* Magazine, Feb. 9, 1931.

12. W. A. Douglas, "Western Arkansas Farmers Watch Food Reserves Dwindle," Baltimore *Sun,* Jan. 13, 1931.

13. New York *Times,* Feb. 4, 1931; see also Arkansas *Gazette,* Feb. 5, 1931.

14. W. A. Douglas, "Snow and Cold Weather Add to Suffering in Arkansas," Baltimore *Sun,* Jan. 14, 1931.

15. Ibid.

16. Ibid.

17. Cited in *Cong. Record,* 71 Cong., 3 sess., vol. 74, pt. 2, 3747.

18. ARC News Service, Jan. 28, 1931, 2, ARC, DR-401.11/7.

19. Ibid., 3–4.

20. W. A. Douglas, "12,838 in Arkansas County Now Being Fed by Red Cross," Baltimore *Sun,* Jan. 30, 1931.

21. W. A. Douglas, "Arkansas Aid is $1 Head for Food for a Month," ibid., Jan. 12, 1931.

22. W. A. Douglas, "20,000 of 28,000 in County of Arkansas Need Relief," ibid., Jan. 11, 1931.

23. ARC News Service, Jan. 16, 1931, 1, 3, ARC, DR-401.11/7.

24. Ibid., 4.

25. Ibid., Jan. 19, 1931, 2–3.

26. Ibid., 4.

27. Ibid., 5.

28. Ibid., Jan. 17, 1931, 4–5.

29. Ibid., Jan. 19, 1931, 5.

30. Ibid., Jan. 20, 1931.

31. Minutes of National Staff Council Meeting, Jan. 7, 1931, ARC, DR-140.04.

32. Daniel, *Shadow of Slavery,* 149–69; Daniel, *Deep'n As it Come,* 105–6.

33. Arkansas County Reports, Jan. 5, 1931, ARC, DR-401.11.

34. Douglas, "20,000 of 28,000 in County of Arkansas Need Relief."

35. Arkansas *Gazette,* Jan. 31, 1931.

36. DeKleine to Fieser, Jan. 14, 1931, ARC, DR-401.11.

37. Statement of W. W. McCrary, Jan. 21, 1931, and statement of R. G. Kirk, ibid. A similar statement was submitted by another planter, J. N. Eagle.

38. Arkansas *Gazette,* Jan. 27, 1931.

39. Ibid., Feb. 1, 1931. Rumors still plagued the area. On February 4 an unknown source spread the word that extra rations would be issued in England and that 600 to 700 people had descended upon the town. After the Red Cross denied the rumors, the crowd peacefully dispersed. Wesselius to Fieser, Feb. 4, 1931, Presidential Papers-Subject File-American National Red Cross, Box 62, Hoover Papers.

40. Arkansas *Gazette,* Feb. 1, 1931.

41. Walls to Joseph Robinson, Feb. 2, 1931, ARC, DR-401.11.

42. McClintock to Evans, Feb. 8, 1931, ARC, DR-401.11/08.

43. McClintock to Baxter, Feb. 7, 1931, ibid.

44. Fieser to Porter Lee, Jan. 28, 1931, ibid.

45. William Pickens to Luther Moore, Jan. 25, 1931, Box C-269, National Association for the Advancement of Colored People Papers, Manuscript Division, Library of Congress, Washington, D.C. The director of publicity for the organization also wrote to Frederick W. Carr, who had written an article in the *Christian Science Monitor* on relief in England. He inquired as to whether any abuses had occurred. Carr replied that the Red Cross had given "bona fide" assistance with no strings attached. Director of Publicity, NAACP, to Carr, Jan. 26, 1931, Carr to Director of Publicity, Jan. 28, 1931, ibid.

46. White to Payne, Feb. 16, 1931, Payne to White, Feb. 17, 1931, ARC, DR-401.02.

47. White to Moore, Feb. 16, 1931, Box C-269, NAACP Papers.

48. Moore to White, Feb. 24, 1931, ibid.

49. "In the Matter of Economic Conditions of Negroes at England, Ark.," Report of the NAACP Subcommittee Appointed to Make Survey, Feb. 2, 1931, ARC, DR-401.02.

50. Ibid.

51. Ibid.

52. Ibid.

53. Payne to White, Mar. 9, 1931, White to Payne, Mar. 10, 1931, ibid.

54. Frank C. Allen to Wesselius, Mar. 27, 1931, ibid.

55. Wesselius to Baxter, Mar. 27, 1931, ibid.

56. Ibid., Mar. 6, 1931.

57. Ibid., Mar. 13, 1931.

58. Ibid., Mar. 28, 1931.

59. Booker and Booker to White, Feb. 20, 1931, Box C-269, NAACP Papers.

60. Report on inquiries made by the National Negro Business League in Arkansas, Mar. 10, 1931, ARC, DR-401.91.

61. William L. Halsey to Warburton, Mar. 5, 1931, ibid.

62. Arkansas *Gazette,* Jan. 31, 1931. A "cant hook" or peavey is a hinged hook device used by lumbermen.

63. "Work Programs Undertaken by Chapters," Feb. 19, 1931, ARC, DR-401. 653.

64. Ibid.

65. A. L. Gray to Dr. E. B. Clements, Feb. 18, 1931, ibid.

66. *Labor,* Feb. 24, 1931.

67. Buxton to Baxter, Mar. 20, 1931, ARC, DR-401.653.

68. Ibid.

69. Hodges to Hyde, Feb. 9, 1931, Presidential Papers-Subject File-National American Red Cross, Box 62, Hoover Papers.

70. Fieser, "Arkansas Trip Report," Feb. 8–16, 1931, ARC, DR-401.11/08. Other officials support this viewpoint. See Reddy to Bondy, Jan. 31, 1931, ARC, DR-401.11/08.

71. Arkansas *Gazette,* Feb. 18, 1931.

7

"Good and Hungry"

Plantation counties in Alabama, Kentucky, Louisiana, Mississippi, and Tennessee also confronted problems in administering relief. Although the drought did not strike these states as extensively as it had Arkansas, they still encountered the economic hardships resulting from southern tenancy. Conditions varied, for not all communities had bank failures, and in some cases planters could furnish their labor force. As in Arkansas, the planter-dominated committees in these states sought to insure that the Red Cross did not feed their croppers too well. Charges of racial discrimination also appeared, especially in Mississippi, and once again black organizations protested alleged violations. By early January the Red Cross had launched an operation in the other Delta states as winter threatened to bring further malnutrition to cropper families.[1]

The evidence concerning the drought in these states has more to do with the limitations of the federal feed and seed loan bill that was passed by Congress in late February than with abuses in the administering of Red Cross relief. The measure was greeted with apathy and disappointment in the cotton country. Although some planters accepted the loans, most viewed the $2,000 limit as inadequate, and tenants tried to gain a waiver of their lien to obtain federal assistance. The owners' refusal to grant waivers proved to be the weakness of the federal measure, for, as conditions worsened, croppers could only turn to the Red Cross.

Accounts from these plantation states described numerous cases of starving cropper families and the inability of localities to meet their needs, much as has been depicted for Arkansas. As resources dwindled in the rural areas, people migrated to nearby cities in search of either work or relief. In Memphis welfare agencies cared for 45,000 applicants, a large percentage of whom were drought sufferers.[2] Hungry farmers also left the hill regions of Louisiana and Mississippi in the early fall, heading for the Delta in hopes of finding jobs as cotton pickers. Since the plantations could not absorb them, hundreds of families lived in vacant shacks with no prospect of food. According to Robert Bondy of the eastern division of the Red Cross, most of the itinerants were poor whites. "Nobody wants them, the planters don't want them, the hill counties don't want them; they are a rather shiftless lot themselves and are developing a very bad reputation among the best white people of Louisiana and Mississippi, as well as among the negroes," he explained. "There are evidences of even greater dishonesty, shiftlessness, irresponsibility, and immorality among many of this poor white group than among the negro population."[3]

By January the Red Cross had stepped up its relief operation as local committees received more extensive grants from national headquarters. In Louisiana state drought Chairman B. F. Thompson estimated he needed $750,000 to $1,000,000 to meet requirements for food and clothing.[4] Since the organization had insisted all along that it possessed sufficient funds to meet the crisis, Thompson promised the applicants that aid would be forthcoming. Unless white farmers in the northern hill counties were allowed to obtain food loans, many would become drifters. "We have a class of people in the north central part of the state quite different to the balance of the state. About 70% are white and even the negroes have been instilled into a certain amount of self-pride and all of them prefer to borrow and pay back rather than be given a dole."[5]

When the relief operation began, most Louisiana Red Cross representatives found the program too generous. The chapter chairman in East Carroll County visited Chicot County in neighboring Arkansas and had been impressed with the wholesale feeding approach there. According to Bondy, he had been "moved by this, as well as some political considerations," to feed the croppers in his area despite the ability of some owners to handle their situation. In Franklin Parish, Louisiana, 600 people lined up in one day to receive rations. According to state Red Cross Chairman E. P. Krick, these represented the poor-white transient class who had become a drain on the community. He believed that references to possible rioting did not seem "far-fetched." To prevent such an incident, the committee followed a rather liberal rationing program.[6] As Bondy saw it, "In Louisiana the feeding program is noticeably affected by a rather wholesale feeding in Arkansas, so that in some Louisiana Parishes feeding approaches a fairly wholesale basis."[7] The Shreveport *Times* supported this viewpoint, insisting that hundreds appeared on relief rolls who should not be there. The paper called upon the committees to use discretion in administering aid.[8]

Not all officials in the state agreed with this assessment. On February 6 Secretary of Agriculture Harry D. Wilson announced that 40,000 families needed aid and that Red Cross funds were not sufficient to meet their requirements.[9] No such controversy existed in neighboring Mississippi, for the 1927 experience had taught the necessity of a conservative relief program—a lesson which many felt Louisiana had not learned.

Prior to January 10 the Red Cross operated on a disaster relief fund of less than $5 million, and then a special drive sought to raise an additional $10 million. Apparently the organization pursued a more conservative policy until additional funds were guaranteed. Field reports from Mississippi revealed a disenchantment with the organization for its lack of adequate assistance. On January 4 field representative Margaret Butler Bishop informed national headquarters that the policy in Mississippi must be changed, for the agency was being criticized by local chapter members and prominent citizens. "It seems to me that we have either got to have more money or we should withdraw." Prominent citizens had told her, "You national folks have boasted that you are chartered by Congress to do Disaster Relief Work, and you have asked all other organizations to [*sic*] hands off when it comes to administration, still you are going to let human beings starve to death while you sit down and say exhaust your local resources." Bishop explained the inability of the organization to ask for public funds at that time. Local chapter officials threatened to resign, for the applicants blamed them for failing to grant aid. With banks in the state closing at a rate of from two to five a day, she saw no hope for local committees since chapter funds vanished with the other deposits. Chairmen from all over the state had called her asking for assistance. One cried "from pure nervousness and over-work." The proposed federal feed and seed loan bill would not benefit 10 percent of the farmers, for many plantations had from one to five mortgages on their land already. Most simply viewed congressional efforts as a "joke." Since Arthur Hyde had maintained in his testimony before the House Appropriations Committee on December 29 that the Red Cross could aid all those not affected by the loan act, Mississippians expected the organization to accept responsibility for relief. Extensive funds should be extended, she concluded.[10]

Bondy replied to her, seeking to explain the role of the organization in Mississippi. He assured her that conditions were no worse there than in Arkansas and Kentucky. National headquarters could not make the mistake of publicly agreeing to feed everyone. "Local resources have not been exhausted in many communities, and they know it and there is no excuse for grumbling. Our expectations are that they will do what they should do themselves before we draw upon our funds to assist them." As soon as the organization was satisfied that local resources had been used, grants would be forthcoming.[11] Despite Bondy's assurances, Bishop persisted in her opinion that more funds must be granted. When informed that national headquarters had refused to honor a request for clothing, medicine, or feed for family cows, she wrote Bondy again. "The people in Mississippi have donated clothing until there is nothing left to give, some of these people are actually suffering from exposure because they have not sufficient clothing. Little children are wearing one thin garment, no under clothing, no shoes and we saw them today with their little bodies blue from cold, due to insufficient clothing." Doctors did render their services free, but they requested the Red Cross to pay for the medicine. The December bills of the Yazoo chapter had gone unpaid because of a bank failure. She urged national headquarters to issue money for clothing and feed for cows to provide milk for children.[12]

After these letters, Dr. William DeKleine visited Coahoma and Bolivar counties and inspected cropper homes. Since bank failures had not been frequent in these counties, planters were better able to care for their labor force. The white transients from the hills presented a greater relief problem than the black croppers. He found conditions in black cabins better than in other areas he had visited, although supplies of meal and flour were extremely low. The owners simply could not furnish the same amount as in normal times. According to one planter, the situation was a reversal from antebellum days, when "planters were so situated that they had to take care of the negroes regardless of their financial circumstances. The negroes are all in debt to them. There is no way of keeping them to work out their indebtedness except by feeding them." The doctor also visited a black school. While the children appeared to be in excellent health, approximately one-third came without lunches. When asked why he did not bring a lunch, one boy replied, "I isn't got the hunger." Despite this assertion, DeKleine could not "quite believe that they isn't." In general he thought the organization was feeding the victims adequately. The flow of requests had just begun to increase in the two counties. The average allowance of $2 per person seemed sufficient to him. So far no chapters had dropped below the $1.50 ration given in Arkansas, which was inadequate. School lunch programs insured that all children would be reached, he concluded.[13]

Bondy agreed that Mississippi conducted an efficient operation. "Mississippi is somewhat in contrast to Louisiana and Arkansas at this time in that dispensing of relief is being more conservatively done, more effectively done and under more able leadership generally." Certainly the agency could be proud of its leadership in Louisiana, but it lacked the extensive contact with the Red Cross that Mississippians had encountered. A determination to accept local responsibility and avoid a massive feeding program was more prevalent in Mississippi than in the other Delta regions. "The need is being met in Mississippi but people are very definitely being put on their own. This is having a very wholesome effect everywhere, particularly resulting in the utmost effort being made by planters and tenants to complete financing arrangements for this year's crop."[14]

The state did seem better organized than the others. The 1927 flood had called into action not only the Red Cross but also the county and home agents as well. Therefore the agents had invaluable experience for the 1930–31 crisis. In Pike County the home agent appointed a woman in each community to get a list of the needy and to guarantee that they received seed for spring gardens. The local chapter, however, informed one of the investigators that only those receiving rations could obtain seeds. According to the demonstrator, "They were not very nice to the women. A great many of the rural families managed to get along without supplies, but begged me pitifully to get seeds, as they had no money. These families were not supplied."

In some counties the home agents had worked to gather food and clothing before the Red Cross began its relief program. When the organization did become involved, the women performed the important task of organizing the farm wives in their clubs to search for hungry families and report their needs to the Red Cross. When seed was distributed, the agents worked with the wives, teaching them better gardening techniques and explaining the benefit of canning fruits and vegetables for the winter. Both black and white agents stressed the significance of a "live-at-home" program whereby the wives planted year-round gardens and canned the produce for winter. Farm agents worked with the husbands, emphasizing the need for crop diversification.[15]

The Mississippi operation did not escape accusations of racial discrimination in administering assistance. When the Hattiesburg Red Cross refused to feed all white applicants prior to aiding blacks, the mayor expelled the chapter from city hall, forcing it into another building. Judge John Barton Payne allowed Walter White to publicize the event in an effort to gain favoritism for the organization among blacks.[16] The fairness of the organization's program was also questioned when James P. Davis, a successful Chicago produce merchant and president of the National Federation of Colored Farmers, insisted that the Red Cross had refused aid to blacks in Mississippi.[17] He also wrote the NAACP, asking that both organizations cooperate to guarantee that black southern farmers receive their share of federal and Red Cross aid.[18] According to the merchant, black farmers in Mississippi had inquired as to whether or not they would be required to work for their rations or repay their owners.[19] Red Cross representative John D. Cremer assured the president no recipient would be forced to work in return for assistance. Acknowledging the "rumors" of such incidents in 1927, he explained that extensive investigations had proven they were without foundation.[20]

In response to Davis's accusations, a Red Cross field representative investigated the policy of the Yazoo chapter and discovered that the particular blacks he mentioned had not applied for relief. She did discover that a person had circulated among blacks advising them how to apply for aid and charging $5 for the service.[21] Davis denied any involvement in such a scheme, explaining that his organization merely encouraged cooperative marketing, charging $5 for annual dues. He considered his group the black Farm Bureau Federation.[22]

If discrimination occurred, no investigation was made and certainly no reports appeared like those in Arkansas. The paucity of sources in the other Delta states makes it difficult to determine the accuracy of the charges. Due to the abuses that had occurred in Arkansas and the Delta states in 1927, despite Cremer's denials, it would be reasonable to assume that the planter-dominated committees protected their own interests. The conservative policy they pursued, which was praised by the Red Cross, could easily have meant that many families who needed assistance did not receive it. The only federal legislation to aid the drought sufferers was the $45-million feed and seed bill. Farmers in the Delta greeted the measure with skepticism. Each planter could borrow up to $2,000—hardly enough to carry his croppers. Smaller farmers were heavily indebted to banks and merchants who refused to waive their first lien, preventing them from applying for a government loan. Finally, croppers could only obtain the loans if their owners waived the lien on their crop, a rare favor. Abuses also occurred as local

135

committees charged processing fees for those croppers who did apply for federal aid. Since local committees consisting of a banker, merchant, planter, and county agent approved the loans, only those considered "respectable" could apply. This system merely allowed for further violations in administering relief.

When Bondy traveled through Louisiana, Kentucky, and Mississippi in late January, he discovered the limitations of the feed and seed loans. According to his investigation, the loan program could not possibly finance the planters; nor were bankers willing to forfeit the first lien on their mortgages. So far the Federal Farm Board and the Intermediate Credit Bank had shown no tendency to ease the credit system. Small farmers suffered especially and would probably lose their land due to their extreme indebtedness.[23]

J. Harrison Heckman found a similar situation in western Kentucky, where farmers who met the requirements of the federal loan act also possessed sufficient collateral to obtain a loan through normal credit channels. As in Mississippi and Louisiana, planters complained that the $2,000 limit was insufficient.[24] In all three states farmers complained that the program had been slow in getting started.[25] Indeed, county agents in some areas had purposely delayed applications for loans, explaining only the hindrances of the measure.

The greatest violations in the program occurred between the committees and the tenants. In order for a renter to obtain a loan, his owner must waive the first lien; few owners were willing to do this. Field representative Helen Wade expressed great concern because landlords in Carlisle, Kentucky, had refused to sign waivers. Several tenants appealed unsuccessfully to the county judge for help.[26] When C. W. Warburton received reports of the planters' refusal, he stressed the inability of the government to aid farmers without a lien. "It is felt that when the Government advances the money with which to make a crop," the extension director naively noted, "there should be no hesitation on the part of the landlord to agreeing that the government should be repaid the money advanced by it, from the proceeds of the crop before the remainder is divided."[27] If owners denied their renters a waiver, then perhaps they could borrow the funds to furnish them, he suggested.[28]

Despite Warburton's restatement of the qualifications for a loan, complaints continued to appear. According to the Benton (Kentucky) *Tribune-Democrat*, it would be to the planter's advantage to waive the first lien, for, if he refused, much of his land would lay fallow. Acknowledging the owner's right to a profit, the newspaper still supported the right of the renter. "But will somebody tell us in the name of the late Samuel Jehosephat Hill how a tenant farmer or sharecropper is going to make a crop unless he has something to make it with? And how is he going to eat and live while the crop is in the making? And just why the man who does all the Work should also take all the *Risk?*" The Red Cross had done all it could, continued the *Tribune,* but it could not finance crops and feed the people indefinitely. All that was needed was a little cooperation from the planters to prevent people from going hungry and naked. "It is no more than right that they should assume some of this responsibility." The Red Cross had already spent $10,000. "Are not the owners of rented farms willing to assume some little risk especially when they stand to win, and as we have said before, assume no responsibility for payment of these loans?"[29]

When renters did obtain loans, the local committees often charged a processing fee, an action not provided for in the act. In Alabama and Tennessee tenants paid 50¢ to apply for a loan, and in Pickens County, Alabama, they paid as much as $2.[30] When informed of the fees, Warburton replied that he saw no objection to charging for the services in order to pay the expense of secretarial help.[31] But $2 or even 50¢ represented a significant sum for a tenant trying to feed a hungry family.

Thus the federal loan program had severe limitations for both planter and tenant. Small farmers also complained of the inadequacies. According to the president of the Farmers' Club in Transylvania, Louisiana, neither the $45-million seed bill nor the $20-million rehabilitation measure would aid the small growers. While planters could borrow through the Staple Growers Association or the Discount Corporation, the smaller tillers had no alternative agency. Since these farmers were unable to meet the mortgage payments on their farms, banks refused to extend them further credit. The Staple Growers Association and the Discount Corporation did not offer a viable alternative, for they required real estate security—either unencumbered or with the mortgage claim waivered—before lending credit. Unless the government administered a liberal program, small farmers would lose their homes.[32] For all of the agricultural classes, the loan program clearly had severe limitations.

From the beginning of the Red Cross program in August, it was understood that the operation would stop by March 1st. At this time planters would begin their normal credit arrangements, and assistance would no longer be needed. While planters might support such a policy, at least one source did not. According to the Jackson (Mississippi) *Daily News,* the announcement of the March closing date was a surprise. "Not only has the measure of relief been inadequate, but the announcement that relief work is to be ended in this state March 1st comes as a distinct shock to those who are acquainted with the dire needs of the people. On what does the Red Cross think the sufferers will subsist until they can at least grow a few vegetables. They can't eat grass," the editor observed, "for not even sheep and goats can exist on the early grazing." So far as he could discern, Herbert Hoover and the Red Cross had failed miserably in the state.[33]

The Red Cross closed its relief program in almost all of the counties in the spring of 1931. James Fieser justified this by arguing that on March 1 the opening up of the normal crop-financing practices, supplemental financing through governmental agencies, and a resumption of some employment had relieved the necessity of Red Cross aid. "Our fundamental policy in all disasters, as is well known, is to dispense relief to meet need, not loss. A basic Red Cross policy is that as soon as a man can help himself, he is no longer in need of charity." Some chapters began to cease relief as soon as they realized that the victims could help themselves, believing a general feeding program "tended to affect aversely the morale of the people."[34]

The Red Cross disaster relief program did administer assistance to 198,539 families in Alabama, Louisiana, Mississippi, and Tennessee. But despite the lack of reports of extensive abuses, as had been the case in Arkansas, violations did occur. In at least one instance Red Cross rations were used to pay men for clearing land for farmers in Humble, Tennessee.[35] There were no accusations of peonage, as during the flood, although James Davis did question the fairness of relief to blacks. Claims by leaders in Louisiana and Mississippi that too many had received aid probably meant that needy victims would lose their rations. The flood experience had taught planters the necessity of a cautious program. More important, the evidence in these states supports the inadequacies of the federal loan program. Although the Department of Agriculture loaned $47 million of the combined feed-seed and rehabilitation bills, most farmers simply lacked the collateral to obtain the money.[36] A Tennessee farmer best summed up the reaction to the federal measure: "I wish that those lawmakers down in Washington would get good and hungry once. I wish they would feel like eating that corn fodder out there. Then they would know what its all about."[37]

Notes

1. The Red Cross aided 30,602 families in Alabama, 73,024 in Louisiana, 46,884 in Mississippi, and 27,029 in Tennessee. *Red Cross Relief Work in the Drought*, 91.
2. New York *Times*, Jan. 22, 1931.
3. Bondy to Smith, Feb. 4, 1931, ARC, DR-401.08.
4. Thompson to Fieser, Jan. 10, 1931, ARC, DR-401.02.
5. Thompson to Warburton, Jan. 19, 1931, ibid.
6. Bondy to Dix and Hurt, Jan. 16, 1931, ARC, DR-401.11/08.
7. Bondy to Fieser, Jan. 31, 1931, ibid.
8. Shreveport *Times*, Feb. 18, 1931, copy in ARC, DR-401.11.
9. New York *Times*, Feb. 7, 1931.
10. Bishop to Dix, Jan. 4, 1931, ARC, DR-401.11/08.
11. Bondy to Bishop, Jan. 8, 1931, ibid.
12. Bishop to Bondy, Jan. 19, 1931, ibid.
13. DeKleine to Fieser, Jan. 20, 1931, ibid.
14. Bondy to Fieser, Jan. 31, 1931, ibid.
15. Home Agent Reports, Mississippi, Feb. 24, 1931, ARC, DR-401.01.
16. Bondy to Dix, Feb. 16, 1931, ARC, DR-401.11/08; Hazel Hart to Cremer, Apr. 6, 1931, ARC, DR-401.91.
17. Mrs. Nettie Hutchins to Bondy, Feb. 13, 1931, ARC, DR-401.91.
18. Davis to NAACP, Jan. 6, 1931, Box 269-C, NAACP Papers.
19. Davis to American Red Cross, Mar. 27, 1931, ARC, DR-401.91.
20. Cremer to Davis, Apr. 17, 1931, ibid.
21. Hutchins to Bondy, Feb. 13, 1931, ibid.
22. Davis to Baxter, ibid.
23. Bondy to Fieser, Jan. 31, 1931, ARC, DR-401.11/08.
24. Heckman to Bondy, Feb. 17, 1931, ibid.
25. Bondy to Smith, Feb. 4, 1931, ibid.
26. Cremer to Warburton, Mar. 19, 1931, ARC, DR-401.001/031.
27. Warburton to Cremer, Mar. 26, 1931, ARC, DR-401.001/9.
28. Ibid., Apr. 3, 1931.
29. "Square Deal for Tenant Farmers or Sharecroppers," Benton (Ky.) *Tribune-Democrat*, copy in ibid.
30. Bondy to Warburton, Mar. 18, 1931, ibid.
31. Warburton to Cremer, Mar. 15, 1931, ibid.
32. President of the Farmers' Club, Transylvania, La., to Warburton, Feb. 14, 1931, Secretary of Agriculture Papers, National Drought Relief Committee, Box 8.
33. Jackson (Miss.) *Daily News*, Mar. 1, 1931, copy in ARC, DR-401.02.
34. Press Release, Mar. 11, 1931, ARC, DR-401.63.
35. Whiteley to Bondy, Mar. 31, 1931, ARC, DR-401.08.
36. Ray Lyman Wilbur and Arthur Mastick Hyde, *The Hoover Policies* (New York, 1937), 400.
37. Arkansas *Gazette*, Jan. 26, 1931.

8
Providence

The Appalachian region of Kentucky, Tennessee, and West Virginia was the other area hit hard by the drought. The factors that distinguished this region from the Delta also created a different attitude toward relief by both administrators and beneficiaries. The obvious distinction was the terrain that sheltered Appalachia's two types of farmers—subsistence growers who usually had a cow, a pig, and a few chickens and stored root vegetables, and the very poor who lived in isolated hollows and ridges. Because of their isolation, mountaineers had not previously encountered outside relief. When the drought destroyed their gardens and they faced starvation, these inhabitants did not expect help from outside. However, once the Red Cross initiated its relief program, the mountaineers willingly accepted the rations. Their fears of starvation overshadowed any concerns for self-reliance and rugged individualism.

Another difference was the attitude of relief committees toward the drought victims. Unlike the Delta, where planters used relief to retain their labor force, the mountain committees, composed of local political and economic leaders, viewed the drought as an act of Providence that would rid the mountains of the poor. Perhaps one reason for this view was the difference in migration patterns in the two regions. In the 1920s sharecroppers had begun to migrate to southern and northern cities, reducing the work force in the rural South. In Appalachia, on the other hand, the population grew by 55 percent between 1900 and 1930, with 16 percent of the increase occurring in the 1920s. Part of this increase was due to the decline in the mining and timber industries, as out-of-work laborers returned to the areas from which they had come. At the same time the birthrate continued to remain very high.[1] Appalachian relief committees did not mind at all the idea of manipulating relief to rid their communities of what they considered to be "excess" people.

Like the Arkansas Delta, by 1930 the mountain counties had experienced the total collapse of their economic structure. Drought and depression only multiplied the widespread hunger and suffering. However, poverty had long been a part of the lives of mountaineers; indeed, Appalachia had for many years been a rich land of poor people. Although wealthy in the natural resources of coal and timber, the region had benefited little from its treasures, for northern and foreign capital had controlled its precious minerals and forests for decades.

Industrial capitalism originally came to the mountains in the 1880s, as the railroad and timber companies invaded first West Virginia and then Kentucky and the other mountain states. Coal companies followed, opening the fields of West Virginia during the first decade of the twentieth century and moving into Kentucky immediately prior to the outbreak of World War I. Industrial capitalism transformed the entire social and economic structure of the mountains: Corporations cheated farmers out of their land; displaced farmers were forced into tenancy or part-time farming combined with seasonal work in the mines or lumber camps.[2] Thousands of other families had no choice but to move to company towns, where they lived at the mercy of the owners (much as sharecroppers owed their existence to the planters). By the early twentieth century Appalachia had become a colony of the coal and timber industries, and colonialism had produced extreme poverty as mountaineers lost control over their very means of subsistence—the land.

Throughout the 1920s the timber and mining industries were in crisis. The wasteful practices of the lumber companies had gleaned the hardwood forests of Appalachia by the time of World War I. The companies had greedily swept through the region, refusing to replenish the woods they had destroyed and leaving behind a path of destruction that resembled Sherman's March to the Sea. Such wholesale destruction raised the ire of environmentalists, and in 1911 Congress passed the Weeks Act, designed to create a national forest reserve in Appalachia. This movement continued throughout the 1920s as thousands of acres were enclosed to form the Great Smoky Mountains and Blue Ridge Parkway Reserves. The decline of the timber industry and the forced migration of families from the federal parks led to the further displacement of mountaineers.[3]

The mining industry also declined in the 1920s. World War I had been a boom time for the coal industry, as the nation geared up to supply the armed forces in Europe. The prosperity lasted until 1923, when European coalfields had returned to production and production declined in the midwestern industries, the major consumers of the area's coal. The result was increased competition between northern and southern coalfields that eventually led to the destruction of the labor unions and to a drastic reduction in miners' wages. Many of the smaller southern companies were driven out of the area by cutthroat competition, displacing more miners. By 1926 the coal industry was in a major depression.[4] The fierce competition in the bituminous coal industry and the introduction of mechanization further reduced the number of men required to dig coal. Since the mines had drawn people away from their farms to live in mining towns (where the soil was unfit for farming), miners were totally dependent upon the company store for food. When the mines shut down, workers had no choice but to return to the land.[5]

The influx of people returning to the land decreased the acreage per family, while the number of farms increased.[6] Of all the areas the Northeastern Cumberland Plateau proved least capable of absorbing the excess population, and by 1930 this region exceeded the national average in the percentage of families receiving an annual income of less than $250; it had the highest relief load throughout the 1930s.[7]

By the winter of 1930–31 the mountaineers' situation was hopeless. Over the years they had been driven from their hollows into the company towns only to be displaced by a depression; their only alternative was to return to a land that could no longer support them. Drought prevented the growth of any food that the poor soil might have produced. There was no other place to go for food except to an outside source. However, the Appalachian economic structure presented problems for any relief program.

First, natural disasters and depressions were not required to disrupt the financial condition of most localities; these were already devastated. An outmoded property tax furnished the major source of revenue, but corporations, which owned most of the land, paid few if any taxes, and the low-income citizens rarely paid sufficient taxes to meet counties' expenses. With the rise in tax delinquency local governments borrowed funds, further increasing indebtedness.[8] Second, the county and state governments were controlled by the corporations. Since these politicians comprised the Red Cross chapters, they would determine, as did Delta planters, the kind and amount of relief extended. The policy of local voluntarism made abuse possible in both regions. Finally, the state and local governments were incapable of handling the increasing demands for relief. For example, the West Virginia legislature, torn between a Democratically controlled house and a Republican-dominated senate, proposed drastic budget cuts to reduce the state's $1,697,091 deficit.[9] As states reduced their allocations, county fiscal wells dried up. An inadequate tax base and austere budgets left the region with no alternative but the Red Cross. However, even if substantial funds had been available, it is doubtful if they would have been used to benefit the people who needed help most. Political favoritism and outmoded stereotypes of relief-seeking families prevented any progressive application of relief, for most local leaders viewed the needy as shiftless and unworthy of assistance. When county aid was granted, the recipients were often required to vote for their benefactors. County governments in the region were clearly "tradition bound, unprofessional, wasteful, and unresponsible."[10]

The Red Cross's relief policy in the fall of 1930 resembled the one adopted in the cotton country—in spite of reports of need, the agency withdrew until the winter. County surveys, conducted in September, predicted tremendous suffering in the winter and the inevitability of a relief program. According to Dr. William DeKleine, "the general feeling in Kentucky does not appear to be as optimistic as it is in Arkansas." Nor did he find the officials worried about publicizing the need for food for fear of ill effects.[11] Maurice Reddy, Kentucky's Red Cross director, substantiated these findings and also found a determination to endure the disaster without outside aid.[12]

This frontier attitude, no matter how admirable, could not feed hungry mouths if no sources existed, and, as Reddy soon discovered, people were already suffering. In October he visited four eastern Kentucky counties. Riding on horseback into the inaccessible places, he found "people getting along as best they could on a very narrow margin, but each day consuming their winter supply which in a normal year would not be touched by this season." Usually they had chickens, hogs, cows, and cellars full of vegetables. However, many had sold their livestock, and the drought had meant no—or few—vegetables for storing. The families derived their entire supply of fat from pigs and cows, and, once these had been sold, malnutrition would develop. Reddy concluded that a very serious problem would confront the Red Cross by November.[13]

Despite Reddy's report, the Red Cross ended its seed distribution program and closed its state relief offices on October 20, announcing the end of its commitment. A memorandum noted that the agency would observe developments in the region but would offer aid only after the exhaustion of state and local funds.[14] When the office closed, the secretary of the state's drought committee, R. W. Scearce, reminded Reddy that the advent of cold weather would bring great need. With a recent freeze and the approaching winter, he feared that the local committees and other relief agencies would "mark time until the need is so great that there will be a tremendous amount of suffering before relief can be secured." The last rain had fallen on September 16, according to Scearce, and the dry spell had destroyed everything.[15]

Although the agency kept some of its agents in the area and provided help for the most needy, by November the workers reported rapid increases in pellagra, hunger, and a need for clothing.[16] Ann Craton, a field representative, warned that in Rowan County the "people will starve to death unless something is done soon. The poverty among the people is everywhere apparent." She believed the situation was worse than any of them had ever imagined. The county judge was committing dependent children to institutions because their parents could not provide for them.[17]

In Morgan County Craton found large numbers who were feeble-minded. "Its people are poor. In normal times there is great poverty and a miserable, low standard of living. Now because of drought and having their normal food supply burned their problem is rapidly approaching the starvation level. Always undernourished and underfed," she continued, "they have less resistance this winter, although inured to hardships, cold, hunger." In the past two weeks three deaths from pneumonia had occurred, no doubt hastened by a low resistance due to lack of food. Most stores had cut off all credit, and people were begging from door to door. "These people are going to starve to death unless something is done soon."[18]

Drought and cold weather added hardship to the usually destitute lives in the eastern Kentucky mountains. Red Cross reports revealed both the poverty that had always existed in the Appalachian region and the degree to which the drought had accentuated it. When corn withered, chickens, cows, and pigs were sacrificed due to lack of feed. No milk or fat meant certain malnutrition. Scorched gardens resulted in empty cellars. Parched crops, dried streams, stagnant lumber yards, deserted mines, and no livestock meant that county taxes could not be paid. Bankrupt counties had no alternative but to ask the Red Cross for relief. Bank failures in late November coupled with extreme cold weather exacerbated the desperate plight of the hill people.[19] On November 27 snow and freezing weather hit the mountain counties of Tennessee,

Kentucky, West Virginia, Virginia, and North Carolina. Ten inches of snow fell in the Great Smoky Mountains, and eight inches in eastern West Virginia. In Kentucky and Tennessee the mercury dropped to 16°, while in Charleston, West Virginia, it reached a low of 9°.[20] The hungry would find it hard to resist disease in such extreme weather.

Facing a harsh winter, agencies scurried to find aid. Kentucky's drought committee announced that it had no funds to alleviate the suffering and asked Governor Flem Sampson to request that the Red Cross reopen its state office. The organization agreed to "be on the job in Kentucky in a short time."[21] A West Virginia drought committee survey estimated that 46 percent of the state's families would lack sufficient potatoes and other root vegetables to carry them through the winter; 39 percent lacked pork and other meats; 40 percent had no poultry. Approximately 9,800 families were "likely to be in such distress as to justify early investigations by the Red Cross or some other special relief agents."[22]

Conditions had reached extreme proportions in the Appalachian hill counties by December. County reports had persistently described the privation that existed in October and predicted grave problems when cold weather arrived. Yet national headquarters publicly continued a conservative relief policy, holding out for the larger winter program that it expected to operate in January. In mid-December Reddy declared that the "picture of distress given by our workers in the eastern part of our state is almost unbelievable. There is a decided lowering of social conditions which were never high in those counties and there is a growing army of itinerants travelling on foot." These tramps slept by the roadside or sought out abandoned mining houses. He also heard stories of people in the rural sections selling their meager household effects to get money for food. Junk wagons purchased the wares and peddled them in nearby towns. Because some counties refused to accept responsibility for relief, their citizens wandered in search of food, presenting problems for neighboring counties. One result was the increase in larceny; for example, highwaymen had robbed tobacco deliverers, cutting the throat of one of the drivers.[23] Health conditions worsened in the hill counties due to the lack of food. Dr. A. T. McCormack of the State Board of Health visited schools and found only green nuts in lunch baskets. A 10 percent increase in the state's infant mortality rate had occurred during the previous four months, largely due to the undernourishment of mothers and children.[24] By December 16

145

Reddy finally reached the conclusion that "we cannot depend upon a further development of local resources in a great many of these counties for such resources have always been limited and this year they are worse than ever." Nor was the situation with the banking system encouraging. "I was told that some of the wealthy people were quietly taking their money to large centers for deposit and this would further weaken the Kentucky financial situation."[25]

As conditions worsened and congressmen debated in December and January the proper means for relieving the victims, concerned citizens, county judges, and other local officials wrote to the Red Cross and their congressmen describing the desperate plight of Appalachia and demanding either federal or Red Cross aid. The reports of total economic ruin resembled those from Arkansas. According to Judge Franklin Rives of Quincy, Kentucky, families lacked food and clothing and could not pay their taxes. "Our farmers heretofore have been able to take care of those in need in their community with what help the county could give, but now they are not able to extend outside help, and my estimate is that unless we can get from two to three thousand dollars outside, some of our people are going to suffer."[26] In Clay County Judge William Spencer described equally dire circumstances in which the combined efforts of the local drought committee and the county government had raised only $430. Due to extreme indebtedness the county could allocate no further funds. "My magistrates tell me that there are hundreds of families bound to suffer if we do not get any relief for them from the Red Cross. . . . We have gone our limit, and our present sums would be exhausted in one day if we should fill all the requests made."[27]

Officials of Cumberland County insisted that words could not describe the serious situation that confronted their people. "We have exhausted all means here to care for them and unless something is done and done at once there will be severe suffering for some in the county." Local committees had raised funds and given away clothing, but resources simply did not meet the demands. A survey revealed that 800 farmers had requested aid; about eighty families lacked food, clothing, and adequate shelter. The recently passed feed and seed loan could not possibly benefit these farmers, for they did not possess collateral. "Everyday brings reports of families that are suffering and we have no relief to offer."[28]

Similar circumstances existed in West Virginia. Boone County reported having twice its usual fifty-five families on relief, and Braxton had 600 requesting help. The county's funds were so overdrawn that it could not meet the demands. Branch Valley in Hardy County had done its best, according to one observer, "but there is a bunch of very poor people in the county and even the better off farmers and businessmen are hard hit this year. In the mountain sections there is no employment of any kind that can be gotten. Many of these people are on little mountain farms and have some livestock but are without feed, money or credit." Caring for 600 families, many containing seven people, had depleted Logan County's resources. With an overdraft of $146,000 the local government needed at least $20,000 to cover its case load. In Marion County the $40,000 allocation for poor relief had been spent and a far greater sum requested from the Red Cross.[29]

Stories of human suffering poured into national headquarters and congressional offices along with the Red Cross county reports. Many families in Mineral County, West Virginia, were reported living in deserted houses without furniture, food, or suitable clothing. A seventeen-year-old girl, wearing her sick mother's dress, a neighbor's coat, and lacking stockings and underwear, walked twenty-three miles to obtain relief for her family only to be denied it after reaching Williamson. An investigator in another area found a family of ten with no food; all the children were barefooted, had no underclothing, and were sleeping in filthy beds. Three had whooping cough and by the time a physician arrived, three others had developed pneumonia. The baby soon died of malnutrition.[30]

From Kentucky came similar demands for food and clothing. The local registrar at Pine Top, Mrs. Minto Tackitt, pleaded with the Red Cross for aid. "There are lots of families going to starve if you can not help us, so if you can do anything to help us take care of them we will be more than glad, as each family has a large crowd of children, and it looks as though they are going to starve and freeze if they can not get a little help." Although neighbors, the court, and magistrates had exerted their full efforts, they had not been able to care adequately for the hungry. "There are about 50 orphan children in this county crying for something to eat. It looks too bad, but we have done all we can for the poor widow women washing by hard day's work trying to get their children something to eat and wear." She described "25 poor children here in sight of me that go from one day to another without a bite to eat unless we divide with them, and you know I can not raise my own family, and these too."[31]

Other reports corroborated Tackitt's observations. Mrs. Mary Breck-inridge of the Frontier Nursing Service described conditions in her 700-square-mile territory of Bell, Clay, Leslie, and Perry counties. She had canvassed her 900 families to determine the exact degree of their food reserves and medical condition. The survey showed 13 percent having no food; 55 percent would have exhausted their resources by spring; the remainder possessed a meager supply still bordering on hunger. "I personally know many of these families, and I know there is nothing whatever in their cabins at the present time," she observed. "In giving Christmas to over 4,000 children, we always give shoes to those that are actually barefoot. This year between four and five hundred children had no shoes at all. When there isn't the money for food, of course there isn't the money for clothing." Timber usually offered a certain amount of income for the mountaineers, but the low water had locked the cut logs upstream. Thus neither employment nor food reserves existed. "In other words, quite plainly and bluntly and frankly, some hundreds of families, to my personal knowledge in southeastern Kentucky face actual starvation this winter unless the matter is handled by the American Red Cross."[32]

A depressed mining industry further complicated the distress in West Virginia. In Monongahela County 500 families needed help due to closed mines and the drought. Some companies allowed miners to work on a limited basis. For example, one coal loader worked two days a week for a daily wage of $4. His expenses for two weeks of powder, coal, rent, blacksmithing, lighting, and other expenses totaled $8.50, leaving $7.50 for a ration of food for his family of ten. One day a coworker discovered that the miner had only cooked potato peelings in his lunch pail, having left the potatoes for his children. Conditions in the Paint and Field Creek mining camps were also reported as serious, with ninety families in actual need of food. Nearly 100 squatter families lived in abandoned coal mining camps, while scores of children lacked clothing and food. One investigator found a woman with pneumonia lying scantily clad in a bed with no mattress.[33]

Living in drafty cabins during the cold winter without sufficient food, water, or clothing naturally led to an increase in disease. Relief investigators reported numerous cases of pneumonia, scarlet fever, trachoma, pellagra, and typhoid. In Saylersville, Kentucky, the county physician encountered an unusual number of sick because isolation could not be enforced. Families with contagious diseases roamed around the neighborhood in search of food and shelter, contaminating other people with whooping cough, diphtheria, smallpox, and chickenpox.[34] Union and Cumberland counties reported a rise in tularemia, a disease contracted while skinning rabbits.[35] When showers finally fell in February, Dr. McCormack of the Kentucky State Board of Health predicted an increase in typhoid and dysentery as the filth rose from underground to the surface of streams and rivers. "The public should realize that never before have so many unusual and unlooked for problems presented themselves, and in many instances, the proper solution has not been found." The child welfare board in Jefferson County, West Virginia, did attempt to confront the sharp increase in children's diseases by establishing an eye, ear, nose, and throat clinic; 3,000 elementary schoolchildren received examinations and treatment.[36] These represented the more fortunate cases, however, for children who lived in the cabins on isolated ridges had few opportunities to encounter either a clinic or a doctor.

Disease, starvation, and cold stalked mountain families during the winter. Some walked miles in the snow seeking relief, while others moved from farm to farm stealing potatoes, chickens, and meat. Horses, cows, chickens, and pigs starved for lack of feed. Officials feared that if the Red Cross did not move in quickly, hundreds of people faced certain death. Hidden away on craggy ridges or on sliding slopes, many mountaineers would not know about aid when it did exist, and some would not request it even after the Red Cross finally began its relief operation. According to one newspaper, these people represented a "patient, fatalistic race, rather shiftless and unable to comprehend the new age. They have seen their woods taken away, the coal companies come into their hills and despoiled their land. They are a fine, brave race, pure Anglo-Saxon and they must be saved. It never occurs to them to ask for assistance. They do not know how."[37] The Red Cross changed this aversion to relief. As field workers rode into the hollows and interviewed families, the mountaineer experienced his first encounter with extensive assistance. For both the field worker and the relief recipient it was a unique experience, and each responded to the other with the logical misunderstandings and suspicions that could have been expected from a middle-class social worker and an isolated mountaineer.

In response to the increasing demand for aid, the Red Cross reopened its Kentucky office in January. Seventeen paid representatives from the national office were sent to Kentucky and eight to West Virginia, who worked with an additional force of 2,103 and 779 volunteers.[38] Red Cross workers quickly discovered sufficient evidence to support the stories of human suffering. According to one supervisor in eastern Kentucky, reports received in the state's drought relief office revealed that the situation had not been exaggerated. "There is a tremendous job ahead to meet the needs of our rural people whose resources are fast being exhausted. The number of families receiving Red Cross aid is increasing weekly and the peak is not yet reached." All reports indicated, however, that Red Cross field representatives had the situation under control.[39]

Field workers faced different problems in organizing the relief effort. Unlike the Delta region, where croppers lived together on plantations, most of the needy were hidden several miles deep in the craggy mountains. To reach these invisible people, investigators had to rely for directions upon local citizens, who, expressing their traditional aversion to "furriners," were often reluctant to aid social workers. Transportation presented yet another problem, and most often field representatives rode mules up the steep mountains and through the coves. One case worker described her experiences in an anonymous eastern Kentucky county that lacked paved roads, railroads, a bus line, and a telegraph line. The county was completely rural and had no incorporated towns or hospitals. "It is desolate, bleak, forbidding. Its 8,000 people are always poor, but with crop failures they are starving. At least twenty percent of its population will be in need of food." Driving in a mule wagon and later riding on the mule, the worker described her encounter with the mountain people. "Everywhere there are barefooted, ragged children, whose parents make no pretense at sending them to school. They have no clothes. They have no shoes. They have nothing to 'put in their buckets.' " Grown-ups appeared equally destitute. "Hollow eyed, half-starved men and women. Their skin is caked with dirt. Their clothing is in rags. Their worn shoes are wrapped in sacking. The children are abjectly miserable." When word spread that the Red Cross had begun a relief program, applicants thronged to the county seat and described their predicament. One woman explained the vicious cycle produced by the drought. "We are on starvation Lady. . . . We didn't raise no crop. All our cabbages, all our potatoes, everything is gone. We haven't got a bite left. The chickens don't lay no eggs, the cows don't give no milk. We haven't got a thing in the world. We are all on sufferance."

The closing of a few small coal mines had added further to the economic depression, and no road work existed. To get a few cents families resorted to selling their beds and stoves for junk. Some slept on the floor, huddled together in an effort to keep warm. Relief workers discovered others living in the cliffs and sleeping on leaves. Roots dug in the woods provided their only source of food. In one cabin a child sat alone with two dead parents. There was no fire or food in the home. County officials had exhausted every means of assistance and sent an urgent request to the Red Cross. "We are all about to starve to death. We have done our best for everybody. We have filled up the poor farm. We have carted the children to orphanages for the sake of feeding them. There is no more room. Our people in the country are starving and freezing."[40]

Yet once field representatives arrived, the local officials did not always offer their full cooperation. Often county judges and magistrates held traditional assumptions about poor relief—those who seek help represent the shiftless; therefore little concern should be given them. According to Red Cross worker Ann Craton, the organization had no idea of the frightful situation that existed in the mountain counties. "We have turned over relief problems to a set of people who have never heard of social work and whose morality is that of the eighteenth century. They are using their power to clean up their communities according to their own standards and their own interpretation." Because of the heavy case loads and the extent and isolation of the area, field workers could not constantly watch the local chapters and committees, but they had to rely on them to carry out the operation. According to Craton, under the guise of Red Cross relief, abuses had occurred "which make your blood run cold. Fortunately it is a naive, unsophisticated part of the world and there is no critical point of view, but at the same time, at almost any minute some of these flagrant things might come to light. If they ever reached the newspapers it would be hideous beyond belief."

Craton offered several examples of the indifferent attitude of local leaders. One feeble-minded family had applied for aid but were not technically drought sufferers or unemployed. Chapter officials defined them as paupers and squatters and refused to grant assistance. Since some of the officials disapproved of the family, they were taken in an automobile to the edge of the woods and left alone to fend for themselves. When the field representative accidentally heard of the incident, she was calmly informed that "they were out in the woods." She ordered the worker to find the discarded group and to bring them in for Red Cross help.

In another county a family's house had burned, and they were living in a cave, sleeping on leaves with a fire for heating. Despite orders to find these refugees, local chapter representatives had simply ignored them. Another chairman had retorted to one prospective beneficiary, "You can freeze and starve for all we are going to do for you." Craton explained that numerous other incidents could be offered to reveal the indifferent attitude of local officials toward the mountaineers. "This set of people are Eastern Kentucky's 'untouchables'—many are hopelessly feeble-minded and many mentally inadequate. The respectables and the church people hate them. The point of view is that God has sent this drought to clean up the Kentucky mountains, to let these people freeze and starve." Unless national headquarters could provide further supervision, Craton was certain that the "bastards, the children of moonshiners, thieves, men in jail, etc." would starve in the name of the Red Cross. "I am giving you the most flagrant examples so that at Washington you may realize what local chapter relief means and what responsibilities we have been forced to put into the hands of well meaning but hopelessly ignorant and begotted people, from a social point of view."[41]

Craton's observations revealed the obsolete attitudes of the local authorities, who in their own way were as backward as those they criticized. When Dr. DeKleine visited counties in the region, he discovered similar conditions; however, his findings reflected an inability to comprehend the culture or the predicament of those he observed. In Boyd County he found small farms on hillsides in the coal region. "They keep a cow or two, a flock of chickens and plenty of children. They do know how to raise children. That seems to be true all over Kentucky. They tell me the families run commonly from 5 to 10, 12 and as high as 15—and a dumber lot I have never seen in my life." In a sense of bewilderment the doctor observed, "I have seen more feeble-minded people or bordering on it, than I have ever seen in so small an area. I am told that 20 percent of the backwoods folks are of that class." DeKleine visited such people. "I saw one family yesterday in Anderson County with four 'dumb Doras,' and all adults. The filth and stench in that house is not describable. I wonder why such folks are permitted to live."[42]

DeKleine decided that families above the "dumb Dora" strata could care for themselves, even during the current crisis. In his eyes these small farmers appeared much hardier and thriftier than the similar classes in the Delta, and he concluded that "the families who are down and out in the hills of Kentucky are *where* they are because of *what* they are." These people on the bottom rung most needed Red Cross help, although he saw no chance of their ever advancing to a better standard of living. Like Craton, he found the usual hostile attitude toward the poor among the general population. "There is a feeling among the better farmers in Boyd County that the drought is providential; that God intended that the dumb ones should be wiped out; and that it is a mistake to feed them. That is not idle talk on my part. I have actually heard that expressed two or three times." DeKleine did not totally disagree with this point of view. Indeed, he believed black croppers had a greater ability to survive and to make food reserves last longer than the poorest hill people. "The negroes are superior in many ways to these white folks. Their homes are cleaner; their children are kept better; they have better cabins (poor as they are) and they are a happier lot. I can well understand why some folks think the 'ornery' ones should be allowed to die off."[43]

Despite Craton's observations, DeKleine insisted that no one had starved to death and no increase in diseases had occurred. However, the Red Cross program was not without its critics. While praising the agency's efforts, Mary Breckinridge described the food ration as inadequate. A survey of 1,175 families conducted by the Frontier Nursing Service revealed that at least one-half or more of the region's 4,000 children lacked milk. Despite the Red Cross's efforts, rations were so low that they kept people barely above starvation. When food was hauled into the region, local merchants passed the expense on to the community. The average ration consisted of a monthly allowance of $2 per person with a maximum of $20 for the largest families that often had twelve or more members. This money purchased store-bought grain of a lower nutritional content. "There is no margin to give a man working-calories, to give children growth, to enable an expectant or a nursing mother to carry her baby, or to stave off the ravaging effects of pellagra and tuberculosis. No provision whatever is made for milk for the young children."[44]

In response to Breckinridge's criticism, Red Cross Supervisor J. Harrison Heckman visited several counties to confirm the accuracy of her report. Regarding the supply of milk, chapter chairmen insisted that a shortage of cows made an adequate milk program impossible. Breckinridge herself had unsuccessfully sought to alleviate this problem for years. According to Heckman, members of the Breathitt County chapter had forgotten how to say no, feeding everyone who appealed. Orders to 1,800 families had already been issued, and 1,000 more had yet to be reviewed. "They have gotten to the point where everybody is

starving and naked in their minds." Several people reported fifty families in Caney Creek had no food and were tying newspapers around
themselves to keep warm. After a visit to the community, Heckman
discovered that the majority of families consisted of penitentiary widows,
the result of a spectacular prohibition raid two years earlier. "Without
doubt, they are in need, but in no case did I see any family without
sufficient meal and lard to last them at least ten days. I saw no one who
actually had suffered or would suffer from lack of clothes. They were
rather hostile to my questions as to the source of their income."[45]

DeKleine also visited Breckinridge's territory and decided that the
Red Cross had, if anything, been too liberal. Breathitt had found the
easiest way out would be to feed everybody. One field representative in
the county firmly stated that 40 percent of those receiving aid did not
need it. Heckman informed the chapter that unless case load was reduced
by at least 50 percent, the agency would cut off future funds. "However,
if their looks is a determining factor, my guess is they won't do much
about it. All of that, of course, is none of my business; but since
everybody appeared to be in the best of health, I had no chance to start
an argument of my own." DeKleine then visited the Breckinridge's
Frontier Nursing Clinic in Leslie County. "As a matter of fact, that is the
only place anybody with a white collar can stay. The pigs are as prominent in the streets as dogs are ordinarily. I saw one trying to get into the
court house, but the judge objected. . . . Pigs are as persistent as bootleg-
gers in this section of the world."

After visiting several homes in Leslie County, DeKleine expressed
surprise at the neat homes and healthy children — much cleaner than
those he had seen in Boyd County a month earlier. "It is possible, of
course, and even probable that the nursing service has made an
enlightening influence on these people. There was not the filth and
squalor I have seen in some of the other homes in other counties and
other states." The people seemed satisfied with Red Cross aid, and no
one was starving. The doctor found it difficult to determine whether the
agency's allowance equaled the normal standard of living. "However,
they all said they had enough to get along with, and that is all they ever
have." According to him, the various chapter chairmen expressed concern over Breckinridge's criticisms. "I am sure they will be able to
convince her where she is at fault."[46]

The Red Cross drought relief program in the Appalachians revealed,
as it had in Arkansas, the severe limitations of local voluntarism. The

most striking characteristic in the mountains was the desire of the local officials to use the disaster to rid their communities of the undesirables. Even DeKleine, although aware of local attitudes, expressed similar prejudices. The Red Cross was not a reformist organization and did not view its responsibility as the alleviation of poverty in the region. However, by dispensing assistance through the local political and economic leaders, the agency could not administer a more adequate program. The hazards of local voluntarism became even clearer when the issue of relief to miners emerged.

Notes

1. U.S. Department of Agriculture, *Economic and Social Problems and Conditions of the Southern Appalachians* (Washington, D.C., 1935), 5. The Appalachian region, especially the Northeastern Cumberland Plateau, had the highest fertility rates in the United States. For example, the birthrate in the region's cities with a population over 10,000 was 339 per 1,000 mothers of childbearing age. However, outside these cities the birthrates soared: Blueridge, 670; Allegheny Plateau, 613; Northwestern Cumberland Plateau, 670; Northeastern Cumberland Plateau, 746. In the valleys the rate was much lower: Southern Appalachian Valley, 532; Central Appalachian Valley, 510; valleys of southwest Virginia, 504. For a further discussion of the social and economic conditions of Appalachia, see Taylor, Wheeler, and Kirkland, *Disadvantaged Classes in American Agriculture.*

2. By World War I, 30 percent of the farmers in one-half of the mountain counties were tenants and in some counties the rate was 50 percent. Eller, *Miners, Millhands, and Mountaineers,* 231. See also Gaventa, *Power and Powerlessness.*

3. Eller, *Miners, Millhands, and Mountaineers,* 86–127.

4. Ibid., 128–60. For a discussion of the mining industry and coal miners, see Corbin, *Life, Work, and Rebellion* (pre-1922 years), and John W. Hevener, *Which Side Are You On? The Harlan County Coal Miners, 1931–1939* (Urbana, 1978).

5. Taylor, Wheeler, and Kirkland, *Disadvantaged Classes in American Agriculture,* 6, 32, 35,

6. Ibid., 5, 16, 19. The average size of farms fell from 109 acres in 1900 to 86 acres in 1930.

7. C. P. Barnes and F. J. Marschner, *Economic and Social Problems and Conditions of Southern Appalachia* (Washington, D.C., 1935), 22; Taylor, Wheeler, and Kirkland, *Disadvantaged Classes in American Agriculture,* 12.

8. Most country revenues went to schools and roads; one-third was used to repay the loans. The tax base in Appalachia registered far lower returns than the national average. For example, the average tax per acre in the United States in 1931 was 24¢ as compared to 58¢ in 1929. In Kentucky the tax amounted to 16¢ and 42¢ and in West Virginia to 13¢ and 49¢, respectively. The average tax per $100 of real estate in the United States in 1913 was 55¢ and $1.19 in 1929, while in Kentucky it amounted to 51¢ and 96¢ and in West Virginia 44¢ and $1.26—20

percent below the national average. Barnes and Marschner, *Southern Appalachia,* 89.

9. Charleston *Gazette,* Dec. 28, 1930, Jan. 4, 1931.

10. Thomas R. Ford, ed., *The Southern Appalachian Region: A Survey* (Lexington, 1962), 152–53.

11. DeKleine, "Report of Visit to Little Rock, Arkansas, and Louisville, Kentucky," Sept. 29, 1930, ARC, DR-401.04.

12. Reddy to Schafer, Oct. 4, 1930, ARC, DR-401.08.

13. Oct. 7, 1930, ibid.

14. American Red Cross, "Kentucky Relief," Oct. 20, 1930, ARC, DR-401.11.

15. Scearce to Reddy, Oct. 21, 1930, DR-401.02.

16. Weekly Report from Kentucky, Nov. 11, 1930, ARC, DR-401.11/08.

17. Craton, Report on Rowen County Chapter (no date), ibid.

18. Ibid.

19. The bank failures of November 22 have been previously cited; see Charleston *Gazette,* Nov. 22, 28, 1930.

20. Ibid., Nov. 27, 28, 1930.

21. Scearce to the Chairmen of the County Drought Relief Committees, Dec. 4, 1930, ARC, DR-401.02.

22. The committee also requested 7,100 carloads of hay, 1,900 carloads of straw, and 3,250 carloads of grass and feed. Howard M. Gore to Hyde, Dec. 6, 1930, Secretary of Agriculture Papers, Acc. 234, Dr. 190.

23. Reddy to Bondy, Dec. 18, 1930, ARC, DR-401.08.

24. McCormack to Kentucky County Judges, Dec. 24, 1930, ARC, DR-401.02.

25. Reddy to Bondy, Dec. 16, 1930, ibid.

26. Rives to McCormack, Dec. 29, 1930, cited in *Cong. Record,* 71 Cong., 3 sess., vol. 74, pt. 2, 1334–35.

27. Spencer to Payne, Jan. 1, 1931, ibid.

28. B. L. Simpson and J. T. McGee to Payne, Jan. 2, 1931, ibid.

29. West Virginia County Reports, 1, 3, 5, no date, ARC, DR-401.11/08.

30. Ibid., 6, 11

31. Tackitt to American Red Cross, Dec. 30, 1931, cited in *Cong. Record,* 71 Cong., 3 sess., vol. 74, pt. 2, 1334.

32. Breckinridge to Alben W. Barkley, Jan. 3, 1931, ibid.

33. West Virginia County Reports, ARC, DR-401.11/08, 6, 4.

34. Bondy to Smith, Jan. 2, 1931, ARC, DR-401.52. The following cases were reported: tuberculosis, 75; pellagra, 50; trachoma, 25; typhoid, convalescent, 25; influenza and grippe, 25. The doctor reported these as additional to the usually high disease rate in a pauper county.

35. New York *Times,* Jan. 1, 1931.

36. Louisville *Courier-Journal,* Feb. 17, 1931.

37. Arkansas *Gazette,* Jan. 19, 1931.

38. Red Cross, *Relief Work in the Drought,* 90.

39. Heckman to Bondy, Jan. 26, 1931, ARC, DR-401.02.

40. "Three Days in the Life of a Red Cross Relief Worker in Eastern Kentucky," Jan. 5, 1931, ARC, DR-401.031.

41. Craton to Bondy, Jan. 20, 1931, ARC, DR-401.11/08.

42. According to Lester V. Berrey and Melvin Van Din Lester in *The American Treasuries of Slang* (New York, 1960), the term "dumb Dora" was first used during the 1920s to refer to the frivolous young women called flappers. Apparently DeKleine used this name to refer to what he viewed as the retarded members of Appalachian families.

43. DeKleine to Fieser, Jan. 24, 1931, ARC, DR-401.11/08.

44. Breckinridge, *The Quarterly Bulletin of the Frontier Nursing Service, Inc.,* 6 (1931), 3–4.

45. Heckman to Bondy, Feb. 14, 1931, ARC, DR-401.11/08.

46. DeKleine to Fieser, Mar. 4, 1931, ibid.

9

Not Taking Care of the Whole People

Appalachian coal miners presented an unusual relief problem for the Red Cross. Unlike hill people who lived scattered about the ridges, miners congregated in villages, living in two- to six-room clapboard houses that rested on piers. Rows of lopsided shacks, often packed so closely together that there was no room for a small garden, lined the muddy trails that served as streets. Like Delta croppers, the miners owed their souls to the commissary, but they saw their supplies deducted daily rather than seasonally. Miners were paid only in scrip, and, since only company stores accepted scrip, prices in them exceeded those in nearby businesses by at least 30 percent. Rent, medical expenses, working materials, and even church fees were extracted from each paycheck. In constant debt to the commissary and the company, miners lived in a condition much like peonage.

When the depression struck, the situation worsened as mines shut down. Although few workers had gardens, the mining counties were classified as part of the drought region and therefore they qualified to receive the federal loans or Red Cross relief — provided the recipients were *farmers* who had suffered a loss due to the *drought.* As the Red Cross moved to aid drought sufferers, it soon encountered demands from the miners. When the pace of union organization increased in the region and strikes occurred, however, the agency refused to become involved in what it viewed as an industrial conflict. Faced with thousands of naked and starving children, the organization confronted a serious dilemma in the winter of 1931. Could evicted families be allowed to starve and freeze to death simply because they lacked gardens and thus could not qualify as farmers suffering from the drought, or would feeding them encourage men to cease work and strike, knowing relief would be provided? In 1928 the Red Cross Central Committee adopted a clear statement of disaster policy: "Such other forms of unemployment and economic maladjustment which may have caused widespread suffering, are not national calamities as contemplated by its charter for which responsibility is imposed upon the Red Cross."[1] Nevertheless, Herbert Hoover once again attempted—unsuccessfully—to involve the Red Cross in providing unemployment relief.

The crisis in the coal industry had already lasted for a decade, for the bituminous coal industry had experienced fluctuations since the end of World War I. No one company dominated the economy; rather, a plethora of large and small companies competed fiercely for the market. Large steel, railroad, and utility corporations manipulated the operators by fixing prices and playing one coal company against another, yet operators continued to maintain high production levels despite the low rates received for their coal. Many mines were eventually forced to shut down, and those that remained open paid extremely low wages.[2] Underemployment had been a major problem throughout the 1920s. For the three decades prior to 1922 bituminous miners had worked an average of 213 days per year. Between 1922 and 1925, however, the average fluctuated from 142 to 195 days of employment. As mechanization increased, more mines closed and fewer diggers worked.[3] Because the mines of West Virginia and Kentucky represented the most recently developed fields, the cutthroat competition of the national market came somewhat later. While the old fields of Ohio and Pennsylvania suffered tremendous reductions in output after 1923, the newer operations in the southern Appalachians expanded, although their production continued to fall below that of the older regions.[4] The depression hit the old fields first, but the Appalachian operators were not far behind.

Miners in West Virginia and Kentucky suffered not only from the economic crash of 1929 but also from a series of natural disasters as well. A flash flood in 1927 had washed out many of the gardens; the drought followed, baking what little top soil the flood had left. As the depression worsened, more mines either shut down or reduced both the number of working days and the wage level. In 1923 the average miner in West Virginia had earned a monthly wage of from $150 to $300. By 1930 a good day's wage was $2.50 to $3. The old rate for loading cars in Logan County had dropped from between 90¢ and $1.10 to 60¢ or 70¢. From the $3 a day earnings, the company deducted 20 percent, excluding rent and commissary fees. One miner's pay envelope showed a total earnings of $45.05 for a half month's work for loading fifty-two cars at 85¢ per car. Deductions included 50¢ a day for transportation to work, $23 for scrip, $8 for back rent, and $3.23 due after other deductions had been made.

159

This process of "overdrafting" represented a major source of contention among miners during 1930–31.[5]

Reduced wages and hours and the injustices practiced by the operators were not the only grievances of miners. In West Virginia a major complaint focused on the need for objective checkweighmen. Company checkweighmen claimed that the weights were broken and that they could simply estimate the tonnage of coal in each loaded car. For example, in a union field the weighman must use the agreed 2,000-pound basis for a ton, while in the unorganized mines he usually estimated on the basis of a 3,000- to 3,500-pound scale.[6] By 1931 the combined impact of the depression, the exploitative practices of the operators, the drought, and the subsequent cold winter created an explosive situation in the West Virginia and Kentucky coalfields.

Labor disturbances erupted throughout the entire year of 1931, though strikes were hardly a new experience for the coalfields of eastern Kentucky and southern West Virginia. Immediately following World War I, in 1919–21, southern West Virginia miners had staged wildcat strikes either to establish the United Mine Workers Union or to retain the union gains that they had made during war. In 1921 a major strike broke out, as miners flocked to Frank Keeney and his West Virginia Mine Workers Union. Coal operators, once wartime restrictions protecting labor had been lifted, sought to break the unions. Before the conflict was over, a virtual civil war had broken out, and President Warren G. Harding was forced to declare martial law to defeat Keeney and the miners. Coal operators used force, intimidation, and eviction during the remaining years of the decade to prevent the miners from organizing.[7]

Union activity met a similar fate in eastern Kentucky immediately following the war as coal operators moved to abolish the unions in their fields. Harlan was the major coal-producing county in the state and during the 1920s ranked as a leading producer. However, the prosperity was achieved at the expense of the miners, as owners reduced their wages and hours, introduced mechanization, and used discharge, eviction, and blacklisting to prevent union activity. By 1929, however, Harlan's steady progress was disrupted, for production levels dropped and unemployment increased. For miners who remained employed, wages decreased to $749 a year, and the workload dropped to 175 days.[8] By 1930 miners in both eastern Kentucky and West Virginia faced either unemployment or reduced wages and a lower number of workdays. Since most lived in company towns, they had no rights and were totally at the mercy of the coal operators for their livelihood. However, coal miners did not accept their predicament complacently.

The strikes that occurred in 1931 were in direct response to the dislocation and deterioration in working conditions that had developed during the 1920s. The strikes of these turbulent months were doomed to failure, for the power of the operators far outweighed that of the strikers. By using troops and the power of eviction, owners once again forced workers to their knees. When operators in the Harlan District slashed wages by 10 percent in February, the United Mine Workers held a meeting in Pineville and urged 2,000 coal diggers to join the union. Immediately the Black Mountain Company fired and evicted 175 families; the Black Star Company fired 35 miners. Three weeks later William J. Turnblazer of the United Mine Workers promised Kentucky diggers food and money if they would strike. Over 11,000 answered the call and immediately the mines shut down. Violence quickly ensued as company-hired guards suppressed the strikers. On May 4 carloads of deputies with rifles and machine guns rode into Evarts and fought with a group of evicted miners. After a thirty-minute barrage three deputies and one miner lay dead. Turnblazer had not kept his promise, and workers frantically searched for food to feed their hungry families. Soon they looted stores and squatted in abandoned mining camps. As the gravity of the situation increased, Governor Flem Sampson made an agreement with Turnblazer to send troops to the region. Turnblazer agreed that the union would welcome troops if food were provided and if the private guards were disarmed and their commissions as deputies withdrawn. On May 6, 400 National Guardsmen descended on Harlan, but the agreement was quickly repudiated. Guards arrested union leaders, and black scabs worked the mines. Sheriff J. H. Blair raided the local union office and discovered material from the radical International Workers of the World. He then charged some union leaders with conspiracy and twenty-eight leaders with the murders in the Battle of Evarts. Defeated, Turnblazer relented and declared the walkout a wildcat strike, ordering the miners back to work. Angry diggers turned to more radical organizations, such as the National Miners Union; however, by the end of 1931 that union, too, had been crushed by local officials and owners.[9]

Destitution among West Virginia miners reached even greater proportions. By 1931 one-third of the state's 112,000 diggers lacked jobs, and another one-third worked only one or two days a week. With cold and hunger widespread, miners decided to organize once again. Keeney, the veteran hero of the great 1920–21 strike, signed an estimated 18,000 to 23,000 workers into his West Virginia Mine Workers Union. In an effort to obtain more hours and better wages, he called a strike during the peak month of July, when operators were filling orders for the Great Lakes bunker trade. Despite his efforts at providing tents and truckloads of food, Keeney could not maintain 8,000 families for a very long time. Like their fellow diggers in Kentucky, the West Virginia workers faced failure from the beginning.[10]

The strikes of 1931 created a dilemma for the Red Cross, for Fred Croxton and Arthur Woods of the president's Committee for Employment were encouraging it to assume responsibility for unemployment relief. The mining situation in West Virginia gave the men an ideal opportunity to insist that the organization represented the only viable vehicle to aid the coal diggers. In addition, in early February John Barton Payne, James Fieser, and Colonel Arthur Woods had agreed that the twenty-four chapters then receiving national funds would make a distinction between the individual who suffered directly from the drought and the person who needed aid due to the depressed mining industry, *when the miner lived on some tillable acreage.* In sections where distress existed and local and state agencies could not adequately handle the situation, Payne agreed that local chapters would render temporary relief without publicity, especially in the Charleston and Clarksburg areas. National headquarters would send workers to these sections to coordinate the various relief agencies in an effort to teach them to handle local needs. In return, the Committee for Employment would contact all relief organizations in the region and encourage them to support the Red Cross and cooperate with the organization in meeting each locality's demands.[11]

Apparently Arthur Woods wanted further assurances that the unemployed miners would receive adequate assistance, for he soon wrote Payne and requested his agency to extend whatever measures were necessary to aid the soft coal district since it lay within the drought region. Payne insisted he could relieve only those who suffered from the drought. Refusing to admit defeat, Woods then visited Hoover and explained the serious condition of the diggers. The president called Payne and requested that he have the Red Cross "see to it very quietly and unobtrusively, supplementing the existing facilities and using them wherever they existed, to relieve the distress." Payne agreed.[12]

In late February Croxton visited the West Virginia mining counties to determine the adequacy of local relief organizations. In a conference with the chairman of the state employment committee, he explained the Red Cross position on relief in the region. "Both he and I were of the opinion that it would be very much more satisfactory if the Red Cross would provide their representatives with rather definite information concerning the enlarged program which they appeared to be ready to edge in on as far as West Virginia is concerned." With this in mind, Croxton and the chairman phoned national headquarters to offer the suggestion but were advised that it would probably not be carried out. Croxton then decided to select the counties experiencing greatest distress and study the adequacy of their relief organization.[13] In each county he discovered the inability of the traditional organizations to handle the increasing demands for aid. Logan County, for example, had completely exhausted its funds and had ceased all relief activities. Six hundred families thus faced the possibility of no income whatsoever. The county had also closed its detention home, and several children lacked homes. Monongahela County faced similar circumstances. Although national headquarters had allocated $2,000 a month for drought relief, destitution was greatest in the mining camps. To alleviate these conditions, Croxton urged local chapter chairmen to wire the Red Cross and request further aid, explaining that he believed national headquarters would be willing to "edge over" and assist local agencies in providing additional aid. Requests should not be phrased in terms of miner relief, he stressed, but as regular relief. After funds had been allocated, he seemed certain the organization would allow some relief to miners. All of the chairmen agreed to this strategy, although Logan County members expressed concern that outside aid might encourage the appearance of more paupers.[14]

While Croxton pursued his investigation, Red Cross field representatives conducted their own surveys. Theo Jacobs visited Cabin Creek, supposedly the most destitute district in the state. After calling on several families in the mining camps that dotted the various branches of the creek, she described a distressing scene. "The general condition in these shacks, picked at random and visited, is most depressing and presents a dreary picture of mere existence in which any sign of comfort or home-like appearance is lacking." The overseer of the poor in Cabin Creek, Mrs. Eskins, had previously distributed a weekly grocery ration of $2 to $5 to several families, but county officials had recently informed her that a lack of resources meant no future provisions would be forthcoming. According to Eskins, the county had never provided for medical supplies, and many families desperately needed them. The county nurse visited only the schools—never the homes.

During Jacobs's visit a miner whose back had been broken in a mining accident came for his ration. Although he had injured himself over a year ago, the company doctor had failed to report it, preventing him from obtaining any compensation. Most miners, Eskins remarked, viewed the compensation act as a curse rather than a blessing. Usually the company granted a small amount of money for a few weeks and then discontinued it. Because of the compensation law, few could secure work after forty-five years of age.

The mine at Wet Branch had gone bankrupt, and miners simply remained in the company houses. In the homes Jacobs found meager furnishings with bed clothes resembling dirty rags, and the walls papered with newspapers to keep out the cold. One man had not worked in eleven months because of illness; his six children could not attend school for lack of shoes, and an ill brother also resided with him. In another house she discovered an old black woman sitting alone before a fire. Only help from generous neighbors had allowed her to survive. Nearby lived a widow with seven children who depended upon the county for her entire income.[15]

West Virginia miners received more public attention in early April, when Brant A. Scott, vice-president of the West Virginia Mine Workers Union, testified before the Senate Committee on Unemployment Insurance. Attacking the Red Cross for refusing to aid the miners, Scott said that when diggers had appealed for assistance in Charleston, the chapter informed them that relief existed only in the city. No aid had been administered in the Kanawha field, according to Scott.[16] He also requested that the Red Cross begin a relief operation for the unemployed workers as soon as possible. Fieser replied that it was not the function of the national organization to care for localized industrial distress; rather the duty rested entirely with the chapters themselves.[17] Judge Payne held a news conference following Scott's testimony and firmly stated that the Red Cross would not administer a program that defined unemployed miners as drought sufferers.[18]

Nevertheless, Croxton joined Scott in calling for additional aid. Returning from his trip to West Virginia, he reported thousands of miners living on a monthly county allowance of $10. "Children and grownups fare alike. The standard food is cornmeal, some flour, and beans. There is no meat and little if any green food." He noted that most

164

of the sufferers were not farmers and thus could not obtain federal loans. "Red Cross chapters in the affected sections have little or no funds with which to grant aid. The result has been that in many sections the counties have been forced to feed the starving and some of these have either run out of money or are about broke." Although the organization had distributed garden seed to the drought victims, none had been given to the miners. Conditions were so bad that Croxton invited two other members of the committee to survey the area with him. "We went into homes and everywhere we could. Some of the conditions found were so bad I hesitate to try to describe them."[19] After Scott's and Croxton's appeals, Hoover once again turned to the Red Cross to administer a program.

On April 4 Hoover wrote Payne and insisted that only his organization could deal with the desperate conditions existing in the soft coal region, for the situation there was part of the whole complex of distress, drought, and depression. "I am wondering whether it would not be wise for the Red Cross to make a statement that it will, through local committees, supplement the local resources in those territories. The problem is nothing like the dimensions represented by agitators," he insisted, "but there is no doubt some real suffering and it is likely to be formulated as a charge that the Red Cross is not taking care of the whole of the people in that area." The president seemed certain that Americans "had no other agency to turn to at the present time to take care of these of our distress problems."[20]

Payne disagreed: "If the responsibility for these situations is accepted by the Red Cross it will involve large sums of money and the difficulty of letting go will be much more serious than if we now refrain from accepting the responsibility." Since most of the men had been periodically unemployed, the judge felt it useless for the organization to attempt to enter a situation plagued by recurrent economic problems. "It is my very strong conviction that unless we adhere with reasonable closeness to our present policy we will be involved in a very serious problem. All of the states affected are in position to help, but they will not help if it is possible to induce the Red Cross to assume the responsibility."[21] According to Payne, the agency would follow the major policy he had outlined in his press conference. "The Red Cross is an emergency organization and has not felt that it was involved in the mining situation. The chapters of the Red Cross locally are now and have been cooperating with other local agencies in an effort to prevent distress. We have offered seed for planting wherever the miners can find land on which to plant. This policy will be continued."[22]

The policy established by Payne continued throughout the labor conflicts of 1931. Red Cross officials maintained that accepting responsibility for relief in coal-mining areas would mean agency involvement in unemployment assistance in other sections of America. Fieser blamed Croxton and the president's Committee for Employment for leading the agitation for extensive aid to the diggers, even though no effort had been made to raise funds in Charleston, Morgantown, and other West Virginia cities. A massive program would create unnecessary problems for local chapters. "In almost every instance our local chapter people, representing the civic leadership of the community, have advised against our undertaking any relief program in mining areas. A number of these have said that they could not go on as chapter officials if we became engaged in these broader industrial issues. Our Chapter Chairman at Harlan, Kentucky, where excellent drouth relief work has been conducted," he continued, "has informed us that in view of the recent agitation in favor of mining relief in an atmosphere of industrial discord, he felt constrained to resign as Chapter Chairman as soon as the drouth relief work was more fully completed. His interests are with the operators." J. George Bender, chairman of the Huntington chapter, called statements on miner distress "propaganda unwarranted by conditions." Fieser mentioned these instances merely to point out that a miner relief program would split local chapters into definite camps—"those who are for and those who are against relief, the latter outnumbering the former since, after all, Red Cross leadership is largely representative of those who have been most successful in life." The bulk of the organization's contributors also fell into the last category. "These, in the main, have led the Red Cross to take the traditional position that it would not engage in relief incident to strikes, lockouts, unemployment and the natural hazards of industry."

Fieser mentioned the current situation in Harlan to demonstrate his point. Hundreds of miners had been evicted because they had attended a union meeting. If the organization undertook a relief program, it would clearly become involved in an industrial conflict. "Unfortunately, the majority of those who urge that the Red Cross depart from its traditional position in this matter, are not major contributors to the Red Cross either in roll call or in its disaster campaigns, and could not, therefore, offset the disgruntlement from more conservative backers." Many of the fields in West Virginia and Kentucky had yet to be organized, and a food program would provide a fertile field for organizers, since the major hindrance in the past had been that if the miners were organized they would expect the union to feed them somehow.

As far as Fieser was concerned, national headquarters had pursued a correct policy by aiding drought victims and encouraging state and local organizations to tackle unemployment relief. "To draw the Red Cross into the [mining] situation is virtually to federalize it, when I am convinced that many of the local communities have not yet exhausted their opportunities for self help." He firmly doubted that Kentucky and West Virginia had fully utilized their resources. "The question is really whether, when local communities and whole states do not undertake to relieve their own situation, the Red Cross nationally should do [so] through funds which must, of necessity, be raised elsewhere." Clearly funds could not be raised locally in Kentucky to aid the miners. In the past these needs had been largely a local and state responsibility. "The serious question is whether they should today be brought out into the open as real federal responsibility even through a non-governmental agency." Fieser concluded that unlike the drought situation, which would clear up, the mining problem would continue due to the economic woes of the industry. Once the organization launched a food program, it would be difficult to withdraw. A liberal seed distribution program presented a feasible alternative, though most of the land surrounding mining towns could hardly be considered tillable. Fieser envisioned extreme difficulties should national headquarters disregard its traditional policy relating to industrial conflicts.[23]

As public attention focused on distress in West Virginia, national headquarters received reports from local chapters describing their efforts to meet the crisis. The county agencies continued to care for the unemployed, allowing the Red Cross to deal strictly with drought victims, but the exhaustion of funds forced the county to request aid from local chapters. Kanawha County alone spent $45,000 on outside poor relief since July. Cabin Creek, one of the most destitute camps, was in this county. Another $20,000 was transferred from other county funds to be expended for further relief. All of the local organizations in each county worked to coordinate their assistance procedures. In Logan County, for example, the Salvation Army confined its efforts to the city, allowing the Red Cross to aid miners in the rural sections. In Marion County the Salvation Army worked the rural sections, leaving the city for the other organizations. It had received funds from the Consolidation Coal Company to supplement relief operations, as had other agencies.[24]

Local chapters reported that in most cases the operators were taking care of the unemployed in their fields. Companies issued scrip at a rate of $1 per day, and many mines were operating for two or three days a week. Distress in all of the counties had been taken care of by either the county, the Red Cross, the operators, or some other agency like the Salvation Army. Although the reports stated no distinct conclusions, they implied that the relief situation was well in hand, despite continuing criticism from the West Virginia Miners Union.[25]

Local chapter reports to the contrary, destitution persisted in the rural mining districts. Harrowing stories of privation continued to appear in the press. Of all those who experienced the shock and dislocation of the depression, children seemed to have fared the worst. They were the first casualties when the economic system collapsed, for when their parents could find no work or relief, they had no choice but to sit, wait, and hope that food would be forthcoming. An agent for the State Board of Children's Guardians described what she encountered on a trip through the area surrounding Kanawha County. In one home she discovered a father cremating his dead infant because he could not afford a funeral. Nearby a mother, supposedly insane from hunger and worry, drowned her two children. On request from a judge, the agent visited another home where the father had been arrested. His ten-year-old daughter had been alone for five days, except for the companionship of a small brown dog and a black hen. The young girl had a cataract in one eye and was almost blind in the other. After she had gone barefoot during the winter, one of her toes had frozen but had healed. She did not recall ever having attended school.[26]

Even when parents lived at home, the children often experienced extreme privation. One family consisted of a father who had a broken hip and his wife who suffered from tuberculosis. Of their seven children, four had hookworm, and an infant had recently died from the disease. None of the children had ever attended school. Although the county had given the family a monthly allowance of $6, that paltry sum ceased when funds gave out. Other children left home, either because their parents had abandoned them or simply because they were hungry. Detention homes and state children's homes were filled to capacity as youngsters from the rural and mining areas sought aid. Some children slept on the floors of these overcrowded institutions, and others went to the county poor farm, even though state laws prohibited young people from living with paupers.[27] These stories did not support the chapter reports that local agencies had the situation under control.

The Red Cross did work closely with various local agencies to coordinate aid both to unemployed miners and to others in the rural sections who for one reason or another did not qualify for drought relief. According to the agreement with the Woods committee, national headquarters had offered to concentrate on two counties, Kanawha and Harrison, by furnishing a worker with an emergency fund. A responsible citizens' group would supposedly work with the organization to coordinate relief and assume full responsibility within two months. Fieser reported that this plan had failed. In Kanawha no local leadership sufficiently conscious of the need for emergency action existed, and the county did not possess adequate funds should it decide to assume the task. Harrison was in a similar position. Fieser firmly insisted that the state had funds to care for the idle and that the Red Cross had fulfilled its responsibility in the region.[28]

The Red Cross encountered another delicate situation in Kentucky during and after the Evarts strike. When operators evicted several hundred families after a United Mine Workers meeting in February, the Labor Department asked the Red Cross on April 8 to approach the owners in an effort to determine their demands for reinstating the workers. Although the organization had consistently refused to become involved in an industrial dispute, Maurice Reddy of the eastern division agreed to meet with members of the union and the operators to determine their demands for a settlement. William Turnblazer assured Reddy that he had no intention of organizing in the Harlan district but had merely sought to counteract the efforts of other organizations in the area. Reddy then conferred with the operators, one of whom had recently resigned as chairman of the Harlan chapter, informing them of the pressure being placed on the Red Cross to feed the evicted workers. According to the operators, these men had been evicted because they had become troublesome after the union meeting rather than because they attended the conference. A large number of them had moved into vacant houses in Evarts. Since they lacked food and work, the owners insisted that these diggers would display radical tendencies. Reddy informed them that public opinion favored the evicted miners and that it was in their best interest to agree to a settlement. According to the operators, if Turnblazer would publicly announce that he did not intend to organize the field, they would formulate a plan for reinstating the men on an individual basis, but they would not explain their position publicly or deal with the union leader directly. After he agreed to the owner's terms, Reddy called Governor Sampson and asked him to complete the negotiations.[29]

Sampson began his negotiations with the operators, but he requested the aid of the Red Cross national headquarters should a reinstatement plan be formed. After the miners returned to work, there would be a time when they would have no income. However, national headquarters refused to aid the diggers even for a short period, believing that such a program would provide an entering wedge for further aid. While the governor pursued a compromise, violence exploded in Harlan on April 18, leaving one guard and one miner dead. Turnblazer wired national headquarters, describing the events at Evarts. Out of desperation these families had planned a march on Harlan to demand food. Fieser and DeWitt Smith suggested that the local chapter be contacted; if local people deemed it necessary, national headquarters would aid the Evarts families. The Washington office then contacted a Mr. Perkins, an operator who had recently resigned as chairman of the Harlan chapter. Perkins reported no violence between the operators and miners; instead a sheriff had attempted to arrest a few miners, and an incident occurred. It would be unwise for the agency to undertake a feeding program, he noted, for the organization would then become an adjunct of the unions in their attempt to enlist diggers. If union organization should continue and the Red Cross conducted a feeding operation, the entire population of 10,000 miners would probably cease work, expecting relief. Reddy inquired as to the status of negotiations between the operators and Sampson, hoping they would soon reinstate the evicted families. In Perkins's opinion, "Governor Flem Sampson has not done anything and won't do anything. I know him and I know he will not." Later in the day field representative W. I. Jones met with local chapter officials who insisted that if the agency undertook a feeding program a new chapter would have to be organized. "In as much as the chapter maintained that there was no need of our extending relief and as Mr. Jones is in close touch with the situation it was decided that the Red Cross could stand by for the time being," reported Reddy.[30] Although the Red Cross refused to administer assistance to the strikers, agents had no qualms about meeting with the operators and local chapters to discover their opinions on relief to the miners. By relying on the operators, the organization made the same mistake that it had done in following the planters' advice in the Delta.

In Bell County the local chapter decided to aid miners. In Pineville over 60 percent of the 425 families receiving Red Cross aid were miners who had lost their gardens. One of the major mines had failed, and about 300 families had no income. Chapter officials had disregarded national headquarters' policy, initiating a feeding program for the unemployed.[31] The activities of the chapters in Harlan and Bell counties offered an interesting comparison regarding attitudes toward relief to miners. In Harlan, where those requesting aid represented the families evicted by the companies, the chapter refused to consider an assistance program. However, in Bell, the needy miners were unemployed because of the inability of the mine to continue its operations rather than as a result of a labor dispute, and the local chapter willingly provided aid. Like Delta planters, the operators condoned relief only when it suited their purposes. Officials at national headquarters were aware of this attitude but continued to allow local chapters to determine their own policies. The surplus of miners in a depression society allowed the owners to dictate every condition under which the men worked. Reddy had hoped the operators would reach an agreement with the strikers and even went so far as to suggest a resettlement plan for the excess miners. "I threw out a little feeler by asking a question rather casually as to how it would work out if a large number of these men could be transplanted to perhaps an agricultural section. I saw that I had touched a very tender spot." Mr. Perkins protested that the men would never know how to do anything but mine coal. "It was very easy to see that the excess number of men in the mining field is very desirous from the operators' point of view."[32]

Faced with similar problems, miners in West Virginia accelerated their organizational efforts. On May 20 Keeney led several hundred evicted families from the Ward district on a twenty-five-mile hunger march to Charleston. They assembled at the Kanawha County courthouse and petitioned the Red Cross for aid. Governor William Conley addressed the group and explained his inability to act. He could make no expenditures except under appropriations authorized by the legislature. "I regret that your governor has not the power to nor the means at hand to help you, but I am going to turn over $10 of my own money to your presiding officers." Conley then expressed optimism about the future of the state. "This is a difficult period through which we are passing, but a better day is ahead, I am sure, because when there have been depressions there have always been better times. It may not come as soon as we want it, but it is sure to come." After reading the constitutional provision prohibiting unauthorized expenditures, the governor assured the gathering, "You wouldn't want us to violate the constitution, because as your representatives have told me, you are good and law abiding citizens." Despite the shortcomings of the government, he insisted it was the best on earth. "We have eliminated all class distinctions, and any man, no matter how humble, may sometime hold high office. It means something to live in a country like this, and your demeanor this morning shows that you appreciate those advantages."[33]

When addressing the marchers, Keeney expressed hope that Conley would do everything in his power to alleviate human suffering. "I don't say the government owes us a living, but I do say the government owes us a manner of making a living." He then mentioned a state law prohibiting operators from compelling miners to trade at company stores and observed that in the Ward fields owners had clearly violated the provision. With the decrease in working days and the closing of mines, Keeney declared that women and children were starving. "We must have some arrangement to relieve the suffering among the women and children if there is to be peace in this state." Charleston attorney Harold Houston then charged operators with causing suffering by cutting wages to reduce costs in their cutthroat competition with other mine owners. Although the majority of marchers belonged to Keeney's union, the 150 members of the United Mine Workers Union in the state issued a resolution on the day of the march, requesting President Hoover to call a conference of coal operators and union officials to discuss the stabilization of the bituminous coal industry.[34]

Since the Red Cross had stated its position regarding relief to miners numerous times, Hoover had no choice but to look for another private agency to administer assistance. After meeting with the president concerning conditions in the bituminous coal fields, Croxton and Grace Abbott of the U.S. Children's Bureau met on May 13 with the board of directors of the American Friends Service Committee. The president suggested that the Friends be asked to administer relief to the idle diggers. A few days later the former chairman of the Friends, Rufus Jones, and two veterans of the organization's post–World War I relief operations, Lucy Biddle Lewis and Harry T. Brown, informed Hoover that their organization had never undertaken only a relief program. According to Jones, "We had always felt that if we should undertake a piece of service where relief was desperately needed we should want to join with it some other aspect of reconciliation or way of life or help to solve the breakdown of civilization at some vital point. Everyone who knows, knows that this is a collapse of civilization at a critical point." They explained that money must be available before a program would be accepted. Hoover then called the Red Cross and told them the Friends needed from $150,000 to $250,000 and assured the Quakers that the Red Cross would come through with the funds.[35]

A few days later the Friends met to discuss a relief program. Jones and others suggested that they select the most destitute valleys in order to experiment with possible ways of handling the work force during an industrial breakdown. One member wondered if such a plan would conflict with Red Cross operations. Jones replied, "The Red Cross is not doing anything, that is why they don't sleep." Hoover had indicated that great assistance would come from the states and counties concerned. "The people," observed Jones, "are extremely ignorant, belong to the poorest part of our citizenship—a broken down type of men, women, and children. We cannot get workers much from the workers themselves. The President really felt that it might be a piece of service that would help solve a desperate problem of civilization."

Another member of the committee, Ray Newton, pointed to the obvious economic conflicts in which the organization would become involved and wondered if Hoover had addressed himself to that dilemma. The president, replied Jones, recognized that there was intensive conflict in the coalfields, but he insisted that the Friends could aid the families. Jones and others saw the solution as one of resettling miners on better farm lands. Lewis described the miner problem as one of the most serious propositions they had ever confronted and any action would bring enormous criticism. According to another member, the task focused on what should be done with the workers of an industry that was no longer economically necessary. "It is a governmental problem, but the government won't do it," added Brown. "The Red Cross sees all that is involved. The problem is how to get these workers out and where to put them." The question of resettlement would not be easy, as Dr. Mary Smity of Bryn Mawr quickly noted. "It is poor food and living conditions which has put them in the poor class they are in. Sending them to farms would involve a great deal of study. The farms there are not inducive to intensive farming. Forestry takes a long time. Dairying requires study. It is too simple to say 'Send them to the farms,'" she concluded. "It will take long time planning to do a constructive and important piece of work." Urging the committee to decide quickly, Biddle observed that children were starving. "It is a question of doing it soon or waiting till the children have died."[36] Unlike the Red Cross, the Friends saw the urgency of providing adequate relief immediately, regardless of the obvious hurdles that had to be overcome.

In June the committee agreed to undertake a few selected rehabilitation programs. While the Friends would not attempt to reconstruct the entire coal industry, they would emphasize relief and rehabilitation work in a limited number of centers in an effort to establish an example for other agencies to follow. "We shall attempt to be unbiased in the treatment of local unions in their relations with each other, in the relation between organized labor and the operators, and in the relations of organized labor to the forces of the State." Ultimately, the program's objective would be the continual rehabilitation of miner families. "If in the course of our work we discover situations which we feel need publicity and which indicate weak spots in our social order, we reserve the right to speak out concerning them."[37]

After the Quakers decided to launch their operation, the concern centered on funds. Hoover had promised that the Red Cross would provide at least $200,000. During the months of June and July the Friends patiently waited for the grant. Finally, on July 3 executive secretary Clarence Pickett wrote to Payne, explaining the proposed plan for West Virginia and Kentucky and requesting a grant of $200,000.[38] Payne immediately contacted Hoover and explained his objections to awarding the money. "For the Red Cross to provide funds for such a demonstration in the face of need in several states would, I fear, involve serious criticism—more than if nothing was done."[39] Without further delay the Quakers initiated their feeding program for the miners' children.

Strikes continued throughout the summer, culminating in the great Harlan strike of 1932. After the Battle of Evarts the radical National Miners Union sought to organize in Harlan. By December the union called for a strike, demanding better wages, freedom to trade with stores outside the company store, and better working conditions. As more miners struck, the conflict became bloodier. Journalists who arrived to publicize the brutality of the operators and the malnutrition of the men, women, and children were beaten, jailed, or run out of town. As before, the power of the operators triumphed over the strikers; by spring the strike had ended.[40]

The conflict in Harlan during the fall and winter of 1931–32 raised once again the question of relief to hungry miners. In the fall of 1931 the Friends initiated its program, feeding 400,000 children within five months. Nor had the Quakers forgotten Hoover's assurances that assistance from the Red Cross would be forthcoming. In October they were still urging the president to obtain the promised allotment from the Red Cross. Although national headquarters never granted the request, it did send Dr. DeKleine into the region in December to ascertain the need for a lunch program for children. He found 70 percent of the children were at least 10 percent underweight.[41] Yet, because of its conservative nature, the Red Cross refused to become involved in the industrial conflict that plagued the coalfields of Appalachia. The Quakers had administered relief to strikers before, particularly the Gastonia, North Carolina, strike of 1929. Their reformist approach made them more inclined to assist the starving miners. All along the Red Cross predicted that once an agency became involved in a relief operation to the region, it would be difficult to withdraw. This proved correct, for the Friends' involvement with the miners lasted throughout the 1930s, and they helped in the resettlement communities of the New Deal years.[42]

The Red Cross experience in the coal region emphasized anew the limits of local voluntarism. Since the organization depended upon wealthy industrialists and prominent citizens for the bulk of its funds, it would not risk alienating contributors with a controversial relief operation. When the organization ended its drought program in June 1931, it had aided but 1,950 families in the Kentucky fields and 585 in the West Virginia districts.[43] These represented families who had subsistence gardens and so could qualify for drought aid. Like the planter-dominated chapters in the Delta, the mine operators agreed to relieve the miners only when it served their own purposes. In not aiding the hungry strikers, the Red Cross became, in effect, a tool of the owners.

Notes

1. Fieser to Payne, Apr. 7, 1931, Presidential Papers—Coal—Box 104, Hoover Papers.

2. Irving Bernstein, *The Lean Years: A History of the American Worker, 1920–1933* (Boston, 1972), 360.

3. Grace Abbott, "Improvement in Rural Public Relief: The Lesson of the Coal Mining Communities," *Social Service Review* 6 (1932), 186. Overextension constituted the major problem in the bituminous region. In 1923 the 9,331 mines reporting to the U.S. Department of Labor employed 704,793 men, while those operating in 1929 employed 502,993—a decrease of 201,800 or 28.6 percent. The decrease in total production, however, was only 5.2 percent, while the average number of employees per mine increased from 76 in 1923 to 83 in 1929. As 35 percent of the operators were squeezed out between 1923 and 1929, the average number of working days per mine increased from 179 days in 1923 to 219 in 1929, a 22.4 percent increase. Nevertheless, the operating mines worked at only 71.1 percent of capacity in 1929 as compared to 75.3 percent in 1923. By 1931 the average number of days had fallen to 187. In West Virginia the number of bituminous mines had decreased from 1,702 in 1923 to 995 in 1928; however, the decrease in number of mines had been accompanied by an increase both in production and days of operation. West Virginia mines in 1928 showed an increase of 53.8 percent in production and of 24.7 percent in days of operation over 1923 levels. The total number of employees in West Virginia mines decreased 5.7 percent in the years 1923–28, though the average number of employees per mine in 1928 was 113 as opposed to 71 in 1923. "Relief Needs in the Coal Mining Areas," Dec. 7, 1931, ARC, DR-419.6/08.

4. From 1920–24, when production in Ohio, Illinois, and Indiana fell 27 percent, it increased 23 percent in Kentucky and West Virginia. Still, tonnage in the older mines exceeded that of the younger. In 1930 Illinois produced a larger tonnage (53,731,000) than Kentucky (51,209,000), and Pennsylvania bituminous tonnage (124,462,000) still exceeded West Virginia's production of 121,473,000 tons. Abbott, "Improvement in Rural Public Relief," 200.

5. "Relief Needs in the Coal Mining Areas," 10.

6. Ibid., 11.

7. Corbin, *Life, Work, and Rebellion,* 195–224.

8. Hevener, *Which Side Are You On?,* 9–10.

9. Bernstein, *Lean Years,* 378–81. The best discussion of the Harlan miners in 1930–31 is Hevener's *Which Side Are You On?*.

10. Bernstein, *Lean Years,* 381–84.

11. Woods, "Memo of Conference with Red Cross," Feb. 2, 1931, ARC, DR-401.02.

12. Woods, "Memo of conversation with Pres. Hoover and Judge Payne," Feb. 11, 1931, PECE/POUR Papers-Central Files of PECE Committee Memo-Arthur Woods Folder, Hoover Papers.

13. The counties selected were Barbour, Boone, Logan, Kanawha, Mingo, Harrison, Marion, Monongahela, and Taylor.

14. Report on West Virginia, Feb. 1931, Croxton Papers-Unemployment and R.F.C. Reports, 1930–31, Box 1, Hoover Papers.

15. Jacobs, "Report on Cabin Creek, Kanawha Co., W. Va.," Jan. 30, 1931, ARC, DR-419.6.

16. Davidson to Fieser, Apr. 6, 1931, ibid.

17. Charleston *Gazette*, Apr. 4, 1931.

18. Ibid., Apr. 5, 1931.

19. Ibid., Apr. 4, 1931.

20. Hoover to Payne, April 4, 1931, Pres. Papers-Coal, Box 104, Hoover Papers.

21. Payne to Hoover, Apr. 7, 1931, ibid.

22. Press interview between Miss Furman of the Associated Press and Judge Payne, Apr. 6, 1931, ibid.

23. Fieser to Payne, Apr. 7, 1931, ibid.

24. "Memo on Unemployment in Mining Communities in W. Va. and What the Red Cross Chapters Are Doing in the Winter Relief Program, 1930–31," ARC, DR-419.6.

25. Ibid.

26. Charleston *Gazette*, Apr. 10, 1931.

27. Ibid.

28. Fieser to Baxter, Apr. 21, 1931, ARC, DR-419.6.

29. Reddy to Bondy, Apr. 14, 1931, ibid.

30. Ibid., Apr. 20, 1931.

31. Ibid., Apr. 14, 1931.

32. Ibid.

33. "A Union in West Virginia?" *New Republic* 66 (Apr. 29, 1931), 281; ibid., 66 (May 20, 1931), 21; Charleston *Gazette*, May 21, 1931.

34. Ibid.

35. Proposal for Work in the Bituminous Coal Regions, American Friends Service Committee Meeting, May 23, 1931, Coal Committee, American Friends Service Committee Papers, Philadelphia.

36. Ibid.

37. "Suggested Principles Governing the Proposed Work of the American Friends Service Committee in the Bituminous Coal Regions," ibid.

38. Pickett to Payne, July 3, 1931, Presidential Papers-Coal, Box 104, Hoover Papers.

39. Payne to Hoover, July 6, 1931, ibid.

40. For a discussion of the Harlan strike, see Hevener, *Which Side Are You On?*

41. Another visitor, a federal labor conciliator, discovered an increase in the number of children in Harlan County who had died of malnutrition-induced diseases. The number of children's deaths had increased from fifty-six in 1929 to ninety-one in 1930 and eighty-four in 1931. Ibid., 11.

42. For the Friends' involvement in the coal region, see Clarence Pickett, *For More Than Bread* (Boston, 1953), 19–40.

43. Red Cross, *Relief Work in the Drought*, 90. In all twenty-three of the drought states, the Red Cross aided a total of 9,056 miners.

Conclusion

The southern drought relief program of 1930–31 represented the largest disaster relief operation in the history of the Red Cross. By the end of the official program, the Red Cross had fed 2,765,000 individuals in twenty-three states at a cost of $10,894,835.62.[1] The magnitude of the task would have strained any agency, but the severe economic conditions of Appalachia and the rural South combined with a national depression created complex problems that meant challenges beyond those of a "normal" disaster. Above all, the drought brought forth questions about the traditional role of the Red Cross as it became embroiled in a national debate over the nature of relief and the role of the federal government in providing relief and unemployment assistance. In fact, the Red Cross found itself adamantly refusing, time and again, appeals from the president on down that it accept responsibility for total relief to depression-stricken America.

Under these circumstances, the organization's efforts at conducting relief were certainly commendable—it raised $10 million in the midst of a national depression and its field agents often acted valiantly as they rode into isolated hollows and bayous in search of the needy or worked conscientiously to prevent landowners from abusing the ration program. In spite of these impressive figures and the dedication of many of its field workers, however, the Red Cross was not totally successful in carrying out its charge to administer disaster aid quickly and equitably.

The central flaw in the program was the rigid adherence of the Red Cross to a concept of local voluntarism, even when its officials knew from the Mississippi flood experience that such an approach would lead to problems in the Delta. Although some agents worked diligently to prevent planters from charging rations to their laborers' accounts as they had done in 1927, the Red Cross still allowed landowners to determine when an assistance program would begin and so indirectly forced sharecroppers to work at reduced wages on empty stomachs. And the Red Cross clearly sided with the coal-mining companies by supporting their representatives on the local relief committees rather than deal with the needs of the hungry miners. Such actions raised questions in many laborers' minds about the impartiality of the organization. Even though no deaths were recorded officially as resulting from the drought, surely many died indirectly from the disaster's long-range effects. How many infants died from lack of milk? How many children died from exposure to the harsh winter? How many elderly died from lack of medicine, adequate food, and clothing? How many sharecroppers succumbed to malnutrition and pellagra because their landowners had refused to participate in the Red Cross ration and yeast program during the fall of 1930? Slow starvation must have been difficult even for a people inured to hardship.

This is not to suggest that the mission of the Red Cross should have been the restructuring of America's economy or that it should have accepted, as President Herbert Hoover had requested, responsibility for all relief. It would have been unfair to expect the agency to cure the social and economic ills of either the southern plantation system or the bituminous coal industry, for the problems confronting these areas were too massive for any private organization to solve. But it was fair to expect the agency to administer aid quickly and equitably, independent of local economic leaders, to prevent unnecessary suffering. Its failure to achieve these ends left the Red Cross open to legitimate criticism that it had not acted autonomously in the interest of all the victims.

Yet the intensity of the criticism hurled at Judge John Barton Payne and the Red Cross never equaled that leveled at Hoover. The president's reputation as the "Great Humanitarian" remained forever tarnished because of his stubborn refusal to support even so conservative a measure as the $60-million feed and seed loan bill. In many ways Hoover was a tragic and complex figure, for, in spite of his public image as cold and distant, he did feel for the victims. When the Red Cross refused to feed the striking miners, he asked the American Friends to help, and his letters to the Quakers revealed his compassion for their plight. Hoover's major problem was his ideological rigidity. Although he knew from his experience that abuses were likely in the Delta and though he had reports describing the tremendous suffering created by the drought and the economic collapse of the plantation and Appalachian regions, Hoover adhered to his belief in local voluntarism and the necessity of the victims to help themselves. Yet he was wrong to think that relief would be administered fairly or that either region had the resources to care for its own people. Perhaps he thought both regions hopeless and feared that extensive aid would be like pouring money down a bottomless barrel. Regardless of his reasoning, though, his policies did nothing to help hundreds of thousands of people who were suffering from the effects of the drought, the depression, or both. In the end Hoover's fear over the emergence of a welfare state outweighed his compassion for the sufferers.

It is important to note that any agency conducting relief in either the rural South or in Appalachia would have encountered nearly insurmountable obstacles. Indeed, the early New Deal agencies followed more nearly the approach of Hoover and the Red Cross than has perhaps been recognized. Thus, planters, merchants, and bankers were initially involved in both the formulation and administration of the agricultural measures of the Roosevelt administration.[2] It is certainly understandable that one of the first major challenges to these federal policies emerged in the Arkansas Delta. When H. L. Mitchell launched the Southern Tenant Farmers' Union in 1934 in Tyronza, he was only a few miles away from England, the home of H. C. Coney.[3] The planters had used the crop reduction measures of the Agricultural Adjustment Administration to drive laborers they no longer needed away from the land, to prepare the way for eventual mechanization, consolidation, and the emergence of full-scale capitalist agriculture.[4]

The drought also revealed the extensive social and economic problems of the rural South. Photographers like Lewis Hines, traveling through the scorched area, portrayed to the nation for the first time the desperate poverty of the region. Their pictures of malnourished children standing in front of dilapidated houses and of men and women who looked years older than their actual age showed a society more akin to an underdeveloped country than to America at mid-twentieth century. Even a depression America must have been stunned by the extreme privation presented in these pictures and, because of them, perhaps, the nation was less surprised when Roosevelt declared the South the nation's number one economic problem in 1933.

The drought also exposed the class relationships of the plantation economy and of the coal industry that were in part causes of the misery.

The plantation economy of sharecropping and tenantry had rested from its beginnings—after the Civil War—on force, intimidation, and racism. And the coal operators had demonstrated continuously their disregard for the rights of the miners during the strikes in the early years of the twentieth century and after World War I. The prospect of an agency rendering relief concerned the planters, who feared that the intervention of any independent organization would upset the delicate relationship with their sharecroppers. To a certain extent, these fears were legitimate, for, once the laborers had an alternative source of subsistence, they were less susceptible to demands that they work at reduced wages. The drought provided yet another example of the exploitative nature of the class relationships in the plantation South before the changes wrought by the New Deal and World War II.

Thus the southern drought ranks with the Dust Bowl as a major event in the history of the American Great Depression. It challenged the traditional notions of relief, revealed the inability of private organizations to feed the millions of hungry and unemployed, and forced the nation into an early debate over the role of the federal government in providing relief. It also disclosed the total collapse of the plantation economy, the crisis in the bituminous coal industry, and the class divisions that characterized both forms of production. As rural southerners and coal miners faced starvation, they looked reluctantly to the federal government. Surely the drought prepared them to accept more easily the unemployment relief measures that would be passed during the New Deal, as it must have softened planter attitudes toward an acceptance of crop production control and the other agricultural measures passed during the Roosevelt years. And perhaps the drought contributed to the increased militancy that characterized the coal miners and tenant farmers during the remaining years of the decade.

At the national level, the drought was the last attempt by the federal government to force a private agency to provide unemployment relief before the emergence of the extensive federal programs of the New Deal era. After 1933 a new concept emerged—that when people are hungry and jobless the federal government has a responsibility to help them. That Hoover never learned this lesson represented a tragedy, not only for his presidency, but also for the millions who suffered because of his intransigence.

Notes

1. Red Cross, *Relief Work in the Drought,* 90.
2. Conrad, *The Forgotten Farmers,* and Grubbs, *Cry from Cotton.*
3. Mitchell, *Mean Things Happening in This Land.*
4. Grubbs, *Cry from Cotton.*

A Selected Bibliography

Books

Abbott, Grace. *From Relief to Social Security: The Development of the New Public Welfare Services and Their Administration.* Chicago, 1941.

Agee, James, and Walker Evans. *Let Us Now Praise Famous Men.* New York, 1960.

Alexander, Donald Crichton. *The Arkansas Plantation, 1920–1942.* New Haven, 1943.

American Friends Service Committee. *Annual Report for 1931–32.* Philadelphia, 1932.

American National Red Cross. *Annual Report, 1930–31.* Washington, D.C., 1931.

———. *Relief Work in the Drought, 1930–31.* Washington, D.C., 1931.

Asch, Berta, and A. R. Mangus. *Farmers on Relief and Rehabilitation.* W.P.A. Research Monograph 8. Washington, D.C., 1937.

Baldwin, Sidney. *Poverty and Politics: The Rise and Fall of the Farm Security Administration.* Chapel Hill, 1968.

Barkley, Alben. *That Reminds Me.* New York, 1954.

Barton, Allen. *Communities in Disaster: A Sociological Analysis of Collective Stress Situations.* New York, 1969.

Beck, P. G., and M. C. Forster. *Six Rural Problem Areas.* W.P.A. Research Monograph 1. Washington, D.C., 1935.

Bernstein, Irving. *The Lean Years: A History of the American Worker, 1920–1933.* Boston, 1960.

Brown, Josephine Chapin. *Public Relief, 1929–1939.* New York, 1940.

Brown, Roy M. *Public Poor Relief in North Carolina.* Chapel Hill, 1928.

Brunner, Edmund deS. *Rural Social Trends.* New York, 1933.

Burner, David. *Herbert Hoover: A Public Life.* New York, 1979.

Campbell, John C. *The Southern Highlander and His Home.* New York, 1921.

Chambers, Clarke A. *Seedtime of Reform: American Social Service and Social Action, 1918–1933.* Minneapolis, 1963.

Clark, Thomas D. *The Emerging South.* New York, 1961.

Colcord, Joanna C. *Emergency Work Relief as Carried out in Twenty-Six American Communities, 1930–31.* New York, 1932.

Conkin, Paul K. *The New Deal.* New York, 1975.

———. *Tomorrow a New World: The New Deal Community Program.* Ithaca, 1959.

Conrad, David Eugene. *The Forgotten Farmers: The Story of Sharecroppers in the New Deal.* Urbana, 1965.

Corbin, David Alan. *Life, Work, and Rebellion in the Coal Fields: The Southern West Virginia Miners, 1880–1922.* Urbana, 1981.

Crews, Harry. *A Childhood: The Biography of A Place.* New York, 1978.

Dabney, Virginus. *Below the Potomac: A Book about the New South.* New York, 1942.

Daniel, Pete. *Deep'n As It Come: The 1927 Mississippi River Flood.* New York, 1977.

———. *The Shadow of Slavery: Peonage in the South, 1901–1969.* Urbana, 1972.

Daniels, Jonathan. *A Southerner Discovers the South.* New York, 1938.

Dodson, L. S. *Living Conditions and Population Migration in Four Appalachian Counties.* Washington, D.C., 1937.

Dulles, Foster Rhea. *The American Red Cross: A History.* New York, 1950.

Dykeman, Wilma. *Seeds of Southern Change: The Life of Will Alexander.* New York, 1962.

Edwards, A. D. *Influence of Drought and Depression on a Rural Community.* Washington, 1938.

Eller, Ronald. *Miners, Millhands, and Mountaineers: Industrialization of the Appalachian South, 1880–1930.* Knoxville, 1982.

Ellis, Edward Robb. *A Nation in Torment: The Great Depression, 1929–1939.* New York, 1970.

Family Welfare Association of America. *Government Relief: A Pathfinding Study.* New York, 1932.

Fausold, Martin, and George T. Mazuzan, eds. *The Hoover Presidency: A Reappraisal.* Albany, 1974.

Feinman, Ronald. *Twilight of Progressivism: The Western Republican Senators and the New Deal.* Baltimore, 1981.

Ford, Thomas R., ed. *The Southern Appalachian Region: A Survey.* Lexington, 1962.

Gaventa, John. *Power and Powerlessness: Quiescence and Rebellion in an Appalachian Valley.* Urbana, 1980.

Gazaway, Rena. *The Longest Mile.* New York, 1969.

Grubbs, Donald. *Cry from the Cotton: The Southern Tenant Farmers Union and the New Deal.* Chapel Hill, 1971.

Hawley, Ellis. *The Great War and the Search for a Modern Order: A History of the American People and Their Institutions, 1917–1933.* New York, 1979.

———, et. al. *Herbert Hoover and the Crisis of American Capitalism.* Cambridge, 1973.

Hayes, E. P. *Activities of the President's Emergency Committee for Employment, 1930–1931.* Concord, N.H., 1931.

Hevener, John W. *Which Side Are You On? The Harlan County Coal Miners, 1931–39.* Urbana, 1978.

Hicks, John D. *Republican Ascendancy, 1921–1933.* New York, 1960.

Hofstadter, Richard. *The American Political Tradition and the Men Who Made It.* New York, 1948.

Holley, Donald. *Uncle Sam's Farmers: The New Deal Communities in the Lower Mississippi Valley.* Urbana, 1975.

Holley, William C., Ellen Winston, and T. J. Woofter. *The Plantation South, 1934–1937.* Washington, D.C., 1940.

Hoover, Calvin B., and U. B. Ratchford. *Economic Resources and Policies of the South.* New York, 1951.

Hoover, Herbert. *American Individualism.* Garden City, N.Y., 1922.

──────. *The Challenge to Liberty.* New York, 1934.

──────. *The Memoirs of Herbert Hoover: The Great Depression, 1929–1941.* New York, 1952.

Hoyt, John C. *The Droughts of 1930–1934.* Washington, D.C., 1936.

Hutchmacher, J. Joseph. *Senator Robert F. Wagner and the Rise of Urban Liberalism.* New York, 1968.

Johnson, Charles S. *The Shadow of the Plantation.* Chicago, 1934.

Jones, John Finbar, and John M. Herrick. *Citizens in Social Service: Volunteers in Social Welfare during the Depression, 1929–1941.* East Lansing, 1976.

Kephart, Horace. *Our Southern Highlanders.* New York, 1926.

Lewis, Helen Matthews, Linda Johnson, and Don Askins, eds. *Colonialism in Modern America: The Appalachian Case.* Boone, N.C., 1978.

Lloyd, Craig. *Aggressive Introvert: A Study of Herbert Hoover and Public Relations Management, 1912–1932.* Columbus, Ohio, 1972.

Loomis, C. P., and L. S. Dodson. *Standards of Living for Four Southern Mountain Counties.* Washington, 1938.

Lubove, Roy. *The Professional Altruists: The Emergence of Social Work as a Career, 1880–1930.* Cambridge, Mass., 1965.

──────. *The Struggle for Social Security, 1900–1935.* Cambridge, Mass., 1968.

Maguire, Jane. *On Shares: Ed Brown's Story.* New York, 1975.

Mangus, A. R. *Changing Aspects of Rural Relief.* W.P.A. Research Monograph 14. Washington, D.C., 1938.

Mann, Arthur. *La Guardia: A Fighter against His Times, 1882–1933.* Chicago, 1959.

Matthews, Elmora Messer. *Neighbor and Kin: Life in a Tennessee Ridge Community.* Nashville, 1965.

Meyers, William Starr, and Walter H. Newton, eds. *The Hoover Administration: A Documented Narrative.* New York, 1936.

Meyers, William Starr, ed. *The State Papers and Other Writings of Herbert Hoover.* Vol. I. New York, 1934.

Mitchell, Broadus. *Depression Decade: From New Era through New Deal, 1929–1941.* New York, 1947.

Mitchell, H. L. *Mean Things Happening in This Land: The Life and Times of H. L. Mitchell, Cofounder of the Southern Tenant Farmers Union.* Montclair, N.J., 1979.

Murchison, Claudius T. *King Cotton Is Sick.* Chapel Hill, 1931.

Nye, Russell B. *Midwestern Progressive Politics: A Historical Study of Its Origins and Developments, 1870–1950.* East Lansing, 1951.

Odum, Howard. *Southern Regions.* Chapel Hill, 1936.

──────. *Systems of Public Welfare.* Chapel Hill, 1925.

Pearsall, Marion. *Little Smoky Ridge: The Natural History of a Southern Appalachian Neighborhood.* Tuscaloosa, 1959.

Perkins, Van L. *Crisis in Agriculture: The Agricultural Adjustment Administration and the New Deal, 1933.* Berkeley, 1969.

Pickett, Clarence. *For More than Bread.* Boston, 1953.

Proceedings of the National Conference of Social Work, 1931. Chicago, 1931.

Raper, Arthur. *Preface to Peasantry.* Chapel Hill, 1936.

_____ . *Tenants of the Almighty.* New York, 1943.

_____ , and Ira De A. Reid. *Sharecroppers All.* New York, 1941.

Recent Social Trends in the United States: Report of the President's Research Committee on Social Trends. New York, 1933.

Robinson, Edgar E. *Herbert Hoover, President of the United States.* Stanford, 1975.

Romasco, Albert U. *The Poverty of Abundance: Hoover, the Nation, and the Depression.* New York, 1965.

Rosen, Elliot A. *Hoover, Roosevelt, and the Brains Trust: From Depression to New Deal.* New York, 1977.

Rosengarten, Theodore. *All God's Dangers: The Life of Nate Shaw.* New York, 1974.

Ross, Malcom. *Machine Age in the Hills.* New York, 1933.

Salutos, Theodore. *Farmer Movements in the South, 1865–1933.* Los Angeles, 1960.

Sanderson, Dwight. *Research Memorandum on Rural Life in the Depression.* New York, 1937.

Schlesinger, Arthur M., Jr. *The Age of Roosevelt: The Crisis of the Old Order, 1919–1933.* Boston, 1957.

Schwarz, Jordan A. *The Interregnum of Despair: Hoover, Congress, and the Depression.* Urbana, 1970.

Sherman, Mandel, and Thomas R. Henry. *Hollow Folk.* New York, 1933.

Smith, Gene. *The Shattered Dream: Herbert Hoover and the Depression.* New York, 1970.

Terkel, Studs. *Hard Times: An Oral History of the Great Depression.* New York, 1970.

Terris, Milton, ed. *Goldberger on Pellagra.* Baton Rouge, 1964.

Tauber, Conrad, and Carl C. Taylor. *The People of the Drought States.* Washington, D.C., 1937.

Taylor, Carl C., Helen W. Wheeler, and E. B. Kirkpatrick. *Disadvantaged Classes in American Agriculture.* Washington, D.C., 1938.

Tindall, George. *The Emergence of the New South, 1913–1945.* Baton Rouge, 1967.

U.S. Agricultural Economics Bureau. *Economic and Social Problems and Conditions of the Southern Appalachians.* Washington, 1935.

U.S. Department of Agriculture. *Agriculture Yearbook, 1931.* Washington, 1931.

Vance, Rupert B. *Human Factors in Cotton Culture.* Chapel Hill, 1929.

Warren, Harris G. *Herbert Hoover and the Great Depression.* New York, 1959.

Weissman, Benjamin. *Herbert Hoover and Famine Relief to Soviet Russia, 1921–23.* Stanford, 1974.

Weller, Jack. *Yesterday's People: Life in Contemporary Appalachia.* Lexington, 1965.

Wilbur, Ray Lyman, and Arthur Mastick Hyde. *The Hoover Policies.* New York, 1937.

Wilson, Joan Hoff. *Herbert Hoover: Forgotten Progressive.* New York, 1975.

Wisner, Elizabeth. *Public Welfare Administration in Louisiana.* Chicago, 1930.

Wolters, Raymond. *Negroes and the Great Depression: The Problem of Economic Recovery.* Westport, Conn., 1970.

oofter, T. J. *Landlord and Tenant on the Cotton Plantation.* Washington, D.C., 1936.

———, and Ellen Winston. *Seven Lean Years.* Chapel Hill, 1939.

Zinn, Howard. *LaGuardia in Congress.* Ithaca, 1959.

Articles

Abbott, Grace. "Improvement in Rural Public Relief: The Lesson of the Coal-Mining Communities." *Social Service Review* 6 (1932), 183–222.

"Anarchy and the Red Cross." *Nation* 132 (Feb. 11, 1931), 144.

Anderson, Paul Y. "A Washington Honor Roll." *Nation* 132 (Jan. 28, 1931), 93–94.

———. "Food and Drink in Washington." *Nation* 132 (Feb. 11, 1931), 150.

"Arkansas's Fight for Life." *Literary Digest* 108 (Feb. 28, 1931), 5–6.

"Back Yonder in the Drought Area." *Literary Digest* 108 (Mar. 21, 1931), 19–20.

Blackburn, Burr. "What the Southern Division Did For the South." *Survey* 53 (Mar. 15, 1931), 760.

Bubka, Tony. "Harlan County Strike." *Labor History* 10 (1970), 41–57.

Carson, William J. "Banking in the South: Its Relation to Economic and Industrial Changes." *Annals of the American Academy of Political and Social Sciences* 153 (1931), 210–23.

Cowley, Robert. "The Drought and the Dole." *American Heritage* 23 (1972), 16–19, 92–99.

Davenport, Walter. "The Drought and Other Blessings." *Collier's* 88 (July 11, 1930), 10–11, 50–51.

"Drought Relief: A Worms Eye View." *New Republic* 55 (1930), 68–70.

"Good and Evil Effects of Drought." *Literary Digest* 106 (Aug. 23, 1930), 5–6.

"Good News From Arkansas." *Literary Digest* 108 (Mar. 28, 1930), 12.

"Great Drought of 1930." *Literary Digest* 106 (Aug. 6, 1930), 5–6.

Grin, Carolyn. "The Unemployment Conference of 1921: An Experiment in Rational Cooperative Planning." *Mid America* 55 (1973), 83–107.

Hamilton, David E. "Herbert Hoover and the Great Drought of 1930." *Journal of American History* 68 (1982), 850–75.

Hawley, Ellis. "Herbert Hoover, The Commerce Secretariat and the Vision of an 'Associative State,' 1921–28." *Journal of American History* 62 (1974), 116–40.

Henry, Alfred T. "The Great Drought of 1930 in the United States." *Monthly Weather Review* 58 (1920), 351–54, 396–401.

"Hoover's Relief Program." *Literary Digest* 107 (Dec. 13, 1930), 7.

"Hoover's Winning Way With Relief." *Literary Digest* 108 (Jan. 1, 1931), 7–8.

Kellogg, Paul U. "Drought and the Red Cross." *Survey* 65 (Feb. 15, 1931), 535–38, 572–76.

Kiessling, O. E. "Coal Mining in the South." *Annals of the American Academy of Political and Social Science* 153 (1931), 84–93.

Lambert, Robert. "Hoover and the Red Cross in the Arkansas Drought of 1930." *Arkansas Historical Quarterly* 29 (1930), 3–9.

Lohof, Bruce. "Herbert Hoover, Spokesman of Humane Efficiency: The Mississippi Flood of 1927." *American Quarterly,* 22 (1970), 690–700.

Murray, Gail S. "Forty Years Ago: The Great Depression in Arkansas," *Arkansas Historical Quarterly* 29 (1970), 291–312.

Nash, Gerald D. "Herbert Hoover and the Origins of the Reconstruction Finance Corporation." *Mississippi Valley Historical Review* 46 (1949), 455–68.

"Now the Farm Breadline." *Literary Digest* 108 (Jan. 24, 1931), 9–10.

Owen, Russell. "Where Drought Sears Land and People." New York *Times Magazine,* Feb. 15, 1931.

"Red Cross Record in Drought Relief." *Review of Reviews* 83 (1931), 33.

Risley, Eleanor. "Drought." *Atlantic Monthly* 147 (May 1931), 627–36.

Robbins, A. "Hunger." *Nation* 132 (Feb. 11, 1931), 151–52.

Roberts, Lydia. "The Nutrition and Care of Children in a Mountain County of Kentucky." *U.S. Children's Bureau,* Publication No. 110. Washington, D.C., 1922.

"Row over Feeding Our Hungry Farmers." *Literary Digest* 108 (Jan. 1, 1931), 8–9.

Schafer, A. L. "When Hunger Follows Drought." *Survey* 65 (Mar. 1, 1931), 581–83.

Shaw, Albert. "The Red Cross and the Treasury." *Review of Reviews* 83 (1931), 28, 31.

"Self-Help Drought Relief Program." *Literary Digest* 106 (Aug. 30, 1930), 9.

Thurston, Elliot. "Senator Joseph T. Robinson." *Forum* 86 (1931), 254–56.

Vaughn, Burton F. "Arkansas Makes a Brilliant Recovery." *Review of Reviews* 83 (1931), 90.

Wickens, David L. "Adjusting Southern Agriculture to Economic Changes." *Annals of the American Academy of Political and Social Science* 153 (1931), 193–201.

Woodruff, Nan E. "The Failure of Relief during the Arkansas Drought of 1930–31." *Arkansas Historical Quarterly* 39 (1980), 301–13.

Zieger, Robert H. "Herbert Hoover: A Re-interpretation." *American Historical Review* 81 (1976), 800–810.

U.S. Congressional Documents

U.S. Congress. *Congressional Record.* 71 Congress, 3 session, Vol. 74, pts. 1–4, 1930–31.

U.S. Congress, House. Committee on Agriculture. *Drought and Storm Relief.* 71 Congress, 3 session, Dec. 5, 1930.

U.S. Congress, House. Subcommittee of House Committee on Appropriations. *Drought Relief for Flood and Storm Stricken Areas.* 71 Congress, 3 session, Dec. 29, 1930.

U.S. Congress, House. Joint Session of the Deficiency and Interior Department Subcommittees of the House Committee on Appropriations. *Senate Amendments to the Interior Department Appropriation Bill for 1932* (H.R. 14675). 71 Congress, 3 session, Jan. 28, 1931.

U.S. Congress, Senate. Committee on Appropriations. *Relief for Farmers in Drought or Flood and Storm Stricken Areas* (H.R. Res. 447). 71 Congress, 3 session, Jan. 5, 1931.

U.S. Congress, Senate. Committee on Appropriations. *La Follette Resolution, Drought Relief and Unemployment.* 71 Congress, 3 session, Jan. 6, 1931.

U.S. Congress, Senate. Committee on Agriculture and Forestry. *Emergency Appropriation for Cooperation with State Health Departments in Rural Sanitation, Etc.* (S. 5440.) 71 Congress, 3 session, Jan. 22, 1931.

Manuscripts

American Friends Service Committee Papers. American Friends Service Committee, Philadelphia.

American National Red Cross Papers. The National Archives, Washington, D.C.

Herbert Hoover Papers. Herbert Hoover Presidential Library, West Branch, Iowa.

The National Association for the Advancement of Colored People (NAACP) Papers. The Library of Congress, Washington, D.C.

Secretary of Agriculture Papers. Record Group 16, The National Archives, Washington, D.C.

Index

Abbott, Grace: meets with Croxton and American Friends Service Committee, 172

Agricultural Adjustment Administration: in the South, 180

Agricultural cooperatives: limitations of in the South, 12; Louisville *Courier-Journal* criticizes, 17; National Drought Conference encourages formation of, 42

Agricultural Credit Corporation: role in drought relief, 85

Agricultural Marketing Act of 1929: importance for farmers, 10

Alabama: rainfall in, 5; conditions in, 42; ARC program in, 130–38 *passim*

Allen, Col. Frank: Payne sends to Arkansas, 120–21

American Friends Service Committee (AFSC): Hoover and, 41; gives relief to miners, 172–73

American Red Cross (ARC): relief in Mississippi River flood (1927), 4; orders surveys of drought region, 7–8; disaster relief policy, 8–9; reserve fund, 11; Hoover asks to assume responsibility for Arkansas, 12; Evans on Arkansas, 16; Arkansas relief surveys, 16–17, 18, 78–81, 116–18; officials struggle with relief policy, 18–19; fall seed distribution program, 22; denies responsibility for plantation workers, 33; relief to Arkansas postponed, 33; Evans visits Arkansas, 32–33; policy in fall of 1930, 34–35; closes relief office in Arkansas, 35; Hoover tries to place unemployment relief on, 41;

on $5 million fund, 44; on fundraising, 44; Tilson on, 48; response to feed and seed loans, 50; Robinson introduces amendment for, 66; Payne rejects unemployment relief as responsibility of, 66; Payne testifies before Senate for, 70–72; $10 million fund launched by, 72; on unemployment relief, 77–78; conducts school lunch program, 79; adequacy of relief questioned, 80–81; responds to criticisms, 81; radio fund drive, 82; composition of Central Committee, 94, 99n91; relief in Arkansas, 100–126; number of families aided by, 100, 101, 138; initiates relief in winter, 103; media campaign, 103–13; follows local customs, 114; on work relief, 123; relief policy in Kentucky, 143; closes state office in Kentucky, 143; relief policy in Appalachia, 145; limitations of program in Appalachia, 154–55; policy toward strikes, 158–59; policy toward coal miners, 158–59, 162, 165–66; conducts surveys in West Virginia, 163; coordinates relief in West Virginia, 169; and Evarts strike, 169–70; limitations of policy in coal fields, 175; total number aided by, 178; cost of relief program, 178; limitations of drought relief program, 178–79

ARC local relief committees: composition of, 12; in Arkansas, 23, 24; refuse aid in Arkansas, 28–30; follow local custom, 79; abuses in

191

A Note on the Author

Nan Elizabeth Woodruff is a member of the department of history at the College of Charleston in South Carolina, where she has been since 1979. She has attended Jacksonville State University (B.A., 1971), the University of Arkansas (M.A., 1973), and the University of Tennessee (Ph.D., 1977). Her previous position was assistant editor on the Booker T. Washington Papers, where she worked on volumes 9 and 10. This is her first book.